A Communicative Grammar

interactions two

A Communicative Grammar

Third Edition

interactions two

Patricia K. Werner

Mary Mitchell Church
Madison Metropolitan School District

Lida R. Baker
Unversity of California, Los Angeles

The McGraw-Hill Companies, Inc.

New York St. Louis San Francisco Auckland Bogotá Caracas Lisbon
London Madrid Mexico City Milan Montreal New Delhi San Juan
Singapore Sydney Tokyo Toronto

This is an  book.

McGraw-Hill

A Division of The McGraw·Hill Companies

Interactions Two
A Communicative Grammar
Third Edition

1 2 3 4 5 6 7 8 9 0   DOC   DOC   9 0 9 8 7 6

ISBN 0-07-069591-1
ISBN 0-07-114376-9

This book was set in Times Roman by Clarinda.

The editors were Tim Stookesberry, Bill Preston, and Steve Vogel; the designers were
Lorna Lo, Suzanne Montazer, Francis Owens, and Elizabeth Williamson; the production
supervisor was Phyllis Snyder; the project editor was Stacey Sawyer; the cover was
designed by Francis Owens; the cover illustrator was Susan Pizzo; the photo researcher
was Cindy Robinson, Seaside Publishing; illustrations were done by David Bohn, Axelle
Fortier, Rick Hackney, Lori Heckelman, and Sally Richardson.

R. R. Donnelley & Sons Company, Crawfordsville, IN, was printer and binder.
Phoenix Color Corporation was cover separator and printer.

Library of Congress Catalog Card Number: 96-75074.

INTERNATIONAL EDITION

When ordering this title, use ISBN 0-007-114376-9

Photo credits: *Page 1* © Frank Tapia; *34* © John Mahler/Stock, Boston; *46* © McLaughlin/The
Image Works; *57* © N. R. Rowan/Stock, Boston; *58* (top) © David M. Grossman/Photo
Researchers, Inc.; *58* (bottom) © Rafael Macia/Photo Researchers, Inc.; *83* © Will & Deni
McIntyre/Photo Researchers, Inc.; *86* © Charles Kennard/Stock, Boston; *87* © Peter
Skinner/Photo Researchers, Inc.; *88* © Owen Franken/Stock, Boston; *91* © John Fung; *101* ©
John Fung; *119* © Tony Freeman/Photo Edit; *122* © Peter Vandermark/Stock, Boston; *128* cour-
tesy of the authors; *129* © UPI/Bettmann; *145* © Kaufman and Fabry Photo/FPG International;

(continued on p. 412)

iv

Contents

Preface to the Third Edition   xiii

CHAPTER one

Education and Student Life   *1*

Review of Basic Verb Forms

TOPIC ONE   Present Verb Forms   2
  A. The Simple Present Tense   3
  B. Adverbs of Frequency and Other Time Expressions   8
  C. The Present Continuous Tense   11
  D. Nonaction Verbs and the Continuous Tenses   13

TOPIC TWO   Past Verb Forms   17
  A. The Past Continuous Tense   18
  B. The Simple Past Tense   21
  C. *Used To*   25

TOPIC THREE   Future Verb Forms   28
  A. *Be Going To*   29
  B. The Simple Future Tense   30
  C. The Future Continuous Tense   32

TOPIC FOUR   Questions and Responses   37
  A. Auxiliary Verbs with *Too, Either, So,* and *Neither*   38
  B. Tag Questions   41
  C. Information Questions; Common Question Words   43
  D. Prepositions   48

focus on testing: verb tenses   55

CHAPTER two

City Life   *57*

Nouns, Adjectives, Articles, and Pronouns

TOPIC ONE   Count Nouns   58
  A. Introduction to Count and Noncount Nouns   59
  B. *A, An,* and *Some*   60
  C. Count Nouns with *There + Be*   62
  D. *Any, Some* and *A lot of*   64

TOPIC TWO   Noncount Nouns (1)   66
  A. Noncount Nouns Versus Count Nouns (1)   68
  B. *How Much* Versus *How Many*   70
  C. Common Units of Measurement   70

TOPIC THREE   Noncount Nouns (2)   76
  A. Noncount Nouns Versus Count Nouns (2)   77
  B. Noncount Nouns with There + Be   78
  C. *(A) Little* Versus *(A) Few; Not Much* Versus *Not Many* 79

TOPIC FOUR   *The* with Locations and Other Special Uses   82
  A. *The* with Locations   83
  B. *The* with the Verb *Go*   85

focus on testing: nouns and articles   89

CHAPTER **three**

Business and Money   *91*

Modal Auxiliaries and Related Structures

TOPIC ONE   Modal Auxiliaries of Request and Permission   92
  A. Introduction to Modal Auxiliaries   93
  B. Making Requests and Giving Permission   94
  C. Making Requests with *Borrow* and *Lend*   96

TOPIC TWO   Modal Auxiliaries and Related Structures of Ability,
            Expectation, and Preference   99
  A. Expressing Ability   100
  B. Expressing Expectations   102
  C. Expressing Preferences   103

TOPIC THREE   Modal Auxiliaries and Related Structures of Advice and Need   106
  A. Giving Advice   107
  B. Expressing Need or Obligation   109
  C. Expressing Lack of Need   109

TOPIC FOUR   Modal Auxiliaries of Possibility, Impossibility, and Probability   111
  A. Expressing Possibility   112
  B. Expressing Impossibility or Disbelief   114
  C. Expressing Probability   115

focus on testing: modals and related structures   118

CHAPTER **four**

Jobs and Professions   *119*

The Perfect Tenses

TOPIC ONE   The Present Perfect Tense   120
  A. The Present Perfect Tense (1)   121
  B. *Ever, Never, Already, Just, Recently, Still,* and *Yet*   125

TOPIC TWO   The Present Perfect Continuous Tense; The Present Perfect Tense (2)   129
  A. The Present Perfect Continuous Tense   130
  B. The Present Perfect Tense (2): The Present Perfect Versus the Present
    Perfect Continuous   133

TOPIC THREE   The Past Perfect Tense   138

focus on testing: the present and past perfect tenses   143

TOPIC FOUR   Review   144

CHAPTER **five**

Lifestyles   *151*

Phrasal Verbs and Related Structures

TOPIC ONE   Inseparable Phrasal Verbs   152
  A. Inseparable Phrasal Verbs (1)   153
  B. Inseparable Phrasal Verbs (2)   155

TOPIC TWO   Separable Phrasal Verbs   159
  A. Introduction to Separable Phrasal Verbs   160
  B. Phrasal Verbs Related to Clothing, Cleaning, and Household Items   163
  C. Phrasal Verbs Related to School or Studies   165

TOPIC THREE   Separable and Inseparable Phrasal Verbs   168
  A. More Separable Phrasal Verbs   169
  B. More Inseparable Phrasal Verbs   170

TOPIC FOUR   Participles and Adjectives Followed by Prepositions   174
  A. Participles Followed by Prepositions   175
  B. Adjectives Followed by Prepositions   178

focus on testing: phrasal verbs and related structures   182

CHAPTER six

The Global Village   *183*

Compound and Complex Sentences (1)

TOPIC ONE   Compound Sentences   184
- **A.** Basic Sentence Structure   185
- **B.** Introduction to Compound Sentences   187
- **C.** Coordinating Conjunctions   188
- **D.** Coordinating Conjunctions with Words and Phrases   190

TOPIC TWO   Complex Sentences   191
- **A.** Introduction to Complex Sentences   192
- **B.** Types of Adverb Clauses   193

TOPIC THREE   Clauses of Contrast (Concession), Reason, and Purpose   197
- **A.** Clauses of Contrast (Concession) and Reason   198
- **B.** Clauses of Purpose   199

TOPIC FOUR   Clauses of Time and Condition: Present and Future time   202
- **A.** Introduction to Clauses of Time and Condition   203
- **B.** Clauses of Time and Condition: Present or Unspecified Time   203
- **C.** Clauses of Time and Condition: Future Time   206

focus on testing: use of compound and complex sentences   213

CHAPTER seven

North America: The Land and The People   *215*

Compound and Complex Sentences (2)

TOPIC ONE   Compound Sentences and Transitions   216
- **A.** Compound Sentences (Review)   218
- **B.** Transitions   219

TOPIC TWO   The Past Perfect Continuous Tense; Time Clauses (1)   224
- **A.** The Past Perfect Continuous Tense   225
- **B.** Time Clauses with the Past Perfect and Past Perfect Continuous Tenses   229

TOPIC THREE   Time Clauses (2)   232
- **A.** Time Clauses with the Simple Past and Past Continuous Tenses   233
- **B.** Time Clauses with the Present Perfect and Simple Past Tenses   236

TOPIC FOUR   Contrast of Simple, Compound, and Complex Sentences   240

focus on testing: use of compound and complex sentences   246

CHAPTER eight

TASTES AND PREFERENCES   247

Clauses and Phrases of Comparison

TOPIC ONE   Positive Adjectives and Participles   248
  A. Participles Used as Adjectives   249
  B. Comparisons with *(Not) As . . . As*   251
  C. Adjectives and Adverbs with *So . . . That*   254

TOPIC TWO   Comparative Adjectives   257
  A. Comparative Adjectives   258
  B. Comparison of Nouns   259
  C. Comparisons with *Than*   260
  D. Comparative Adverbs   262

TOPIC THREE   Superlative Forms   266

TOPIC FOUR   Review   273

focus on testing: review of problem areas
from chapters five through eight   279

CHAPTER nine

Discoveries   281

The Passive Voice

TOPIC ONE   The Passive Voice with Simple Tenses   282
  A. Introduction to the Passive Voice   283
  B. The Passive Voice with the Simple Present and Past Tenses   284
  C. Uses of *By* + Agent   286
  D. *It* with the Passive Voice   288

TOPIC TWO   The Passive Voice with the Present Perfect Tense   291

TOPIC THREE   The Passive Voice with the Present Continuous Tense   296

TOPIC FOUR   The Passive Voice with Modal Auxiliaries   301

focus on testing: use of the passive voice   305

CHAPTER ten

Medicine, Myths, and Magic

307

Adjective Clauses

TOPIC ONE   Adjective Clauses with *That*   308
A. Introduction to Adjective Clauses   309
B. Clauses with *That:* Replacement of Subjects   309

TOPIC TWO   Adjective Clauses with *Who, Which,* and *Whose*   312
A. Clauses with *Who* and *Which:* Replacement of Subjects   314
B. Clauses with *Whose:* Replacement of Possessives   315
C. Restrictive Versus Nonrestrictive Clauses   316

TOPIC THREE   Adjective Clauses with *That, Which,* and *Who(m)*   318
A. Clauses with *That* and *Which:* Replacement of Objects   319
B. Clauses with *Who(m):* Replacement of Objects   320

TOPIC FOUR   Adjective Clauses with *When* and *Where*   323

focus on testing: use of adjective clauses   327

CHAPTER eleven

The Media

329

Gerunds, Infinities, and Related Structures

TOPIC ONE   Gerunds   330
A. Introduction to Gerunds and Infinitives   331
B. Uses of Gerunds   331
C. Gerunds After Prepositions   332
D. Common Verbs Often Followed by Gerunds   335
E. Common Verbs Often Followed by Gerunds or Infinitives (1)   336

TOPIC TWO   Infinitives   338
A. Uses of Infinitives   339
B. Common Verbs Often Followed by Infinitives   342
C. Infinitives with *Too* and *(Not) Enough*   344
D. Infinitives of Purpose   346

TOPIC THREE   Infinitives Versus Gerunds   348
Common Verbs Often Followed by Infinitives or Gerunds (2)   351

TOPIC FOUR   Causative and Structurally Related Verbs; Verbs of Perception   354
A. Causative and Structurally Related Verbs   356
B. Verbs of Perception   358

*focus on testing: use of gerunds, infinitives,
and other verb forms*   363

CHAPTER twelve

Prejudice, Tolerance, and Justice **365**

Hope, Wish, and Conditional Sentences

TOPIC ONE   *Hope* and *Wish*: Present and Future   366

TOPIC TWO   Conditional Sentences: Present or Unspecified Time   372

TOPIC THREE   Past Wishes and Conditions   376
  A. Perfect Modal Auxiliaries   377
  B. Past Wishes   381
  C. Conditional Sentences: Past Time   382

TOPIC FOUR   Review   384

focus on testing: review of problem areas from
chapters nine through twelve   390

Appendix   393
Index   407

Preface
to the Third Edition
The Interactions Two Program

The Interactions Two program consists of five texts and a variety of supplemental materials for low-intermediate to intermediate students seeking to improve their English language skills. Each of the five texts in this program is carefully organized by chapter theme, vocabulary, grammar structures, and, where possible, language functions. As a result, information introduced in a chapter of any one of the Interactions Two texts corresponds to and reinforces material taught in the same chapter of the other four books, creating a truly integrated, four-skills approach.

The Interactions Two program is highly flexible. The texts in this series may be used together or separately, depending on students' needs and course goals. The books in this program include:

- **A Communicative Grammar Book.** Organized around grammatical topics, this book includes notional/functional material where appropriate. It presents all grammar in context and contains many types of communicative activities.

- **A Listening/Speaking Skills Book.** This book uses lively, natural language from various contexts, including dialogues, interviews, lectures, and announcements. Listening strategies emphasized include summarizing main ideas, making inferences, listening for stressed words, reductions and intonation. A variety of speaking activities complement the listening component.

- **A Reading Skills Book.** The reading selections contain sophisticated college-level material; however, vocabulary and grammar have been carefully controlled to be at students' level of comprehension. The text includes many vocabulary-building exercises and emphasizes reading strategies such as skimming, scanning, guessing meaning from context, understanding the structure and organization of a selection, increasing reading speed, and interpreting the author's point of view.

- **A Writing Process Book.** This book uses a process approach to writing, including many exercises on prewriting and revision. Exercises build skills in exploring and organizing ideas; developing vocabulary; using correct form and mechanics; using coherent structure, and editing, revising, and using feedback to create a final draft.

- **A Multi-Skills Activity Book.** New to this edition, this text gives students integrated practice in all four language skills. Among the communicative activities included in this text are exercises for the new video program that accompanies the Interactions Two series.

Supplemental Materials

In addition to the five core texts outlined above, various supplemental materials are available to assist users of the third edition, including:

Instructor's Manual

Extensively revised for the new edition, this manual provides instructions and guidelines for using the five core texts separately or in various combinations to suit particular program needs. For each of the core texts, there is a separate section with answer keys, teaching tips, additional activities, and other suggestions. The testing materials have been greatly expanded in this edition.

Audio Program for *Interactions Two: A Listening/Speaking Skills Book*

 Completely re-recorded for the new edition, the audio program is designed to be used in conjunction with those exercises that are indicated with a cassette icon in the student text. Complete tapescripts are now included in the back of the student text.

Audio Program to Accompany *Interactions Two: A Reading Skills Book*

 This new optional audio program contains selected readings from the student text. These taped selections enable students to listen at their leisure to the natural oral discourse of native readers for intonation and modeling. Readings that are included in this program are indicated with a cassette icon in the student text.

Video

New to this edition, the video program for Interactions Two contains authentic television segments that are coordinated with the twelve chapter themes in the five texts. Exercises and activities for this video are in the Multi-Skills Activity Book.

Interactions Two: A Communicative Grammar, Third Edition

Rationale

Interactions Two: A Communicative Grammar, Third Edition introduces, practices and applies grammatical structures through meaningful, relevant contexts. The text progresses with the intermediate-level student by gradually shifting from basic structures and conversational topics to complex structures and academic topics. The first several chapters review basic use of articles, prepositions, and modal auxiliaries in conversational context such as student life, money and banking, and city living. Later chapters treat more complex structures through more sophisticated topics such as traditional and modern medicine, discoveries in the known universe, and the history and traditions of North America. Thus, in *Interactions Two: A Communicative Grammar,* form and content are never separated: What we express and how we express it are the combined focus of the text.

Chapter Organization and Teaching Suggestions

All chapters are divided into four grammar topics, many of which include related subtopics.

Each grammar topic opens with artwork and a short passage or conversation that introduce the target structures and the theme. The topic openers can be used to introduce key vocabulary and to make sure the students have a basic understanding of the content. They can be covered with the class as a whole, or they can be used as homework assignments, timed readings, or listening comprehension exercises.

All structures are presented in boxes that include general rules and examples. Also included when necessary are notes on particular usages and variations, spelling, punctuation and pronunciation guidelines, and exceptions to the general rules. Grammar explanations can be assigned as homework, or they may be covered briefly in class. We do not recommend long, detailed presentations in class.

Every topic includes a variety of exercises and activities that are sequenced to progress from more-controlled to less-controlled practice of the target structures. The exercises are both traditional and innovative, including transformations, sentence completions, cloze exercises, and questions. Most exercises may be used for either oral or written work; they may be done as a class, in pairs, in small groups, or as homework. Three specific types of exercises are clearly labeled: **Rapid Oral Practice, Error Analysis,** and **Review. Rapid Oral practice** and **Error Analysis** exercises are included periodically to focus on common problem areas. Review exercises appear frequently throughout the text, recycling previously-studied material and integrating it with newly practiced material. In addition, Chapters Four, Eight, and Twelve each include an entire section devoted to review.

Finally, every chapter offers a wealth of speaking and writing activities found in sections called "Using What You've Learned." The activities in these sections range from minidramas and language games to formal presentations and compositions. These activities are optional, but we recommend using as many as possible. They are designed to encourage the use of target structures and vocabulary in natural, personalized communication. Moreover, they help to form a bridge between the controlled, structured language of the classroom and real-life language outside the classroom.

Flexibility

Students come to a course with varying skills, attitudes, needs and time available for study. Likewise, ESOL courses vary greatly in length, number of contact hours, and focus. Therefore, *Interactions Two: A Communicative Grammar* includes more material than may be necessary for many courses. If you do not want or have time to cover all the material in the text, be selective. Cover the structures that the majority of your students have the most difficulty with, and omit the structures that most already have a command of. You may also want to omit diagnostic or review material, reading passages, and activities. Of course, the extra material may be assigned to those students who need additional work with given structures, or the material may be used as the basis for quizzes and exams. We heartily encourage using as many of the activities as possible, though. They are stimulating and lively ways of allowing students to communicate more authentically within the classroom.

New to the Third Edition

1. **Streamlined Design.** The new edition features an attractive two-color design and an extensively revised art program. These changes were initiated to make the books more appealing, up-to-date, and user friendly. In addition, we made the books easier to use by simplifying some explanations, highlighting explanations in shaded boxes and charts, numbering exercises and activities, and using icons to signal group activities.
2. **New Chapter Theme on the Global Village.** The new edition features an entirely new theme for Chapter Six: The Global Village. The chapter covers types of compound and complex sentences through thematic material relating to recent worldwide changes in politics, economics, demography, and communications.

3. **Review Sections Every Four Chapters.**
While many structures are periodically recycled and reviewed throughout the text, the third edition provides even more systematic integration through special review sections in Chapters Four, Eight, and Twelve. These review sections have a variety of cumulative exercises that can be used in class, for homework, or as the basis for quizzes.

4. **Focus on Testing.** These new boxed features in every chapter are designed to help students prepare for standardized grammar and usage tests like the TOEFL. Most chapters have a short **Focus on Testing** box which highlights structures covered in the particular chapter. However, Chapters Four, Eight, and Twelve have slightly longer boxes that include test items on structures from a variety of chapters. Through repeated exposure to and practice with this standardized test format, students will hopefully gain more confidence and experience less anxiety in actual test-taking situations.

5. **Reference Appendix.** All key reference material—including spelling rules and irregular forms, irregular verb forms, verbs + gerunds and/or infinitives, special uses of *the,* and so on—has been moved to an appendix, making it easier to find.

Acknowledgments

A very special thanks to Maria Pace and Stella Blanco for their help during the completion of this book. In addition, our thanks to the following reviewers whose comments, both favorable and critical, were of great value in the development of the third edition of the Interactions/Mosaic series:

Jean Al-Sibai, University of North Carolina; Janet Alexander, Waterbury College; Roberta Alexander, San Diego City College; Julie Alpert, Santa Barbara City College; Anita Cook, Tidewater Community College; Anne Deal Beavers, Heald Business College; Larry Berking, Monroe Community College; Deborah Busch, Delaware County Community College; Patricia A. Card, Chaminade University of Honolulu; José A. Carmona, Hudson County Community College; Kathleen Carroll, Fontbonne College; Consuela Chase, Loyola University; Lee Chen, California State University; Karen Cheng, University of Malaya; Gaye Childress, University of North Texas; Maria Conforti, University of Colorado; Earsie A. de Feliz, Arkansas State University; Elizabeth Devlin-Foltz, Montgomery County Adult Education; Colleen Dick, San Francisco Institute of English; Marta Dmytrenko-Ahrabian, Wayne State University; Margo Duffy, Northeast Wisconsin Technical; Magali Duignan, Augusta College; Janet Dyar, Meridian Community College; Anne Ediger, San Diego City College; D. Frangie, Wayne State University; Robert Geryk, Wayne State University; Jeanne Gibson, American Language Academy; Kathleen Walsh Greene, Rhode Island College; Myra Harada, San Diego Mesa College; Kristin Hathhorn, Eastern Washington University; Mary Herbert, University of California, Davis; Joyce Homick, Houston Community College; Catherine Hutcheson, Texas Christian University; Suzie Johnston, Tyler Junior College; Donna Kauffman, Radford University; Emmie Lim, Cypress College; Patricia Mascarenas, Monte Vista Comunity School; Mark Mattison, Donnelly College; Diane Peak, Choate Rosemary Hall; James Pedersen, Irvine Valley College; Linda Quillan, Arkansas State University; Marnie Ramker, University of Illinois; Joan Roberts, The Doane Stuart School; Doralee Robertson, Jacksonville University; Ellen Rosen, Fullerton College; Jean Sawyer, American Language Academy; Frances Schulze, College of San Mateo; Sherrie R. Sellers, Brigham Young University; Tess M. Shafer, Edmonds Community College; Heinz F. Tengler, Lado International College; Sara Tipton, Wayne State University; Karen R. Vallejo, Brigham Young University; Susan Williams, University of Central Florida; Mary Shepard Wong, El Camino College; Cindy Yoder, Eastern Mennnonite College; Cheryl L. Youtsey, Loyola University; Miriam Zahler, Wayne State University; Maria Zien, English Center, Miami; Yongmin Zhu, Los Medanos College; Norma Zorilla, Fresno Pacific College.

CHAPTER **one**

Education and Student Life

Review of Basic Verb Forms

Topic One: Present Verb Forms
Topic Two: Past Verb Forms
Topic Three: Future Verb Forms
Topic Four: Questions and Responses

in this chapter

TOPIC one

Present Verb Forms

Setting the Context

previewing the passage How do you usually feel during your first few days at a new school? Share your ideas and experiences while answering these questions about the picture.

- Who are these people, and where are they?
- Describe the two young men in the center of the picture. What problem does one of the students have? How will he solve it?

THE FIRST DAY

STEVE: Do you need some help? You seem lost.

MIGUEL: Thanks, I *am* lost! I'm looking for the foreign student office. Can you help me?

STEVE: Sure, I'm going near there. Do you want to come with me? By the way, my name's Steve. What's yours?

MIGUEL: I'm Miguel.

STEVE: Where do you come from, Miguel?

MIGUEL: I come from Colombia. I'm here to study architecture. Are you from here?

STEVE: No, I'm not from Madison. I'm from Canada, from Toronto. I started college in Canada, but I'm finishing my degree here.

MIGUEL:	What are you studying?
STEVE:	I'm majoring in engineering. I'm taking a lot of computer courses now. They're very crowded this semester.
MIGUEL:	Do you live in a dorm?
STEVE:	No, I don't. I'm here with my wife and baby daughter. We have an apartment on the other side of town. Where do you live?
MIGUEL:	I was in a hotel, but I'm moving into Meyer Dormitory this afternoon.
STEVE:	There's the foreign student office. Good luck!

discussing ideas

What is Miguel looking for? What is Steve majoring in? What are dormitories? Are you living in one now?

A. The Simple Present Tense

The simple present tense can describe habits, routines, or events that happen regularly. It can also express opinions or make general statements of fact.

uses	examples	notes
Statements of Fact	I **go** to City College. He **goes** to City College.	Time expressions such as the following often appear with this tense: *always, every day, in general, never, often, rarely, sometimes, usually.*
Opinions	I **like** my classes. He **doesn't like** his classes.	
Regular Events, Habits, or Routines	I **have** classes every day from 9 to 3. He **has classes** two days a week.	

The Verb *Be*

forms	affirmative statements	negative statements
Long Forms	I **am** a student. She **is** at the college. We **are** in the library.	I **am not** a teacher. He **is not** at the college. They **are not** in the library.
Contracted Forms	I**'m** here. She**'s** here. We**'re** in the library.	I**'m not** there. He **isn't** there. They **aren't** in the library.

	questions	possible answers
Yes/No Questions and Short Answers	**Am** I late?	Yes, I **am.** No, I**'m not.** Yes, you **are.** No, you **aren't.**
	Is she at the college? **Are** they in the library?	Yes, she **is.** No, she **isn't.** Yes, they **are.** No, they **aren't.**

The Verb *Have* and Other Verbs

forms	affirmative statements	negative statements
Long Forms	I **have** class every day. I **study** a lot. She **has** classes every day. She **studies** a lot.	They **do not have** class every day. They **do not study** a lot. He **does not have** class every day. He **does not study** a lot.
Contracted Forms		They **don't have** class every day. He **doesn't study** a lot.

	questions	possible answers	
Yes/No Questions and Short Answers	**Do** I **have** classes tomorrow? **Do** I **study** a lot? **Does** she **have** classes tomorrow? **Does** she **study** a lot?	Yes, I **do.** Yes, you **do.** Yes, she **does.**	No, I **don't.** No, you **don't.** No, she **doesn't.**

Note: See Appendix pages 396 to 397 for spelling rules for the *-s* ending. See pages 37–54 of this chapter for more information on questions and responses.

 **exercise 1** Underline all uses of the simple present tense in the conversation "The First Day" on page 2.

 **exercise 2** We often use the simple present tense to give information about ourselves. Complete the sentences with appropriate forms of the following verbs. Use each verb at least once.

be	be interested in	come	have	live

1. His name _____ Miguel.

2. Miguel _____is_____ Colombian.

3. He _____ from Bogotá.

4. He _____ in Meyer Dormitory.

5. He _____ an American roommate.

6. He _____ architecture.

7. Their names _____ Steve, Nancy, and Barbara.

8. They _____ Canadian.

9. They _____ from Toronto.

10. They _____ in an apartment.

11. My name _____ Francesca Espinoza.

12. I _____ Italian.

13. I _____ from Florence.

14. I _____ with my uncle and aunt in a house.

15. I _____ art history.

 **exercise 3**   Complete the conversation here and on the next page with the simple present form of the verbs in parentheses. Use contractions when possible.

MARIA: Hi, Daniel! How _____*are*_____ (be) you? _____*It's*_____ (be) good to see

you!

DANIEL: Hi, Maria! I _____ (be) fine. And you?
                              1

MARIA: Great! Daniel, I _____ (want) to introduce you to Isabelle. She
                                    2

_____ (come) from France. She _____ (have) a scholar-
        3   4

ship to study here. Her brother _____ (live) here, too, but she
                                              5

_____ (not have) any other relatives here.
        6

DANIEL: It _____ (be) nice to meet you, Isabelle. How _____ you
_____7_____   __8__
_____ (like) the United States?
____9____

ISABELLE: I _____ (like) Madison a lot. It _____ (be) very pretty. I
____10____   __11__
_____ (not know) about other places, though. I _____
____12____   __13__
(hope) to visit many places with my brother.

DANIEL: My brother _____ (be) here, too. We _____ (share) an
____14____   __15__
apartment with another student.

MARIA: _____ you _____ (have) classes now? Let's all go to the
__16__   __17__
Student Union for lunch. They _____ (make) great hamburgers,
__18__
and the food there _____ (not cost) very much.
____19____

In pairs, make statements, questions, and responses in the simple present tense
using the following cues. Use the examples as models.

examples: I / have a professor for history class
              a teaching assistant
          A: **I have a professor for history class. Do you have a
             professor, too?**
          B: **No, I don't. I have a teaching assistant.**

              my brother / study here
              a technical school
          A: **My brother studies here. Does your brother study here,
             too?**
          B: **No, he doesn't. He studies at a technical school.**

1. I / live in a dorm
   an apartment
2. I / have classes every day
   three days a week
3. my roommate / come from the United States
   Canada
4. my roommate / always study at the library
   in our apartment
5. my neighbors / play the stereo all night
   go to bed early
6. my professors / assign work every night
   about twice a week
7. I / always do my homework at the last minute
   ahead of time
8. my math teacher / have office hours three times a week
   once a week

 **exercise 5**   Sit with a partner. Ask each other the questions below. Write your partner's answers.

1. What's your full name?

2. Where do you come from?

3. Where do you live here?

4. Do you have a roommate?

5. What is your major?

6. Do you have classes every day?

7. What special thing do you hope to do here?

Now introduce your partner to the class.

example: **I want to introduce you to my partner Francesca. Her full name is Francesca Irina Espinoza. She comes from Italy. She lives in a house with her aunt and uncle. She doesn't have a roommate. Her major is economics. She doesn't have classes every day—just four days a week. One special thing she hopes to do here is visit the national parks. She loves camping and all outdoor activities.**

B. Adverbs of Frequency and Other Time Expressions

A common use of the simple present tense is to describe habits or routines. The following adverbs and time expressions are often used with this tense to indicate frequency.

ADVERBS	TIME EXPRESSIONS
100% ↑ 0% ↓ always, usually, often, frequently, normally, sometimes, occasionally, seldom, rarely, hardly ever, almost never, never	100% ↑ 0% ↓ all the time, most of the time, in general, generally, once (twice, etc.) a week (month, etc.), from time to time, (every) now and then, off and on, once in a while

Guidelines for Placement of These Expressions

uses	examples	notes
With the Verb be	I am **usually** on time. She is **rarely** late.	One- or two-word adverbs of frequency come after *be*.
With All Other Verbs and Verb Tenses	I **seldom** go to class late. She **rarely** goes to class. He has **never** been late.	One- or two-word adverbs of frequency normally come before the main verb or between the auxiliary and main verbs in a statement.
Longer Time Expressions with All Verbs	They are late **once in a while.** **Once in a while** they come late.	Longer time expressions usually come at the beginning or end of a sentence.
Ever with Questions and Negatives	Is he **ever** late? Do you **ever** come late? I don't **ever** skip classes.	*Ever* means "any time." *Ever* and other adverbs of frequency come after the subject in a question.

exercise 6

Fill in the blanks with adverbs of frequency that fit the context as in the examples. In some cases there may be more than one correct answer.

1. I'm a terrible student. I'm _never_____ late for class. I'm _____ on time. I _____ turn in my homework late. I _____ get As on tests. In fact I fail at least one class almost every semester. I hate school.

2. I'm a good student, but I like to have fun too. I'm _____ on time for classes. I don't get very many "As," but I _seldom_____ fail a test. I _____ forget to do my homework. I _____ go out on Saturday nights, and _____ I go out on weeknights too— if I don't have too much homework.

3. I love school. I'm an excellent student; in fact, I _____ get straight As. When I'm not in class, I am _____ in the library studying. I _hardly ever_____ go out. My friends say I am too serious, but I love to study and learn new things.

exercise 7

What kind of student are you? Tell about yourself by completing the following. Add other information if you like.

I'm a _____ student. I'm _____ late for class. I'm _____ on time. I _____ do my assignments. I _____ fail tests. I go out on weekends _____ , and I _____ go out on weeknights, too. I go to the library _____ .

exercise 8

Use the cues in each picture, here and on the next page, to make complete statements about these people.

example: **Paul almost always does his assignments. Every now and then Christine forgets assignments.**

Do my assign-
ments? Almost
always...

Forget assign-
ments? Every
now and then.

Am I on time? As a rule, yes... Late? Well, occasionally.

1.

_____

_____

_____

_____

Study at the library? Hardly ever. The library? Off and on.

2.

_____

_____

_____

_____

Go to the language lab? Once in a while. Language lab? Almost never.

3.

_____

_____

_____

_____

Do I write my family and friends? Never! Call? Always. Call my parents? Rarely. Too expensive.

4.

_____

_____

_____

_____

exercise **9** Most colleges and universities have a variety of facilities, such as libraries, sports centers, theaters, and museums. In pairs, ask one another the following questions.

1. How often do you study at the library? Do you ever check out books?
2. How frequently do you use the language lab?
3. Do you ever go to movies or plays on campus?
4. Do you usually buy your lunch at the campus cafeteria?
5. How often do you use the gym? The pool? The tennis courts?
6. Do you ever go to a museum on campus? Which one?

The Present Continuous Tense

The present continuous tense can describe activities at the moment of speaking, activities currently in progress, or plans for the future.

uses	examples	notes
Activities at the Moment of Speaking	I**'m doing** my homework now. She**'s studying** at the library.	Time expressions often used with the present continuous tense include *now, right now, at the moment, today, this week (month, year), these days, currently, nowadays.*
Activities Currently in Progress	I**'m taking** math this semester. He**'s majoring** in chemistry.	
Plans for the Future	We **aren't moving** tomorrow. We**'re moving** on Saturday.	

forms	affirmative statements	negative statements
Long Forms	I **am studying** now. She **is working** today. They **are taking** math.	I **am not studying** now. She **is not working** today. They **are not taking** math.
Contracted Forms	I**'m studying** now. She**'s working** today. They**'re taking** math.	I**'m not studying** now. She **isn't working** today. They **aren't** taking math.

	questions	possible answers	
Yes/No Questions and Short Answers	**Am** I **studying** now? **Is** she **studying** now? **Are** they **studying** now?	Yes, I **am.** Yes, she **is.** Yes, they **are.**	No, I**'m not.** No, she **isn't.** No, they **aren't.**

Note: See Appendix pages 396–397 for spelling rules for the *-ing* ending.

exercise  Underline all uses of the present continuous tense in the conversation on pages 2 and 3. Tell whether the activities are happening at the moment of speaking, are currently in progress, or are plans for the future.

exercise 11 Look at the picture on page 2 and describe what is happening in it. Use the following cues to help you.

> **example:** look at a map
> **Miguel is looking at a map.**

1. look for the foreign student office
2. try to help Miguel
3. ride bicycles
4. carry books
5. read a college catalog
6. talk in front of the student union

exercise 12 Complete the following conversation with present continuous forms of the verbs in parentheses. Use contractions when possible. Pay close attention to the spelling of the -ing forms.

DANIEL: How _are_____ your classes _going_____ (go), Maria?

_____ you _____ (take) a lot of different subjects?
        1   2

MARIA: Well, this semester I _____ (finish) all the basic psychology
                  3

courses, so I _____ (take) six classes. I _____ (try) to
          4   5

find a part-time job, too. This afternoon, I _____ (interview) for a
                                 6

job at a psychology lab.

DANIEL: You _____ (work) too hard! I _____ (not study) as much
        7   8

this semester, and I _____ (enjoy) life much more. My brother
              9

and I _____ (play) on a soccer team, and we _____
     10   11

(learn) about photography. We _____ (plan) some trips, too. Next
                        12

weekend, we _____ (visit) some friends in Chicago.
          13

MARIA: That's great! Maybe next semester I'll take it easy.

In pairs, take turns asking and answering questions in the present continuous tense using the following cues. Use the example as a model.

> **example:** you / live in the dorm this semester
> in an apartment
> MARIA: **Are you living in the dorm this semester?**
> DANIEL: **No, I'm not. I'm living in an apartment now.**

1. you / take Russian history this semester
   European history

2. your roommate / still major in economics
   political science

3. your friends / still learn word processing
   data processing

4. your boyfriend (girlfriend) / study African history this semester
   African languages

5. you / work in the library
   computer center

6. your family / come to visit you during Christmas vacation
   during spring break

7. we / have lunch together today
   tomorrow

8. your sister / graduate at the end of winter quarter
   spring quarter

D. Nonaction Verbs and the Continuous Tenses

Certain verbs are not normally used in continuous tenses, or they are used only in very specific cases.

Feelings, Opinions, or Thoughts

examples	verbs		notes
I **don't understand** your question. What **do** you **mean?** I **want** to know. **Do** you **mind** explaining it? *Compare:* I**'ve been meaning** to call you. I**'ve been wanting** to talk to you about that.	appear appreciate be believe dislike hate know like love	mean need prefer recognize remember seem sound understand want	Verbs that express feelings or thoughts are not normally used in continuous tenses. In certain cases, however, *mean, need,* and *want* appear in the present perfect continuous tense.

Possession

examples	verbs		notes
She **owns** a house. She also **has** a car. *Compare:* She**'s having** problems with her car. We**'re having** lunch at 6:00.	belong to have	own possess	The *-ing* form is used with *have* in some idiomatic expressions.

Perceptions (Senses)

examples	verbs		notes
This pizza **tastes** good. It **smells** delicious. *Compare:* I **am tasting** the pizza now. We**'ve been hearing** stories about you.	hear look see	smell taste	The *-ing* form is used to express a specific action. Note that *hear* and *see* can sometimes be used in the present perfect continuous tense.

 **exercise 13** Complete the conversation on the opposite page with appropriate forms of the verbs in parentheses.

DORM FOOD

DANIEL: This food _smells_____ (smell) awful!

MARIA: If you _____ (think) that it _____ (smell) bad, wait
⠀⠀⠀⠀⠀⠀⠀⠀⠀⠀⠀⠀1⠀⠀⠀⠀⠀⠀⠀⠀⠀⠀⠀⠀⠀⠀⠀⠀2
until you _____ (taste) it!
⠀⠀⠀⠀⠀⠀⠀⠀⠀3

DANIEL: Why _____ this cafeteria _____ (have) such
⠀⠀⠀⠀⠀⠀⠀⠀⠀⠀⠀⠀⠀⠀⠀⠀⠀⠀⠀⠀⠀⠀⠀⠀⠀⠀4
terrible food? I _____ (remember) the food at the cafeteria at
⠀⠀⠀⠀⠀⠀⠀⠀⠀⠀⠀⠀5
my university. It was much better than this. I _____ (not
⠀⠀⠀⠀⠀⠀⠀⠀⠀⠀⠀⠀⠀⠀⠀⠀⠀⠀⠀⠀⠀⠀⠀⠀⠀⠀⠀⠀⠀⠀⠀⠀⠀6
understand)! Why _____ the cook at this dorm
_____ (use / always) so much grease? And, why
⠀⠀⠀7
_____ they _____ (cook) everything too long?
⠀⠀⠀⠀⠀⠀⠀⠀⠀⠀⠀⠀⠀⠀⠀⠀⠀⠀⠀8

MARIA: Well, if you _____ (not like) greasy, tasteless food, this
⠀⠀⠀⠀⠀⠀⠀⠀⠀⠀⠀⠀⠀⠀9
_____ (not be) the place to eat. Today they _____
⠀⠀⠀10⠀⠀⠀⠀⠀⠀⠀⠀⠀⠀⠀⠀⠀⠀⠀⠀⠀⠀⠀⠀⠀⠀⠀⠀⠀⠀⠀⠀⠀⠀⠀11
(serve) "mystery meat" again. _____ you _____
⠀⠀⠀⠀⠀⠀⠀⠀⠀⠀⠀⠀⠀⠀⠀⠀⠀⠀⠀⠀⠀⠀⠀⠀⠀⠀⠀⠀⠀⠀⠀⠀12
(see) my roommate over there? She _____ (try) to cut the meat
⠀⠀⠀⠀⠀⠀⠀⠀⠀⠀⠀⠀⠀⠀⠀⠀⠀⠀⠀⠀⠀⠀⠀⠀13
with a plastic fork. Good luck!

DANIEL: I _____ (not want) to eat here tonight, that _____
⠀⠀⠀⠀⠀14⠀⠀⠀⠀⠀⠀⠀⠀⠀⠀⠀⠀⠀⠀⠀⠀⠀⠀⠀⠀⠀⠀⠀⠀⠀⠀⠀15
(be) for sure! I _____ (get) a stomachache just looking at this
⠀⠀⠀⠀⠀⠀⠀⠀⠀⠀⠀16
food.

MARIA: I _____ (have) an idea. How about getting a hamburger some-
⠀⠀⠀⠀⠀17
where?

DANIEL: That _____ (sound) like a great idea. Let's go.
⠀⠀⠀⠀⠀⠀⠀18

Using What You've Learned

 **activity 1** **Getting to Know Your Classmates.**   Take this opportunity to get to know more about your new classmates. Make a chart like the one below and use it to find classmates with similar backgrounds and interests. Use the following cues to help you to form complete questions:

Name	(What . . . ?)
Age and date of birth	(How old . . . ? When . . . ?)
Hometown (country)	(Where . . . ?)
Native language	(What . . . ?)
Reason for studying English	(Why . . . ?)
Length of time studying English	(How long . . . ?)
Education, major, occupation, plans	(What . . . ?)

name	birthday	family	education	interests	other
José Rico	May 2	single 2 brothers	B.A. in French	playing guitar	works in an ice cream factory

After you finish, give a brief summary of all the interests you share with other students.

> **example:**   Toshio and I have the same birthday! Also, both of us play tennis and golf . . .

 **activity 2** **Expressing Opinions.**   What are your opinions about American food, or food at your school cafeteria or nearby lunch spot? Make at least five original statements using the following verbs: *like, dislike, appear, look, seem, smell, taste.*

Past Verb Forms

Setting the Context

Is homesickness a problem for you? Share your ideas and experiences while answering the following questions about the picture.

- Who is the young man in the picture? Where is he?
- What is he thinking about?
- How is he probably feeling?
- What can he do about this problem?

STUDYING ABROAD

Over 300,000 foreign students are studying in the United States, and homesickness is often a problem. Having a friend to talk to is sometimes the best remedy for it.

TOM: Hi, Miguel! How is it going?

MIGUEL: Well, . . . okay, . . . no, terrible. I was thinking about home, and I was getting a little homesick.

TOM: I know what you mean. I'm homesick, too.

MIGUEL: You know, a year ago now, I was studying at the university. I was really busy. While I was taking classes, I was also working for my father on weekends.

TOM: Why did you leave your country, then? Didn't you get a degree there?

MIGUEL: When I won a scholarship to study here, I decided to leave. It was a great opportunity. And, of course, I wanted to have the experience of studying abroad. I made the right decision, but sometimes it's hard.

discussing ideas What was Miguel doing a year ago? Why did he leave his country? Are you studying away from home? Do you get homesick? What do you miss the most about your hometown or country?

A. The Past Continuous Tense

The past continuous tense describes activities that were happening or in progress in the recent past, at a specific time in the past, or during a period of time in the past. It often describes or "sets" a scene.

uses	examples	notes
Activities in the Recent Past	I **was watching** the news a moment ago. The announcer **was** just **telling** about the fire.	Time expressions often used with the past continuous tense include *just a minute (moment, week, month) ago, at that time, at this time last week (month, year), in (during, by) the summer (June, etc.), all day (morning, week, etc.).*
Activities at a Specific Time in the Past	John **was studying** at the library at the time of the fire. At 8:00, he **was writing** his composition.	
Activities During a Period of Time in the Past	My classmates **were working** on the project all summer. I **was doing** homework during the morning.	

forms	affirmative statements	negative statements
Long Forms	I **was studying** then. She **was working** then. They **were taking** math.	I **was not studying** then. She **was not working** then. They **were not taking** math.
Contracted Forms		I **wasn't studying** then. She **wasn't working** then. They **weren't taking** math.

	questions	possible answers	
Yes/No Questions and Short Answers	**Was** I **studying** then? **Was** she **working** then? **Were** they **taking** math?	Yes, I **was**. Yes, she **was**. Yes, they **were**.	No, I **wasn't**. No, she **wasn't**. No, they **weren't**.

Note: See Appendix pages 396 to 397 for spelling rules for the *-ing* ending. See pages 13 to 14 for information on verbs that do not normally appear in the continuous tenses. See pages 37 to 54 for more information on questions and responses. Chapter Seven includes information on the use of the past continuous with *when* and *while*.

 **exercise 1**   Use the following cues to form sentences with the past continuous tense and various time expressions.

> example: a year ago / Miguel / study at the university in his country
> **A year ago, Miguel was studying at the university in his country.**

1. in 1994 / Miguel / still live in Colombia
2. at that time / he / study at the university
3. he / not work
4. he / live / with his family
5. by June of 1995 / Miguel / live in the United States
6. during the summer of 1995 / Tom / travel in Europe
7. two other friends / travel / with him
8. by the end of the summer / all of them / start to get homesick

exercise 2   Use the cues to describe the scene of a special evening Miguel had a year ago. Use the past continuous tense in your sentences.

> example: Last December 12 / my girlfriend and I / celebrate her birthday
> **Last December 12, my girlfriend and I were celebrating her birthday.**

1. we / sit / in our favorite restaurant
2. she / wear a beautiful black dress
3. I / wear / my best suit
4. we / hold hands and drink champagne
5. the waiters / smile at us
6. the band / play romantic music

Suddenly, the lights went out . . .

exercise 3   Use the cues to form questions with the past continuous tense. Then use the questions to interview a classmate.

> example: **In the summer of 1994 Lina was living in Cairo, Egypt. She was living with her family. She wasn't traveling or studying. She was working in a travel agency and getting ready to come to the United States to study English.**

In the summer of 1994 . . .

1. where / you / live?
2. who / you / live with?
3. you / study? Where?
4. you / work? Where?
5. you / travel? Where?

Finally, tell the class about your partner.

exercise 4   Tom is complaining that nothing in his life ever changes. Use the following cues to compare past and present activities in Tom's life.

> example: study chemistry
> **A year ago I was studying chemistry, and I'm still studying chemistry.**

1. try to decide on a major
2. live in the dorm
3. save money for a car
4. look for a part-time job
5. plan to learn French

exercise 5   What were you doing a year ago? Is your life basically the same or has it changed? Give five original sentences comparing your situation then to your situation now.

> example: **A year ago I was studying English, and today I'm still studying English.**
> **A year ago I was living in Tokyo, but now I'm living in Canada.**

B. The Simple Past Tense

The simple past tense describes actions or situations that began and ended in the past.

uses	examples	notes
Past Actions	I **studied** at a Japanese university for three years. I **won** a scholarship a year ago.	Time expressions often used with this tense include *yesterday, last week (month, year, Monday, weekend, etc.), a week (month, etc.) ago.*
Past Situations	He **enjoyed** his classes. He **didn't like** math.	

forms	affirmative statements	negative statements
Long Forms	I **studied** for an hour. It **worked** yesterday. They **took** math last year.	I **did not study.** It **did not work** yesterday. They **did not take** math.
Contracted Forms		I **didn't study.** It **didn't work** yesterday. They **didn't take** math.

	questions	possible answers	
Yes/No Questions and Short Answers	**Did** I **study** for an hour? **Did** it **work** yesterday? **Did** they **take** math last year?	Yes, I **did.** Yes, it **did.** Yes, they **did.**	No, I **didn't.** No, it **didn't.** No, they **didn't.**

Note: See Appendix pages 396 to 397 for spelling rules for the *-ed* ending. See Appendix pages 394 to 395 for a list of irregular past verbs. See pages 37–54 for more information on questions and responses. Chapter Seven includes information on the use of the simple past tense with *when* and *while.*

 **exercise 6** Miguel's roommate, Tom, is from the U.S. Midwest. Tell a little about Tom's life by forming complete sentences with the cues given here and on the next page. Pay careful attention to the spelling and pronunciation of the verb endings.

example: Tom / enjoy his childhood a lot
Tom enjoyed his childhood a lot.

1. Tom / live with his parents until college
2. Tom / attend a public high school

3. He / play many sports in high school
4. He / work in a restaurant during high school
5. He / save money from his job
6. Tom / travel a lot during high school
7. He / apply to three universities
8. Tom / want to study business
9. He / decide to go to a large, public university
10. He / hope to get a scholarship.

 **exercise 7**

Miguel is a Colombian studying at a large U.S. university. Tell about Miguel's life by forming complete sentences with the following cues.

example: Miguel / grow up in Colombia
Miguel grew up in Colombia.

1. his parents / meet each other in Bogotá
2. they / get married in 1960
3. they / have six children
4. Miguel / go to a bilingual school
5. he / become fluent in English
6. he / begin university studies in Bogotá
7. he / take a test for a scholarship
8. Miguel / win the scholarship
9. he / choose to study architecture in the United States
10. he / leave Colombia to complete his education

exercise 8

Complete the following conversation with the simple past form of the verbs in parentheses or a form of *do* + simple verb.

TOM: Miguel, guess what? Your sister _called_____ (call) an hour ago.

MIGUEL: Really? From Colombia?

TOM: Yes, and she _____ (speak) to me in English. Her English is very
      1
good.

MIGUEL: It should be good. She _____ (study) here, too. At first, she
        2
_____ (plan) to stay for only one summer, and she just
   3
_____ (take) English courses. She _____ (become)
   4   5
fluent very fast. Then she _____ (apply) to the University of
                              6
Texas. They _____ (accept) her and she _____ (begin)
              7   8
studying there that fall.

TOM: She must be very smart. What _____ she _____
                                     9   10
(major) in?

MIGUEL: When we _____ (be) small, she _____ (tell / always)
11   12

everyone that she was going to be a scientist. Well, she _____
13

(start) in engineering, but she _____ (change) majors. In the end,
14

she _____ (get) her degree in computer science—with honors!
15

We all _____ (feel) very proud of her.
16

 **exercise 9**   Interview beginning a classmate about his or her experiences in high school. Write
eight questions beginning with *Did*. Then ask your partner the questions.

examples: **Did you take calculus in high school?**
Did you ever fail a class?
Did you study English?
Did you study any other language?

Then write eight sentences about your partner.

example: **Mei Lin didn't take calculus in high school. She never failed a
class. She studied English for four years. She also studied
French for two years.**

exercise 10   Fill in the blanks using the words in parentheses. Use the simple past or past
continuous forms of the verbs.

ANA: What _____ were _____ you _____ doing _____ (do) two hours ago?

MAY: I _____ (sleep), of course. It was only six-thirty A.M.!
1

ANA: _____ you _____ (feel) the earthquake?
2   3

MAY: Earthquake! No! I _____ (not feel) anything. I
4

_____ (not know) there was an earthquake. I _____
5   6

(not hear) about it on the news.

ANA: Well, there was. I _____ (feel) it. It _____ (start) at
7   8

exactly six thirty-eight. I _____ (do) my exercises at the time.
9

Suddenly the floor _____ (start) to move. It _____
10   11

(last) for about fifteen seconds.

MAY: _____ you _____ (have) any damage in your
12   13

apartment?

ANA: No. I guess it _____ (not be) a very big earthquake.
14

MAY: _____ (be) you afraid?
15

ANA: No. To tell you the truth, I _____ (enjoy) it!
16

Complete the following letter with the simple present, simple past, present continuous, or past continuous forms of the verbs in parentheses.

Madison

September 10

Dear Mom and Dad,

 I __miss__ (miss) all of you, and I _____ (hope)
 ₁

everything _____ (be) fine at home.
 ₂

 Let me tell you about my first few days. I _____ (arrive)
 ₃

in Madison three weeks ago. At that time it _____ (rain) a
 ₄

lot. My first few days _____ (not be) very good because I
 ₅

_____ (feel) depressed and homesick. I immediately
 ₆

_____ (notice) a lot of things that _____ (be)
 ₇ ₈

new to me. The students, especially, _____ (seem) so dif-
 ₉

ferent from students at home. Students here _____
 ₁₀

(wear / usually) very casual clothing, and there _____ (be)
 ₁₁

some students who _____ (not take) school very seriously.
 ₁₂

To give you an idea, I'll describe one situation. Last Monday I

_____ (study) in the library. I _____ (try) hard
 ₁₃ ₁₄

to concentrate, but several students around me _____ (talk)
 ₁₅

and some _____ (laugh). I _____ (get) upset. But
 ₁₆ ₁₇

then I _____ (ask) them to be quiet, and they
 ₁₈

_____ (be) very nice about it.
 ₁₉

 Now I _____ (understand) that at first I _____
 ₂₀ ₂₁

(be) just too nervous about going to school in a new country. And, I

_____ (begin) to enjoy my life here. It _____
  22   23
(be) autumn, and the leaves on the trees _____ (change)
                                                24
color. Right now some students _____ (play) football—
                                      25
American football—outside. Yesterday, my roommate Tom _____
                                                              26
(ask) me to play with them, and I _____ (score) two touch-
                                          27
downs! But we _____ (lose) anyway.
                  28
    This _____ (be) all for now. I _____ (have) to
            29   30
study. My teachers _____ (give / always) us a lot of homework.
                          31

Love,
Miguel

C. Used To

Used to + simple form of the verb describes activities or situations that were true or happened regularly in the past but that no longer exist now.

uses	examples	notes
Past Situations	I **used to live** in a small town. (Now I live in a big city.)	Time expressions that often appear with _used to_ include _not anymore_ and _every week (month, summer, year, etc.)_.
Past Habits	He **used to play** tennis on Monday. (Now he plays on Tuesday.)	
Repeated Actions in the Past	My family **used to rent** a cabin every summer. (We don't anymore.)	

forms	affirmative statements	negative statements
Long Forms	I **used to study** every night. He **used to work** every weekend.	I **did not (didn't) use to study.** He **did not (didn't) use to work.**

questions		possible answers
Yes/No Questions and Short Answers	**Did** you **use to study** every night? **Did** he **use to work** every weekend?	Yes, I **did.** No, I **didn't.** Yes, he **did.** No, he **didn't.**

exercise 12

Marie is a freshman in college. The sentences below tell about her life when she was in high school. Restate the sentences below with *used to*.

example: In high school, Marie wore a uniform to school every day.
           Marie used to wear a uniform to school every day.

1. When she was in high school, Marie lived at home with her parents.
2. She had her own room.
3. She didn't have a lot of homework.
4. She had a lot of time to watch television and talk on the phone with her friends.
5. Her father woke her up for school every morning.
6. Her mother helped her with her chemistry homework.
7. She and her friends spent a lot of time at the shopping mall.
8. She didn't have to take responsibility for herself.

exercise 13

Now tell about your own life in high school. Use the sentences in Exercise 12 as a model. You may add sentences to make your writing more interesting.

example: When she was in high school, Marie lived at home with her parents. She had her own room.
           When I was in high school, I used to live at home with my parents.
           I didn't use to have my own room. In fact, I had to share a room with my two younger brothers!

exercise 14

Use the cues below to form questions with *used to*. Then use the questions to interview a classmate about what he or she used to do during the summer in his or her country.

example: go to the beach every day
           A: **Did you use to go to the beach every day during the summer?**
           B: **No, I didn't use to go to the beach, but I used to go swimming at the public swimming pool all the time.**

1. go to the mountains
2. see a lot of movies
3. read a lot of books
4. visit your relatives in other cities
5. travel with your family
6. work part-time
7. get bored
8. play with the kids in your neighborhood
9. visit museums
10. look forward to the first day of school

Using What You've Learned

Storytelling.   Go back to Exercise 2, on page 19. Write a story about what happened to Miguel and his girlfriend after the lights went out in the restaurant. You can begin like this:

> On December 12, 1994, Miguel and his girlfriend Ana were sitting in their favorite restaurant and celebrating Ana's birthday. She was wearing. . . . He was wearing. . . . They were feeling completely happy together.
> Suddenly, the lights went out. . . .

Sharing Memories.   Do you have special memories from your childhood? Your memories may be of the place where you grew up, the friends that you used to play with, or the games that you used to play, for example. Choose one special memory and describe it in a short composition. Then work in small groups and take turns telling your stories.

example: **When I was a child, we used to play outside a lot during the winter. We loved the snow, and we used to build igloos and forts and slides. One winter, we built a very long slide down the hill behind our house. All of us remember that slide very well because while my cousin was going down the slide, she hit a tree. . . .**

Describing Schools.   Sit with three other classmates and tell one another about the similarities and differences between the school you are attending now and the last school you attended in your country. You may also talk about your personal experiences at both schools. A few discussion points are listed below, but feel free to add to the list:

- the types of schools (for example, a high school versus an intensive English program)
- the types of students
- the number of hours of instruction per week
- subjects taught
- homework, tests
- relationship between students and teachers
- your purpose in attending both schools
- your success

TOPIC **three**
Future Verb Forms

Setting the Context

previewing the passage

Have you ever taken a lecture class? Are classes in your native country primarily lectures or small group discussions? Share your ideas and experiences while answering the following questions about the picture.

- Who is the man walking into the room?
- What kind of a class is this and what are these students going to learn?

COMPUTER SCIENCE 104

"Good morning. This is Computer Science 104. My name is John Andrews, and I will be your instructor for this course. Tomorrow I am going to choose two teaching assistants who will teach the discussion sections and help grade the assignments. I will introduce the new T.A.s to you at our next meeting.

5   "During the course, you'll be learning about three important computer languages: BASIC, PASCAL, and FORTRAN. For the next three weeks, we will be spending a lot of time on BASIC. You are going to write programs in BASIC first. Then we'll begin PASCAL. There will be a midterm and a final exam. If you do well on the programming assignments, you will have no
10 trouble with the tests.

"Are there any questions before I begin today's lecture?"

discussing ideas

- What is a lecture? What is a discussion section?
- What is a teaching assistant? Do you have T.A.s in any of your courses? What will they be teaching?

A. Be Going To

Be going to + verb often expresses specific future plans or intentions. It is common in conversation and often sounds like "gonna" or "gunna."

uses	examples	notes
Future Plans	I**'m going to** study tonight. She**'s going to** help me with my work.	Future time expressions such as *later, this afternoon (evening, weekend), tomorrow, etc.* are often used with *be going to*.
Future Intentions	I**'m going to** get good grades this term. I**'m not going to** go to so many parties.	

forms	affirmative statements	negative statements
Long Forms	I **am going to** study tonight. She **is going to** work. They **are going to** leave now.	I **am not going to** study tonight. She **is not going to** work. They **are not going to** leave now.
Contracted Forms	I**'m going to** study tonight. She**'s going to** work today. They**'re going to** leave soon.	I**'m not going to** study tonight. She **isn't going to** work today. They **aren't going to** leave soon.

	questions	possible answers	
Yes/No Questions and Short Answers	**Am** I **going to** study tonight? **Is** she **going to** work today? **Are** they **going to** leave soon?	Yes, I **am.** Yes, she **is.** Yes, they **are.**	No, I**'m not.** No, she **isn't.** No, they **aren't.**

Note: See pages 37–54 for more information on questions and responses.

Use *be going to* with the following cues to ask your teacher questions about your English course. Then ask your teacher at least five additional questions about plans for this quarter or semester.

example: you / assign homework every night
Are you going to assign homework every night?

1. we / finish this book
2. we / have many tests
3. you / give homework on the weekends
4. the class / take any field trips
5. we / have any class parties
6. there / be any guest speakers
7. we / see videos in class
8. you / correct our grammar mistakes

When students begin a new quarter or semester, they usually have good intentions to study a lot, to get good grades, and so forth. List four things that you are going to do this semester and then list four things that you are *not* going to do. You may use the following cues or form your own sentences.

examples: I'm going to study every night.
I'm not going to go to parties during the week.

- go to the language lab every week
- study my notes after every lecture
- wait until the last minute to begin studying for exams
- visit my professors during office hours
- do my homework with the TV on
- turn assignments in late
- fall asleep in class

B. The Simple Future Tense

Like *be going to,* the simple future tense expresses future intentions. In some cases, *will* and *be going to* are interchangeable. However, *will* (not *going to*) is normally used to express offers, predictions, promises, and requests. In spoken English, the contracted forms are common.

uses	examples	notes
Intentions *Offers* *Predictions*	I**'ll work** much harder from now on. Mary **will find** some books for you. I**'ll get** a better grade by studying more.	Time expressions often used with this tense include *tomorrow, next week (month, year, Monday), from now on, in the future.*
Promises *Requests*	I**'ll do** a better job next time! **Will** you **help** me with my work?	

forms	affirmative statements	negative statements
Long Forms	I **will study** tonight. It **will work** very well. They **will take** math next term.	I **will not study** tonight. It **will not work** very well. They **will not take** math next term.
Contracted Forms	I**'ll study** tonight. It**'ll work** very well. They**'ll take** math next term.	I **won't study** tonight. It **won't work** very well. They **won't take** math next term.

	questions	possible answers
Yes/No Questions and Short Answers	**Will** I **study** tonight? **Will** it **work**? **Will** they **take** math?	Yes, I **will.** No, I **won't.** Yes, it **will.** No, it **won't.** Yes, they **will.** No, they **won't.**

Note: See pages 41–47 for more information on questions and responses. Chapter Six includes information on the use of the simple future with *if, unless, when* and other conjunctions.

exercise 3   Mothers always worry when their children go away to school. In pairs, take turns asking and answering this worried mother's questions. You may give short or long answers.

> example: study hard
> A: **Will you study hard?**
> B: **Yes, Mom, I'll study very hard.**

1. get plenty of sleep
2. eat well
3. go to bed early
4. do all of your assignments
5. be polite in class
6. ask a lot of questions
7. send us postcards
8. phone once a week
9. let us know if you need money
10. take good care of yourself

exercise 4   Robert is having trouble in his history class. He decides to visit his teacher in her office. Fill in the blanks here and on the next page with *will* or *be going to*. In some cases both forms are correct. Use contractions when possible.

ROBERT: I got a "D" on the last exam. Do you have time to talk to me about it?

TEACHER: I _____ (be) in my office on Wednesday afternoon from
1:00 to 4:00. Come by then and I _____ (go over) your test
with you, OK?

ROBERT: Thanks. I _____ (be) there around 1:30.

Later . . .

ROBERT: I don't understand what's wrong with my answer to question number 2.

_____ you _____ (explain) it to me?
₄   ₅

TEACHER: Let's see. Well, you didn't answer the question completely. The question says to tell what happened and list the reasons. You didn't talk about the reasons.

ROBERT: I see. Well, on the next test I _____ (read) the questions more carefully. And next time I _____ (not start) studying at 11 o'clock on the night before the test.

TEACHER: You sound very motivated to improve, Robert. I'm sure that you _____ (get) a better grade on the next test. Good luck!
₈

 C. The Future Continuous Tense

The future continuous tense normally describes actions that will be in progress in the future. This means that they will begin before, and perhaps continue after, a specific time in the future.

uses	examples	notes
Actions in Progress in the Future	At this time tomorrow, **I'll be taking** a test. **Will** you **be taking** the test, too? A week from today, we**'ll be flying** home.	Specific time expressions such as *at 3:00 (noon), at that time, at this time tomorrow (next week), the day after tomorrow, a week (month) from today* often appear with this tense.

forms	affirmative statements	negative statements
Long Forms	I **will be studying** this weekend. It **will be working** at noon. They **will be taking** the exam on Saturday.	I **will not be studying** this weekend. It **will not be working** at noon. They **won't be taking** the exam then.
Contracted Forms	I**'ll be studying** at 6. It**'ll be working**. They**'ll be taking** the exam at 2.	I **won't be studying** at 6. It **won't be working** then. They **won't be taking** the exam at 2.

	questions	possible answers
Yes/No Questions and Short Answers	**Will** I **be studying** there? **Will** it **be working** at noon? **Will** we **be taking** the exam then?	Yes, I **will.** No, I **won't.** Yes, it **will.** No, it **won't.** Yes, we **will.** No, we **won't.**

Note: See Appendix pages 396–397 for spelling rules for the *-ing* ending. See pages 37–54 of this chapter for more information on questions and responses. See pages 13–14 for a list of verbs that do not normally appear in the continuous tenses.

 Underline all uses of the future continuous tense in the passage "Computer Science 104" on page 28. Pay attention to the time expression used in each case.

 Robert wants to make another appointment to see his history teacher in her office. Unfortunately she is very busy. Look at the teacher's schedule and make sentences using the future continuous tense.

example: Tuesday / 1 to 3 P.M. / attend a faculty meeting
On Tuesday from 1 to 3 P.M., she'll be attending a faculty meeting.

1. Monday / teach all morning
2. Monday from 12 to 1 P.M. / have lunch with the chairman of the history department
3. Monday afternoon / writing a report
4. Tuesday / teach from 9 to 11 A.M.
5. Tuesday / observe a student teacher from 11 to 12:30
6. Tuesday from 1 to 3 P.M. / attend a faculty meeting
7. Tuesday / write an exam from 3 to 5 P.M.
8. Wednesday / attend meetings all day

 With a partner, take turns interviewing one another about your schedules for the rest of this week. Ask at least eight questions.

examples: **What will you be doing at 6 A.M. tomorrow?**
Will you be working in the library on Saturday?

 Use the following syllabus to describe the coursework expected in Computer Science 104. Use *going to*, the simple future, and the future continuous to form at least ten sentences.

Week 1 - read Chapters 1, 2, 3 of text; form study groups for research projects
Week 2 - read Chapters 4, 5 of text; hand in outline for the research project; start the first program in BASIC
Week 3 - critique outlines; finish the first program in BASIC
Week 4 - work on the research project; read Chapters 6, 7 of text; write a program in PASCAL
Week 5 - review for the exam; complete first draft of the research project
Week 6 - take midterm exam; read Chapter 8 of text

examples: **In the first week, we are going to read Chapters 1, 2, and 3 of the text.**
During the first week, we will be forming study groups.
There will be a midterm exam the sixth week.

 **exercise 9**   **Review.**   Review all the tenses in this chapter by using appropriate forms of the verbs in parentheses. In some cases, more than one form may be appropriate. Be prepared to explain your choices.

FOREIGN STUDENTS IN THE UNITED STATES

The first foreign students _____ (come) to the United States to study over two hundred years ago. For two centuries, until World War II, the percentage of foreign students in the United States _____ (stay) about the same. Then, after the war, foreign student enrollment _____ (start) to change. In the 1950s, the number of foreign students _____ (begin) to increase tremendously. This trend _____ (continue) through the 1960s and 1970s. During 1980 and 1981, for example, more than 300,000 foreigners _____ (study) in U.S. schools. At that time, 47,000 _____ (be) from Iran and almost 20,000 _____ (be) from Taiwan. As a region, South and East Asia _____ (send) the greatest number of students in 1980.

Nowadays, some nations, such as the OPEC countries, _____ (send) fewer students than they did in the past. The Asian countries, on the other hand, _____ (sponsor) more students than ever. In fact, more than 60% of all the international students studying in the U.S. _____ (come) from Asia. The largest number _____ (come) from China. Japan is second, and Taiwan is third. Almost half of these foreign students _____ (major) in either business or engineering.

In the future, the number of foreign students in the United States _____ (continue / certainly) to grow. It is estimated that, by the year 2000, more than half a million students from foreign countries _____ (study) in the U.S. Of these, more than half _____ (be) graduate students.

Using What You've Learned

Fortune-Telling. Imagine that you are going to a fortune-teller to ask questions about your future. Work with a partner. Ask and answer questions using the simple future, *going to,* and the future continuous. The customer can ask questions about family, money, health, work, and so on.

example:

CUSTOMER: **Where will I be living five years from now?**
FORTUNE-TELLER: **Five years from now you will be living in Paris, France.**
CUSTOMER: **Will I be married?**
FORTUNE-TELLER: **You will be married to a man from Morocco, but you won't have any children yet.**

activity **2**

Describing Educational Experiences and Plans. Sit in groups of three or four. Take turns talking about your educational history. Tell your classmates:

- where you went to school in the past
- why you are taking English courses now
- what you plan to do or accomplish in the future

Try to use all the verb tenses you have reviewed in this chapter.

TOPIC **four**

Questions and Responses

Setting the Context

*previewing
the
passage*

At Miguel's university, every foreign student has an advisor. Do you have an advisor or counselor at your school? Share your information about advisors while answering the following questions about the picture.

- Where is Miguel?
- What kinds of questions do you think the advisor is going to ask Miguel?

THE FOREIGN STUDENT ADVISOR

ADVISOR: It's nice to meet you, Miguel. Now, tell me a little about yourself. First of all, you're from Colombia, aren't you? Did your family come with you?

MIGUEL: Yes, I'm from Colombia. And, no, my family didn't come with me. They're in Bogotá now. My sister studied in the United States several years ago, though. She won a scholarship to study here, and so did I.

ADVISOR: That's great, Miguel. Well, this is your first visit to the U.S., isn't it? When did you arrive? How do you like it so far?

MIGUEL: I arrived on Saturday, August 28th. It was a long trip, and I finally got here at 11:00 P.M.. This is my first visit to the States, so I'm a little nervous, of course! But I know that I'm going to like it here a lot.

ADVISOR: How many hours does it take to fly here from Bogotá?

MIGUEL: Well, it normally takes about twelve hours.

ADVISOR: That's a long trip! Now, tell me about your university work. You began your studies in Colombia, didn't you? Where did you study? How many semesters did you complete? I have a copy of your transcripts, don't I? . . .

What questions did Miguel's advisor ask? What are some other questions that advisors might ask students? What questions would you like to ask your advisor?

exercise 1

Review. Two roommates are talking. Use the cues below to write complete questions and short answers. Then work in pairs and take turns asking and answering your questions.

example: studying accounting this semester / yes
    A: **Are you studying accounting this semester?**
    B: **Yes, I am.**

1. want to see a movie tonight / sorry, but no
2. going to study tonight / yes
3. have a lot of work to do / yes
4. get a bad grade on your accounting test yesterday / yes
5. test difficult / yes
6. know where Jack is / no
7. Jack say where he was going / no
8. Sally still at the library / yes
9. you be here when I get back / yes
10. studying tomorrow night too / yes

A. Auxiliary Verbs with *Too, Either, So,* and *Neither*

If two sentences have different subjects but the same verb, you can shorten the second sentence by using an auxiliary verb (*do, did, was, will,* etc.) + *too, so, either,* or *neither.*

	Two Complete Sentences	Complete Sentence + Shortened Sentence	
Affirmative	I like to study. John likes to study.	I like to study. John **does, too.** I like to study. **So does** John.	*Too* follows the auxiliary verb or *be* in the shortened sentence.
	I am a teaching assistant. John is a teaching assistant.	I am a teaching assistant. John **is, too.** I am a teaching assistant. **So is** John.	The auxiliary verb or *be* follows *so* in the shortened sentence.
Negative	You don't like to study. Mary doesn't like to study.	You don't like to study. Mary **doesn't either.** You don't like to study. **Neither does** Mary.	*Either* follows the auxiliary verb or *be* in the shortened sentence.
	Mary isn't a good student. I'm not a good student.	Mary isn't a good student. I'm **not either.** Mary isn't a good student. **Neither am** I.	The auxiliary verb or *be* follows *neither* in the shortened sentence.

exercise 2   Complete the following with the appropriate auxiliary verb and *too* or *either*.

example: My sister hates to study, and I <u>do</u>   <u>too</u>   .

She doesn't get good grades, and I <u>don't</u>

<u>either</u>   .

1. My sister always gets C's, and I _____ _____.

2. I'm not a good student, and she _____ _____.

3. I got bad grades last semester, and she _____ _____.

4. I wasn't serious enough, and she _____ _____.

5. I'm starting to feel worried, and she _____ _____.

6. She's planning to work harder, and I _____ _____.

7. I'll go to the library every night, and she _____

_____.

8. I won't go to parties every night, and she _____

_____.

Work in pairs and take turns making statements and responding. Use the words in parentheses to give short responses with *so* or *neither*.

examples: The textbook for chemistry is expensive. (the lab manual)
A: **The textbook for chemistry is expensive.**
B: **So is the lab manual.**

The books for math are not expensive. (the books for English)
A: **The books for math are not expensive.**
B: **Neither are the books for English.**

1. My dormitory is always noisy. (my apartment building)
2. The dorm food isn't very good. (the cafeteria food)
3. Gino's has good pizza. (the student union)
4. The student union wasn't crowded last night. (Smith Library)
5. A lot of foreign students study at Smith Library. (many graduate students)
6. Smith Library closed early last night. (the language lab)
7. Ali is going to study in the library tonight. (his roommate)
8. Professor Shaw will not have office hours this Wednesday. (Professor Marcus)

 **exercise 4**

In pairs, take turns making true statements and responding with *too, so, either,* or *neither.* Follow the examples.

examples: I (don't) like the food at the student union.
A: **I don't like the food at the student union.**
B: **Oh, really? I do.** *or*
I don't either. / Neither do I.

I'm (not) going to bed early tonight.
A: **I'm going to bed early tonight.**
B: **So am I.** *or* **I am, too.**

1. I (don't) like the food at the dormitory.
2. I'm (not) going to eat at the dorm tonight.
3. I'm (not) going to study after dinner.
4. I'll (I won't) finish everything tonight.
5. I (don't) have a car.
6. I (don't) think chemistry (biology, English grammar, etc.) is interesting.
7. I got (didn't get) a good grade on the last test.
8. I had (didn't have) a great time during my last vacation.

B. Tag Questions

Tag questions are short questions at the ends of sentences. They use the same auxiliary verbs as yes/no questions. If the statement is affirmative, the tag question is negative. If the statement is negative, the tag question is affirmative. In general, people use tag questions when they expect a certain response. A negative tag question normally receives an affirmative response. An affirmative tag question normally receives a negative response.

	affirmative statement + negative tag; expected response	negative statement + affirmative tag; expected response
Simple Present and Past Tenses	"You study a lot, **don't you?**" "Yes, I do." "You studied a lot, **didn't you?**" "Yes, I did."	"You don't study a lot, **do you?**" "No, I don't." "You didn't study a lot, **did you?**" "No, I didn't."
The Verb be; Present and Past Continuous Tenses; be going to	"You're a student, **aren't you?**" "Yes, I am." "She's studying, **isn't she?**" "Yes, she is." "They were, **weren't they?**" "Yes, they were." "He's going to study, **isn't he?**" "Yes, he is."	"You aren't a student, **are you?**" "No, I'm not." "She isn't studying, **is she?**" "No, she isn't." "They weren't, **were they?**" "No, they weren't." "He isn't going to study, **is he?**" "No, he isn't."
Simple Future and Future Continuous Tenses	"You will study, **won't you?**" "Yes, I will." "He'll be studying, **won't he?**" "Yes, he will."	"You won't study tonight, **will you?**" "No, I won't." "He won't be studying, **will he?**" "No, he won't."

 **exercise 5**   In pairs, take turns making statements with tag questions and giving short responses.

examples: A: You aren't studying now, <u>are</u>   <u>you</u>   ?

B: <u>No,</u>   <u>I'm</u>   <u>not</u>   .

A: Your roommate is studying now, <u>isn't</u>   <u>she</u>   ?

B: <u>Yes,</u>   <u>she</u>   <u>is</u>   .

1. Your friend Paulette is at the library, _____ _____ ?

2. She was studying at the library last night, _____ _____ ?

3. You're not going to play soccer tonight, _____ _____ ?

4. We're playing soccer tomorrow, _____ _____ ?

5. Your friends aren't coming tonight, _____ _____ ?

6. They were here last night, _____ _____ ?

7. You'll wait for me after class, _____ _____ ?

8. You won't forget, _____ _____ ?

9. You'll be working in the language lab tonight, _____ _____ ?

10. You're not going away this weekend, _____ _____ ?

 **exercise 6**   Work in pairs. Use the cues below to form tag questions and the expected answers. Expand the answers with an explanation or additional information.

    examples: always ask a lot of questions
            A: **You always ask a lot of questions in class, don't you?**
            B: **Yes, I do. I don't always understand everything.**

            not eat lunch in the cafeteria yesterday
            A: **You didn't eat lunch in the cafeteria yesterday, did you?**
            B: **No, I didn't. I took a bag lunch.**

1. got an A on the last English test
2. absent last Friday
3. not go out much at night
4. not enjoy writing essays
5. not study next Friday night
6. not like American food
7. have classes every day
8. have an account at the computer center

 **exercise 7**   When we make questions with tags, we expect a certain answer, affirmative or negative. However, sometimes listeners give answers that are different from what we expect. For example:

    QUESTION: You're from Taiwan, aren't you?
     ANSWER: No, actually I'm from the People's Republic of China.

                                           Interactions Two • Grammar

Sit with a classmate that you don't know very well. Take turns asking each other affirmative or negative tag questions about the topics below. Answer the questions truthfully.

examples: native language
A: **Your native language is Chinese, isn't it?**
B: **Yes, it is.** *or* **No, actually it's Malaysian.**

if your partner lives alone
A: **You don't live alone, do you?**
B: **No, I don't. I live with my uncle and aunt.** *or* **Yes, I do.**

1. native country
2. native language
3. where your partner lives
4. what kind of transportation your partner uses to come to school
5. if English is very easy for your partner to learn
6. major
7. if your partner failed the last test
8. if your partner is a U.S. or Canadian citizen

C. Information Questions; Common Question Words

Information questions ask *who, what, when, where, why, how, how often,* and so on. In most information questions, the auxiliary verb comes *before* the subject. However, in questions about the subject (with *who, which,* and *what*) there is *no* auxiliary verb.

Information Questions with *When, What Time, Where, Why,* etc.

	question word	auxiliary verb	subject	main verb
***With be and* will**	**When**	**is**	Kim	**coming?**
	What time	**is**	she	**going to arrive?**
	Where	**was**	she	**going?**
	What	**will**	she	**do** here?
	How long	**will**	she	**be staying** in Dallas?
With Other Verbs	**When**	**does**	the bus	**arrive?**
	How long	**does**	the trip	**take?**
	How	**did**	the accident	**happen?**
	Where	**did**	it	**happen?**
	Which hospital	**did**	Kim	**go** to?

Information Questions About the Subject with *Who, Which,* and *What*

	question word	verb
With All Verbs	Who Who Who Which person What	**was hurt** in the accident? **is** in the hospital? **saw** the accident? **was driving?** **happened?**

Common Question Words

examples	notes
how	asks about manner
how . . . like	asks for an opinion
how + *adjective or adverb* 　how cold (hot, far, late, fast, slow, etc.) 　how long 　how many 　how much 　how often	asks about a characteristic (such as temperature, distance, or speed) asks about length of time asks about quantity (count nouns) asks about quantity (noncount nouns) asks about frequency
what	asks about things
what . . . be like	asks for a description*
what + noun 　what kind of 　what color (country, size, etc.)	 asks about category asks for specific details
what time	asks for a specific time
when	asks about time (specific or general)
where	asks about place or direction

*What does she (he, it) look like?　asks for a physical description
　What is he (she, it) like?　　　　asks about qualities or characteristics (*interesting, nice, fun,* etc.)

examples	notes
which (+ *noun*) which book (city, one, etc.)	asks about a specific person, place, or thing
who(m)	asks about people
whose	asks about ownership or possession
why	asks for reasons

exercise 8   Miguel is talking to his advisor. Complete their conversation with question words.

> **example:**   ADVISOR: Tell me, Miguel . . . _____ *What*'s new?
> MIGUEL: I have a lot to tell you about!

1. ADVISOR: _____ are your classes like?

   MIGUEL: They're all interesting, but my English class is difficult.

2. ADVISOR: _____ English class are you taking?

   MIGUEL: English 117.

3. ADVISOR: _____ is your instructor?

   MIGUEL: Professor Burnson.

4. ADVISOR: _____ does it seem difficult?

   MIGUEL: Because we have to do a lot of writing.

5. ADVISOR: _____ of assignments does he give?

   MIGUEL: The assignments are long essays, but I'm learning a lot from them.

6. ADVISOR: I suggest that you talk to Professor Burnson. _____ is his office?

   MIGUEL: It's in Smith Library.

7. ADVISOR: _____ does he have office hours?

   MIGUEL: From 10:00 A.M. to noon on Tuesdays.

8. ADVISOR: Now, please tell me about your other classes. _____ history class are you taking?

   MIGUEL: Dr. Fendler's.

exercise 9   Complete the following questions with *how* or with *how + adjective* or *adverb*.

example: MIGUEL: Tom, <u>how far</u> is the Science Center from here?
TOM: About five blocks.

1. MIGUEL: _____ computers do they have at the Science Center?

TOM: About fifty, I think.

2. MIGUEL: _____ does it cost to use a computer?

TOM: Three dollars an hour, I think.

3. MIGUEL: _____ can you use a computer there?

TOM: As often as you want, but you should make a reservation first.

4. MIGUEL: _____ can you work at one time?

TOM: Two hours is the maximum time, I think.

5. MIGUEL: _____ do I get to the Science Center from here?

TOM: Walk straight down Broadway Avenue.

6. MIGUEL: _____ do you like using a computer?

TOM: I really like it. I can work much faster.

Read the following short news item. Use a dictionary or ask your teacher about any unfamiliar vocabulary words. Then write information questions to match the answers below.

STUDENTS DEMAND RIGHTS—TO CHEAT

DHAKA, BANGLADESH (Reuters)— Hundreds of students at a Bangladesh secondary school assaulted teachers and burned a school building in a demonstration in which they demanded the right to cheat during examinations.

Officials said the protests held last Wednesday in Shibganj, in the northern part of the country, began when students marched out of an examination hall shouting, "We seek the right to copy!" and "Allow friends to help us!"

Startled authorities called in police to break up the protests, in which students tore up examination papers, assaulted monitors, and set a building on fire.

Police refused to intervene, however, saying any action on their part could spark protests in other examination centers.

---

1. Q:
A: Hundreds of students at a Bangladesh secondary school.

2. Q:
A: They demanded the right to cheat during examinations.

3. Q:
A: The protests were held in Shibganj in northern Bangladesh.

4. Q:
A: The protests started when students marched out of an examination hall shouting.

5. Q:
A: Last Wednesday.

6. Q:
A: The authorities called in the police.

7. Q:
A: The students tore up examination papers, assaulted monitors, and set a building on fire.

8. Q:
A: The police refused to intervene.

9. Q:
A: The police refused to intervene because they were worried that their action might lead to protests in other examination centers.

D. Prepositions

Common Prepositions of Time

QUESTION: When (What time) did Kim arrive?
RESPONSE: She arrived **in the morning.**

examples	notes
in (during) the morning (July, the summer, 1984)	Use *in* or *during* with periods of time.
during the week (the month, the year)	
on Tuesday (August 13)	Use *on* with days or dates.
at 3:00 (noon, midnight, the beginning, the end)	Use *at* with specific times. *Exception: at* night
from 9:00 **to (until, till)** 5:00	Use *from . . . to (until, till)* with beginning and ending times.
for eight hours (three days)	Use *for* with durations of time.

Common Prepositions of Place and Direction

QUESTION: Where did you see Kim?
RESPONSE: I saw her **in** class.

examples	notes
in class (Ellison Hall, Santa Barbara, California, the West, Canada)	Use *in* with buildings, cities, states, regions, and countries.
on Milpas Street (the Ohio River, Lake Michigan, the East Coast, the Pacific Ocean)	Use *on* with streets and bodies of water.
at 423 Orilla Drive (the corner, home, work, school, church, the office)	Use *at* with specific addresses and certain idiomatic expressions.

Other Prepositions of Place and Location

QUESTION: Where is the book?
RESPONSE: It's **next to** the typewriter.
QUESTION: Where is the market?
RESPONSE: It's **across (up, down)** the street from the theater.

above	down	over
across	in front (back) of	under
beside	near	up
by	on top of	

Use the catalog page below to fill in appropriate prepositions of time in the following sentences.

Biology	100	T TH	1:20
	lab[1]	M	7–10 P.M.
		T	7–10
		W	2–5
		TH	7–10
Business	100	M–F	9:20
	110	T TH	8:20
	210[2]	T TH	10:30
Chemistry	101	T TH	11:20
	210	T TH	9:20–11:20
		M W	7–9
		T TH	7–9
English[3]	101	M–F	9:20
	102	MTWTH	10:30
	225	T TH	12:00–1:30

[1]Open hours, biology lab: January 15–March 15
April 15–June 1
June 15–July 15
September 10–December 10
[2]Not offered in summer or winter.
[3]Open hours, language lab: M–F 6–10   Sat 8–12

example: Chemistry 210 has one section _in (during)_ the morning and

two sections _at_ night.

1. Biology lab meets _____ three hours _____ Wednesday afternoon.

2. Business 210 is offered _____ the spring and _____ the fall.

3. English 225 starts _____ noon and goes _____ an hour and a half.

4. The biology lab is not open _____ August.

5. Most biology labs are held _____ the evening.

6. The language lab has open hours _____ 6:00 _____ 10:00 P.M. _____ the week and _____ 8:00 _____ 12:00 P.M. _____ Saturday morning.

Use the catalog from Exercise 11 to make complete sentences about the following. Use negatives when necessary.

> example: Biology 100 / T TH
> **Biology 100 meets on Tuesday(s) and Thursday(s).**

1. Biology 100 / 1:20
2. Chemistry 210 / M W / 7–9
3. Chemistry 210 / two hours
4. English 101 / M–F / 9:20
5. English 225 / 90 minutes
6. language lab / Sunday
7. biology lab / March 16–April 16
8. Business 210 / summer or winter

Complete the following with appropriate prepositions of place or direction. Use the map to help you.

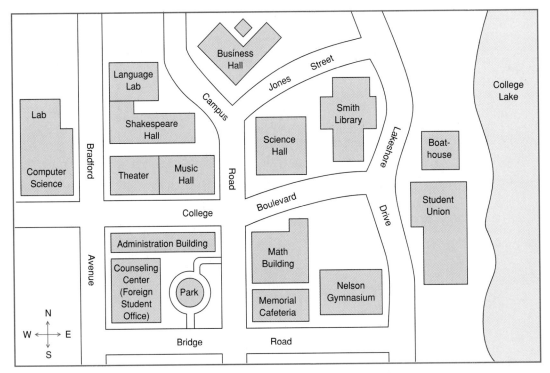

> example: "Excuse me. Where is the administration building?"
>
> "It's _____at_____ 200 College Boulevard."

1. "Excuse me. Where is the computer science building?"

    "It's _____ the corner _____ College Boulevard and

    Bradford Avenue. It's _____ the street _____ the theater."

2. "Excuse me. Could you tell me where the foreign student office is?" "It's

_____ the counseling center. That's _____ Bradford

Avenue _____ the administration building."

3. "Excuse me. Do you know where the boathouse is?"

"It's _____ Lakeshore Drive _____ the student union."

4. "Excuse me. How do I get _____ Smith Library _____

here?"

"Let's see. We're _____ the counseling center now. First, go out

the front door and turn _____ your right. Turn right again

_____ College Boulevard and walk _____ the lake. Smith

Library is _____ the corner _____ College Boulevard and

Lakeshore Drive. It's _____ the street _____ the

boathouse."

exercise 14   Use the map to form true sentences about the locations below.

    example: Boathouse / College Lake
                   The boathouse is next to College Lake.

1. Student Union / Lakeshore Drive
2. Math Building / Memorial Cafeteria
3. Foreign Student Office / park
4. Memorial Cafeteria / Science Hall
5. Computer Science building / Theater building
6. Counseling Center / Bradford Avenue / Bridge Road
7. Language lab / Shakespeare Hall
8. Student Union / Boathouse

exercise 15   **Review.** Miguel is visiting his foreign student advisor again. Complete their conversation by circling the appropriate words here and on the next page. Be prepared to explain your choices.

ADVISOR: Hello, Miguel. Have a seat. How are you (do / (doing))? ((How) / What kind)

         are your classes? You are taking some difficult classes, (are / aren't) you?
                                                         1

MIGUEL: Well, I (want / am wanting) to talk to you about that. I (don't know / am
                              2   3

         not knowing) what to do about my calculus class. I (am not understand-

         ing / don't understand) many things. (Neither / either) do many of my
         4   5

         classmates.

ADVISOR: (Did / Were) you talk to your professor about this?
              6

MIGUEL: It's difficult to talk to him because he (is / is being) very busy. He
arrives (at / on) 9:20, exactly, and he (always leaves / leaves always)
(in / at) the end of class.

ADVISOR: He has office hours, (doesn't / has) he?

MIGUEL: Yes, he (does / do). I (am going to / am going) make an appointment
with him.

ADVISOR: That's good. Now tell me about your other classes.

MIGUEL: I (enjoy / enjoyed) them very much. I have classes (from / for) 9:20
(at / until) noon (on / in) Monday, Wednesday, and Friday. Tuesdays, I
have a lab (for / to) two hours (in / on) the evening. I (usually go / go
usually) (at / to) the library every night . . .

exercise 16   **Review.**   The following conversation takes place on the first day of school. Fill in
the blanks with the missing verbs and question words.

STUDENT: Excuse me. I'm lost. _____ is the math building?

TEACHER: It's right over there. I _____ (go) there too. _____
(you, take) the mathematics placement exam?

STUDENT: Yes, I am. How about you?

TEACHER: I _____ (be) a teaching assistant here.

STUDENT: Oh, really? In which department?

TEACHER: In the math department, actually.

STUDENT: Oh. Maybe I _____ (be) in your class.

TEACHER: It's possible. _____ are you from?
           6

STUDENT: From Egypt.

TEACHER: That's interesting. _____ did you arrive here?
           7

STUDENT: Just two weeks ago.

TEACHER: You _____ (speak) English very well. _____ did
             8   9
you learn it?

STUDENT: In school. In my country we _____ (start) learning English in
                                          10
fourth grade. I always _____ (study) hard because I
                            11
_____ (want) to go to college in the U.S.
     12

TEACHER: _____ are you living? In the dorms?
             13

STUDENT: No, actually I _____ (stay) with my cousins. They
                            14
_____ (have) a house near the campus. It's cheaper for me to
     15
live with them.

TEACHER: I _____ (know) what you mean. Well, here's the math
             16
building. I _____ (see) you around. By the way, my name is
               17
Tom Jenkins.

STUDENT: I'm Ahmed Khalifa. _____ (you, be) in the Ph.D. program?
                                18

TEACHER: Yeah. I _____ (graduate) in June. At this time next year I
                     19
suppose _____ (I, look) for a job.
             20

STUDENT: Well, good luck.

TEACHER: Good luck to you, too.

Using What You've Learned

Comparing Schedules. In pairs, take turns asking and answering questions
about your weekly schedules. Include questions about the following topics:

- your English class(es)
- other classes
- language lab
- work (if you have jobs)
- free time

Use the following calendar to help you. Include specific days and times in your answers.

example: A: **When do you usually go to the language lab?**
B: **I usually go to the lab on Monday and Wednesday at 3:00.**

	monday	tuesday	wednesday	thursday	friday	saturday	sunday
8:00							
9:00							
10:00							
11:00							
12:00							
1:00							
2:00							
3:00							
4:00							
5:00							
Evening							

 **Giving Directions.** Get a map of the campus or area where you are studying. Work in pairs and take turns asking for and giving directions from your building or location to another location that your partner chooses.

example: A: **How do I get to the language lab from here?** *or*
Where is the language lab?
B: **Just go straight up Campus Road. You'll pass the music building on your left. Then you'll see Shakespeare Hall on your right. The language lab is in Shakespeare Hall.**

 **Discussing Educational Issues.** Reread the newspaper article on page 47. Then discuss the following questions in groups.

1. Are "copying" and "helping" your friends on tests the same as cheating?
2. Do students have a "right" to cheat, in your opinion?
3. What do you think happened *before* the protests described in the story? In other words, what events might have led up to the violence?
4. Has anything similar to this ever happened in your country?
5. Is cheating a big problem in your country? What "techniques" do students use?
6. In your country what happens to a student who is caught cheating?
7. Do you know the cheating policy at the school you are now attending?
8. There is a saying in English: "Cheaters never prosper." Do you agree or disagree with this statement?

Verb Tenses

Problems with verb tenses are usually found on standardized tests of English proficiency. After you review the verb tenses, check your understanding by completing the sample items below.

Remember that . . .

- Many verb tenses have a variety of uses.
- Every sentence must have a subject and a verb. A singular subject takes a singular verb, and plural subjects take plural verbs.
- The continuous tenses are used for actions in progress at a certain time. Nonaction verbs are not used in continuous tenses.
- Word order is important with *so* and *neither*.

Part 1. Circle the correct completion for the following.

example: The sun _____ in the east.
       a. rise
       b. is rising
       c. rises
       d. rising

1. After Miguel _____ his test, he left school.
   a. failed
   b. was failing
   c. was failed
   d. failing

2. Steve _____ many people in Meyer Dormitory.
   a. know
   b. is knowing
   c. is know
   d. knows

3. Daigoro _____ in Tokyo seven years ago.
   a. was used to live
   b. used to lived
   c. used to live
   d. living

Part 2. Circle the letter below the word(s) containing the error.

example: Maria <u>is having</u> a large party. Daniel <u>is knowing</u> about it,
            A   Ⓑ

but Miguel <u>doesn't</u>.
C   D

1. The food <u>at</u> Pizza House <u>is tasting</u> good, but the <u>dorm</u> food <u>is</u> like
            A   B   C   D

paper.

2. Tami, Ya-Wen, and Yvonne <u>are going</u> <u>to</u> go to the library <u>after</u> class,
                              A   B   C

<u>don't they?</u>
D

3. Miki <u>didn't know</u> the answers <u>on</u> the test and John <u>didn't</u> <u>neither</u>.
        A   B   C   D

CHAPTER two

City Life

Nouns, Adjectives, Articles, and Pronouns

Topic One: Count Nouns

Topic Two: Noncount Nouns (1)

Topic Three: Noncount Nouns (2)

Topic Four: *The* with Locations and Other Special Uses

in this chapter

57

Setting the Context

Have you ever been to New York City? What have you seen or heard about it? Share your experiences while answering these questions about the pictures.

- What is happening in each picture?
- What does commuting mean? What are some common methods of commuting?

IN PRAISE OF NEW YORK CITY

When people talk about New York City, they usually mean Manhattan. Manhattan is a narrow rock island twelve miles long. Although two million men and women work on this little island, only half a million of those who work there live there. As a result, a million and a half commuters have to get
5   on the island every morning and off it every night. Twenty-eight bridges and tunnels connect Manhattan to the rest of the country. Every day thousands of cars, trucks, buses, motorcycles, and bicycles carry residents, workers, and tourists to and from this financial and cultural center of the United States.

Andy Rooney

discussing ideas

Compare the number of commuters and the number of residents in Manhattan. What kinds of problems does the number of commuters cause? Is this true of most large cities?

A. Introduction to Count and Noncount Nouns

A noun can be a person, place, thing, idea, emotion, or quantity. There are two basic noun groups: those you can count (count nouns) and those you cannot count (noncount nouns). This chapter begins with count nouns. Noncount nouns are covered later. Here are some examples of each kind.

noncount nouns	count nouns		count nouns with irregular noun plurals			
	Singular	*Plural*	*Singular*	*Plural*	*Singular*	*Plural*
air	book	books	child	children	person	people
economics	box	boxes	deer	deer	series	series
furniture	city	cities	fish	fish	sheep	sheep
love	class	classes	foot	feet	species	species
news	key	keys	goose	geese	tooth	teeth
rice	student	students	man	men	woman	women
traffic			mouse	mice		
water			ox	oxen		

Note: See Appendix pages 396 to 397 for spelling rules for *-s* endings.

Write the plural forms of these count nouns.

1. watch _watches_

2. bus _____

3. woman _____

4. shelf _____

5. person _____

6. thief _____

7. tooth _____

8. radio _____

9. child _____

10. mouse _____

11. ski _____

12. monkey_____

13. loaf _____

14. box _____

15. tree _____

16. tomato _____

17. city _____

18. piano _____

19. ghetto _____

20. subway _____

21. church _____

22. ferry _____

B. A, An, and Some

A or *an* with a singular count noun means "one" or refers to a person or thing that is not specific. The article *a* comes before a consonant sound, and *an* comes before a vowel sound. *Some* often appears with plural nouns.

singular nouns	plural nouns
I have **a car.** Is there **a house** for rent nearby? There is **an apartment** above the store. It takes him **an hour** to get to work.	They don't have **cars.** Are there **some houses** for sale around here? There are **some apartments** next door. It sometimes takes **hours** to get home.

exercise 2   Add *a, an,* or *some* to the following list.

1. _____ house

2. _____ apartment

3. _____ churches

4. _____ elevator

5. _____ tunnels

6. _____ taxis

7. _____ condominium

8. _____ shopping mall

9. _____ museums

10. _____ art gallery

11. _____ building

12. _____ offices

13. _____ island   **15.** _____ commuter

14. _____ airport   **16.** _____ headache

exercise 3 Complete the following conversation with the appropriate singular or plural forms of the nouns in parentheses. Include *a* or *an,* if an article is necessary.

AGENT: Could I help you?

ELLEN: Yes, I'm looking for <u>an apartment</u> (apartment). Is it possible

to find _____ (apartment) or _____
             1   2

(studio) for under seven hundred dollars _____ (month)?
                                                         3

AGENT: Well, I occasionally have _____ (apartment) that rents
                                              4

for less than eight hundred dollars _____ (month). Right
                                                    5

now I have _____ (townhouse) available on the east side.
                        6

It is renting for seven hundred and thirty-five dollars a month plus

_____ (utility). And I often have _____
             7   8

(studio) available. In fact, right now there is _____ (studio)
                                                              9

downtown for six hundred and ninety dollars. It's in _____
                                                                        10

(eight-story building) with good security. It's _____
                                                              11

(very nice place) with _____ (large kitchen), and it's in
                                   12

_____ (interesting neighborhood).
             13

ELLEN: Let me think about it and call you tomorrow. Thanks.

exercise 4   Add *a*, *an*, or *some* to the following.

GETTING SETTLED IN A NEW CITY

Finding _____ *a* _____ good place to live in _____ new city
                                                        1

can be difficult. _____ cities have plenty of reasonably priced apart-
                            2

ments and houses, but others don't. In that case, finding _____
                                                                        3

apartment or _____ house can be very difficult, unless you have
                        4

lots of money for rent.

Price isn't the only thing _____ newcomer should think about,
                                            5

though. _____ other considerations are finding _____
                    6   7

safe neighborhood, being close to _____ bus or _____
                                            8   9

subway line, and having _____ grocery store or _____
                                10   11

laundromat nearby.

If you have _____ friends in the new city, you are
                        12

_____ lucky person. Your friends can probably give you
        13

_____ idea of the best places to start looking. If you don't have
        14

friends yet, get advice from people you can trust.

C. Count Nouns with *There + Be*

You can form statements and questions with *there + be (there is / are, was / were, has been / have been)*. When *there* begins a sentence, the verb agrees with the noun that follows it.

forms	affirmative statements	negative statements
Long Forms	**There is** an island in the river. **There are** islands in the river.	**There is** no tunnel to Connecticut. **There are** no tunnels to Connecticut.
Contracted Forms	**There's** an island.	There **isn't** a tunnel. There **aren't** tunnels.

	questions	possible answers
Yes/No Questions and Short Answers	**Is there** a bridge across the East River? **Are there** bridges across the East River?	Yes, **there is.** No, **there isn't.** Yes, **there are.** No, **there aren't.**

exercise 5 Form complete sentences by using *there is + a / an* or *there are* with the following. (Use the map to help you.)

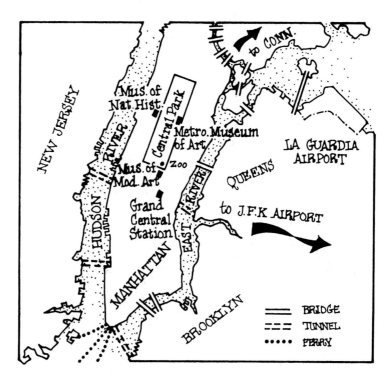

example: subway in New York City
There is a subway in New York City.

1. several tunnels to New York City
2. large park in Manhattan
3. museum in Central Park
4. two museums near Central Park
5. two large airports in New York City
6. island in the East River
7. several bridges across the East River
8. two rivers around Manhattan
9. zoo in Central Park
10. train station in Manhattan

D. Any, Some, and A Lot Of

Some and *a lot of* can appear with plural count nouns. *Any* can appear with singular or plural count nouns. *Any* is often used in questions and in negative statements. The three expressions are also used with noncount nouns (see pages 68 and 70).

singular nouns	plural nouns
Is there **any apartment** for rent now? There isn't **any house** for rent nearby.	Are there **any houses** for sale nearby? There aren't **any apartments** available now. Are there **some (a lot of) houses** for sale around here? There are **some (a lot of) apartments** nearby.

exercise 6   In pairs, ask and answer questions about the map on page 63. Use *any* in your questions and *some* or *not any* in your responses.

> **example:**   ferries to Manhattan
> A: **Are there any ferries to Manhattan?**
> B: **Yes, there are some.**

1. tunnels to New Jersey
2. bridges to New Jersey
3. ferries to Manhattan
4. airports in Manhattan
5. tunnels under the Hudson River
6. museums in Manhattan
7. rivers around Manhattan
8. islands in the Hudson River

exercise 7   Complete the following passage with either *is* or *are*.

ELLEN: Hello, I talked to you yesterday about rentals. __Is__ there still a townhouse for rent?

AGENT: Yes, there _____ . As I said yesterday, there _____ two bedrooms. The
<u> </u>1   2

         townhouse has two floors. Upstairs there _____ a full bath, and downstairs
                                                3

         there _____ a half bath. There _____ four closets, but there _____ a very
                4   5   6

         small kitchen. In the kitchen, there _____ only two cupboards and one
                                            7

         large cabinet. The rent _____ six hundred thirty-five dollars a month.
                            8

         Utilities _____ not included. Would you like to see it?
                9

ELLEN: Yes, I think that I would. _____ there a chance I could see it this after-
                                  10

         noon?

 **exercise 8**   First, read the following story for meaning. Then, circle the correct form from
each pair of verbs in parentheses.

TOUGH LIFE

    My neighborhood (is / are) a tough neighborhood, and it (isn't / aren't) a
                                                                        1

very pretty one. There (is / are) a lot of apartment buildings and parking lots,
                        2

but there (isn't / aren't) any real parks left. There (was / were) some stores
               3   4

nearby until last year, but they (is / are) closed now. There (was / were) too
                              5   6

many robberies. A typical apartment around here (is / are) small and run-down.
                                                7

Some of the apartment buildings (is / are) full, but a lot of them (is / are)
                                      8   9

abandoned. People (is / are) trying to move away because there (is / are) a
                        10   11

lot of problems here. It (is / are) a dangerous neighborhood, and the police
                              12

(doesn't / don't) come here very often. There (isn't / aren't) a lot of families
             13   14

left anymore. There (was / were) a park down the street a few years ago,
                         15

but no one took care of it. Now it (is / are) just a garbage dump. There
                                      16

(isn't / aren't) any flowers or bushes left. There (isn't / aren't) any benches or
swings for the kids. Today there (is / are) just broken bottles and papers and
cans everywhere. There (was / were) a church too, but even the church
(is / are) closed now. It's so sad to see a neighborhood die. I wish I could
move. I don't feel safe here.

Using What You've Learned

Spelling Bee.   Divide into two teams and make lines down each side of your
classroom. Your teacher will give you singular nouns, and you should give the
plural spelling. If you give the correct answer, move to the end of the line. If not,
sit down and study your spelling rules!

Describing Your Neighborhood.   What is your neighborhood like? Are there
houses or apartment buildings? Are there any stores or shopping centers nearby?
First, make a list of eight sentences that describe your neighborhood. Then, work
in pairs. Ask and answer questions about your neighborhoods, using *there is* and
there are as often as possible.

> example: **In my neighborhood, there are a lot of apartment buildings,
> but there aren't any houses.**

Complaining.   You have just rented a furnished apartment. The rental agent gave
you a full description of the apartment, but you did not go in to see it because the
renters were still there. When you go to the apartment for the first time, you find
that it is a mess! You return to the rental agent with a list of your complaints. In
pairs or in groups of three, role-play a scene complaining to the rental agent. You
can begin with "When I rented my apartment, you told me there was (were) . . . ,
but there isn't (aren't). . . ."

Other situations for role-plays in pairs or groups of three:

- You are on a trip and you are staying at a "bargain, no frills" motel. Unfortunately, your "bargain" motel is missing many of the things that were advertized. You go to the manager with a list of complaints: no swimming pool, no donuts for breakfast, no TV, no microwave, no soap, no towels. You can begin with "When I made my reservation, I was told there was (were) . . . , but there isn't (aren't). . . .
- You've made arrangements to rent a van for a two-week trip with your friends. Unfortunately, when you pick up the van, it isn't what you'd expected. You go to the manager of the rental agency with your complaints: no power windows, no air conditioning, no AM-FM radio, no cassette player, no cassette tapes, no CD player, no CDs, no sunroof, no luggage rack, no refrigerator. You can begin with, "When I called to rent this van, I was told there was (were) . . . , but there isn't (aren't) . . . .

TOPIC two
Noncount Nouns (1)

Setting the Context

previewing the passage

Have you ever fixed up a house or an apartment? What are some of the things you often have to do when you move into a new place? Share your experiences while answering these questions about the picture.

- Where are the young women? What are they doing?
- What do they still need to do?
- Do they have a lot of food in the apartment?

ELLEN: May, after we clean the kitchen, let's go shopping. There's no food to eat at all, and we need a little more paint and a few more cleaning supplies.

MAY: And some furniture! So let's make a list. How much paint do we need and how much food should we buy?

ELLEN: We need another gallon of white paint for the living room and a quart of blue paint to finish the bathroom. As for food, let's get a few necessities today and wait to do the rest.

MAY: Okay. Let's see . . . . A dozen eggs. A pound of butter. Two loaves of bread. A jar of peanut butter. Some orange juice. A few bars of soap. A tube of toothpaste. A few rolls of paper towels. Anything else?

ELLEN: Are those what you call necessities? What about milk, cheese, . . .

MAY: Well, just add them to the list.

discussing ideas

Which items are necessities for May? What items does Ellen add to the list? What are ten to fifteen items that are necessities for you?

A. Noncount Versus Count Nouns (1)

Noncount nouns include ideas *(history, knowledge)*, emotions or feelings *(love, peace)*, activities *(tennis, swimming)*, or mass nouns—things that you can measure *(gasoline, rice)* or group together *(furniture)*. The most common mass nouns are names of foods.

	examples	notes
Noncount Nouns bread coffee butter meat cheese rice	We need **bread.** There isn't **any coffee** left. Is there **some rice?**	Noncount nouns are singular and take singular verbs. Do not use *a* or *an* with noncount nouns, however. Instead, you can use adjectives such as *some* and *any*.
Noncount or Count Nouns business a business chicken a chicken glass a glass glasses	We're having **chicken** for dinner. Have you ever held **a chicken?** We need **glass** for the window. Could I have **a glass** of water?	Some nouns are either count or noncount, depending on their meaning. *A* or *an* can be used with these nouns when they are count nouns.

Write *C* in front of the count nouns and *N* in front of the noncount nouns.

1. __C__ egg
2. _____ apple
3. _____ rice
4. _____ sugar
5. _____ chocolate

6. _____ cheese
7. _____ spoon
8. _____ fork
9. _____ milk
10. _____ flour

11. _____ grapefruit
12. _____ salt
13. _____ sandwich
14. _____ potato
15. _____ cereal

exercise 2   The following sentences contain nouns that can be either count or noncount. Complete the sentences with *a* or *x* to indicate that no article is necessary.

examples: This morning, my mother made __(a)__ pie.

Generally, I like __(x)__ pie for dessert.

1. I like tea with _____ lemon.

   Did you remember to buy _____ lemon?

2. I smell _____ gas.

   Neon is _____ gas.

3. Real estate is _____ good business.

   _____ business is good this year.

4. All animals are afraid of _____ fire.

   There was _____ fire in our kitchen this morning.

5. I caught _____ fish yesterday.

   Many people prefer _____ fish to beef.

6. He doesn't like _____ chocolate cake.

   For her birthday, her mother baked her _____ cake.

7. _____ fruit is healthy.

   Is an avocado _____ fruit?

8. Would you like _____ glass of juice?

   Where can I buy _____ glass to repair the window?

9. Fondue is _____ traditional food from Switzerland.

   Everyone needs _____ food to survive.

10. Many people eat _____ turkey on Thanksgiving.

    My uncle has _____ turkey on his farm.

B. *How Much* Versus *How Many*

How much is used to ask questions with noncount nouns. *How many* is used to ask questions with count nouns. Answers to these questions often include indefinite pronouns or adjectives. They may also include units of measurement, such as *a pound of . . .* or *a bottle of . . .*

	examples	notes
Noncount Nouns	**How much bread** do we have? We have **a little bread.** We don't have **any bread.**	Answers to questions with noncount nouns may include a variety of indefinite adjectives such as *a lot (of), lots of, some, much, (a) little* or *not . . . any.*
Count Nouns	**How many loaves of bread** should I buy? Don't buy very **many loaves.** Buy **a few loaves** of bread.	Answers to questions with count nouns may include a variety of indefinite adjectives such as *a lot (of), lots of, some, many, (a) few,* or *not . . . any.*

Note: The expressions *some, (not) any, a lot of,* and *lots of* may be used with both count and noncount nouns. The expressions *(a) little, (a) few, (not) much,* and *(not) many* are covered later.

exercise    Complete the following questions with *how much* or *how many.*

1. How much _____ bread should I buy?

2. _____ apples do we have left?

3. _____ milk do we need?

4. _____ toothpaste should I buy?

5. _____ boxes of detergent should we get?

6. _____ rice do you need for that recipe?

7. _____ water do you drink every day?

8. _____ cups of coffee do you drink?

C. Common Units of Measurement

To give specific amounts of either count or noncount nouns, use the following units of measurement. *Of* follows all the expressions except *dozen.*

bag	sugar, potato chips, potatoes
bar	candy, hand soap
bottle	detergent, ketchup, juice, soda, other liquids
box	cereal, detergent
bunch	bananas, carrots, grapes, green onions, flowers
can	soup, beans, tuna, soda
carton	eggs, milk
cup, tablespoon, teaspoon	all liquid and dry recipe ingredients
dozen∗	eggs, bakery products, fruit and vegetables
gallon, quart, pint	all liquids, ice cream
head	lettuce, cabbage
jar	mayonnaise, peanut butter, jam, mustard, other foods that are spread
loaf	bread
package	potato chips, spaghetti
piece	cake, bread, pie, meat, etc.
pound, ounce	meat, poultry, fruit, vegetables, cheese
roll	paper towels, toilet paper
six-pack, twelve-pack, case	beer, soda
stick	butter
tube	toothpaste

∗*Dozen* does not use *of.* Compare: *I bought a dozen eggs. I bought a carton of eggs.*

exercise 4   Use the picture to complete the list of things that May and Ellen bought at the grocery store.

example: <u>one bunch</u> of grapes

1. _____ of ketchup

2. _____ of eggs

3. _____ of milk

4. _____ of lettuce

5. _____ of green onions

6. _____ of mayonnaise

7. _____ of potatoes

8. _____ of laundry detergent

9. _____ of toothpaste

10. _____ of paper towels

11. _____ of hand soap

12. _____ of soda

exercise 5   Look at the following advertisements for "specials" at local supermarkets. In pairs, take turns asking and answering questions with *how many,* using the cues.

example: pounds of bananas / less than $1
     A: **How many pounds of bananas can you buy for less than $1?**
     B: **You can buy three pounds.**

1. gallons of milk / less than $5
2. boxes of crackers / less than $5

3. heads of lettuce / less than $2
4. pounds of Swiss cheese / less than $7
5. tubes of toothpaste / less than $6
6. bottles of ketchup / less than $2
7. quarts of ice cream / less than $3
8. jars of mayonnaise / less than $3
9. bags of potato chips / $2
10. six-packs of soda / less than $5

DAIRY SPECIAL!

milk 1^{98}/gallon
ice cream 2^{29}/quart
Swiss cheese 3^{49}/lb

MUNCHIES!

crackers 1^{39}/1-lb box
potato chips 1^{26}/8 oz.

Superwhite toothpaste 1^{89}
daisies 2^{50}/bunch
soda 2^{19}/six-pack
hand soap 3 bars/1^{00}
SPECIAL! eggs 1^{19}/carton

mayonnaise 1^{19}
ketchup 1^{29}
lettuce 79¢/head
bananas 39¢/lb

---

exercise  In pairs, practice making questions with *how much*. Take turns asking and answering questions about the ingredients in the recipe.

example: salt
A: **How much salt do you need to make chocolate fudge?**
B: **You need an eighth of a teaspoon of salt.**

1. sugar
2. cocoa

3. milk
4. butter

5. vanilla

⊙⊙⊙⊙⊙**Chocolate Fudge**⊙⊙⊙⊙⊙⊙

cocoa :   6 tablespoons
sugar :   2 cups
butter :   3½ tablespoons
salt :   ⅛ teaspoon
milk :   ¾ cup
vanilla :   1 teaspoon

In pairs, take turns asking and answering questions. Following the examples, make short conversations about the items.

examples: album (count noun)
A: **I bought some new albums today.**
B: **How many albums did you buy?**
A: **I bought three.**

cheese (noncount noun)
A: **I bought some Swiss cheese today.**
B: **How much did you buy?**
A: **I bought two pounds.**

1. Costa Rican coffee
2. gas for the car
3. tickets for the jazz concert
4. detergent
5. fresh fruit

6. strawberry ice cream for dessert
7. carrots
8. wine glasses
9. chicken
10. bananas

Use the charts here and on the next page to convert the items below from British units of measurement to metric units of measurement and vice versa.

example: two gallons of gas
Two gallons of gas is approximately equal to seven liters of gas.

1. one quart of milk
2. five pounds of cheese
3. 72 degrees Fahrenheit
4. five yards of rope
5. one cup of sugar
6. thirty miles

7. 1 liter of soda pop
8. 1 kilogram of hamburger
9. 2 kilometers
10. 3 meters of string
11. 450 grams of butter
12. 25 centimeters of string

Basic Units

Length	meter = about 1.1 yards
	centimeter = .01 meter = about .4 inch
	kilometer = 1,000 meters = about .6 mile
Volume	liter = about 1.06 quarts
	milliliter = 0.001 liter
	5 milliliters = 1 teaspoon
Weight	30 grams = 1.1 ounces
	kilogram = 1,000 grams = 2.2 pounds
Temperature	Celsius: 0° C = 32° F
	37°F = 98.6°F

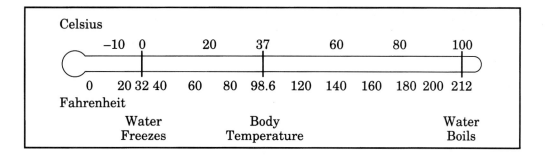

Celsius

−10 0 20 37 60 80 100

0 20 32 40 60 80 98.6 120 140 160 180 200 212

Fahrenheit

Water
Freezes

Body
Temperature

Water
Boils

Using What You've Learned

Shopping Lists.   Do you need to go grocery shopping soon? What do you need to buy? Make a shopping list and then work with a partner. Take turns asking and telling about the items on your list.

If you went grocery shopping recently and don't need to go again soon, then make a list of the items you bought on your last shopping trip.

Giving Recipes.   Do you know how to make an omelette? Do you know how to make a hamburger or a chocolate milkshake? Or perhaps you know how to make something more exotic, such as coq au vin or paella or kushi katsu.

Think of a recipe that you know and make a list of the ingredients. Then work in pairs or small groups and explain your recipes and their ingredients. Even better, prepare the dish for your classmates and let them sample as you explain!

Note: You may want to make a collection of class recipes.

Playing a Memory Game.   All members of the class should sit in a circle. One student will begin the game by saying, "I went to the supermarket, and I bought *a bottle of ketchup*." The next student must repeat the first student's item and add one; for example: "I went to the supermarket, and I bought *a bottle of ketchup and a jar of peanut butter*." The third student will repeat the first two items and add one. You may not write anything, and you are "out" if you forget any of the items *or* if you make a mistake in grammar!

Noncount Nouns (2)

Setting the Context

previewing the passage

City living has both good points and bad points. Share your ideas about cities while answering these questions about the picture.

- Who is the man in front of the apartment building? What is his job? Who is the man on the far right?
- Describe other parts of the picture. What can you do in a big city? What are some things that are difficult to do?

CITY LIFE

Living in a big city has both advantages and disadvantages, but many people think of the disadvantages first. For example, it is often difficult to find good housing in a large city. Apartments are expensive, and there are very few houses available in safe locations. Employment is another problem. Jobs are

5 hard to find in many cities. Transportation is also difficult. Bicycles can be dangerous, buses are not always on time, and parking is expensive.

  City living also has advantages, however. Shopping is much better in a city. There are special stores for everything imaginable. There are restaurants, delicatessens, and grocery stores with food from every part of the world. And,

10 of course, entertainment is one of the biggest advantages of city life. There are art galleries, museums, clubs, plays, concerts, and shows for everyone's taste.

discussing ideas

What are two advantages of life in a big city? What are two disadvantages? Why is housing often a problem in large urban areas?

A. Noncount Versus Count Nouns (2)

Abstract nouns are another common type of noncount noun. Abstract nouns may be ideas, activities, or emotions. They often refer to categories or groups that include count nouns. Compare:

noncount nouns	count nouns
employment	jobs occupations professions
homework	assignments exercises
information	facts statistics
love	dates feelings
news	broadcasts programs
violence	arguments fights wars
weather	climates storms tornadoes

 **exercise 1** **Rapid Oral Practice.** Ellen lives in a large eastern city. Her family lives in the West. She teaches at a public elementary school. Using the following cues, form sentences about Ellen's opinions by adding *is important* or *are important*.

examples: Friends **are important.**
Good transportation **is important.**

1. Free time . . .
2. Honesty . . .
3. Warm clothes . . .
4. Patience . . .
5. Money . . .
6. Neighbors . . .
7. Friends . . .
8. Letters . . .
9. Accurate information . . .
10. News from home . . .

Dear Ann—
—I got your letter today!
Thanks for writing.
News from home is
so important to me!
I miss everyone a lot.
—I'll write soon to
tell you about our new
apartment & about life
in the big city.
love, Ellen

Ann Smith
734 San Rafael
Stanford, CA
94305

 **exercise 2** Fill in each blank with one word from the following list. Some blanks have more than one correct answer.

cities   parking   transportation   housing
area   homes   life   jobs

 Life   in a big city has both advantages and disadvantages. There

are usually many apartments for rent. However, _____ can be very
                                                         1
expensive. For example, very few people can afford to buy _____ .
                                                                    2
Additionally, it is difficult to find housing in a safe _____ .
                                                            3
   Employment is another problem. _____ are hard to find in many
                                           4
_____. _____ is also difficult. Bicycles can be dangerous,
     5   6
buses are not always on time, and _____ is expensive.
                                         7

 B. Noncount Nouns with *There + Be*

There + be is also used with noncount nouns. With noncount nouns, the verb *be* is always singular: *there is, there was, there has been.* Indefinite articles *(a, an)* are not used.

	singular	**plural**
Noncount Nouns	**There is** always good entertainment in New York.	
Count Nouns	**There is** a good play on tonight.	**There are** good plays on every night.

 **exercise** In pairs, take turns making comments and contradicting them. Form complete sentences from the cues. Each set of cues includes one count and one noncount noun. Be sure to use the correct form of the verb with each.

example: cars / heavy traffic
A: **In big cities, there are always a lot of cars.**
B: **That's not true. There isn't always heavy traffic in a big city.**

1. buses / convenient transportation
2. cheap apartments for rent / inexpensive housing
3. shows and concerts / good entertainment
4. poor people / poverty
5. international restaurants / international food
6. unusual buildings / interesting architecture
7. dirty streets and dirty air / serious pollution
8. robberies and assaults / violent crime

C. *(A) Little* Versus *(A) Few; Not Much* Versus *Not Many*

A few, few, and *not many* are used with count nouns. *A little, little,* and *not much* are used with noncount nouns. *A few* and *a little* mean "some" (but not a large amount). *Not many, few, not much,* and *little* mean "a small amount" (perhaps not enough). *Not many* and *not much* are more common in conversational English than *few* and *little.*

with count nouns		**with noncount nouns**	
a few	There are **a few** apples left. (There are some apples left.)	a little	There is **a little** milk left in the carton. (There is a small amount of milk left.)

with count nouns		with noncount nouns	
few	**Few** apples are left. (There is a very small number of apples, probably not as many as we want or need.)	little	There is **little** milk left. (There is a very small amount of milk left, probably not enough.)
not many	There are**n't many** apples left.	not much	There is**n't much** milk left in the carton.

 **Rapid Oral Practice.** Go through the following list and add *a little* or *a few* before each word.

example: friends
a few friends

1. problems
2. time
3. money
4. assignments
5. homework

6. news
7. furniture
8. clothes
9. advice
10. dollars

11. pizza
12. candy
13. facts
14. arguments
15. information

 Add *a few* or *few* before count nouns and *a little* or *little* before noncount nouns.

ELLEN: What will we eat for breakfast tomorrow? Maybe we need to go shopping and buy _____ things at the store.
1

MAY: We have very _____ money, but I think we have enough for
2
groceries for tomorrow's breakfast.

ELLEN: Luckily, we have _____ apples, _____ eggs, and
3   4
_____ butter. All we need is _____ bread and
5   6
_____ jelly for breakfast.
7

MAY: But what about lunch and dinner? We have _____ needs, but we
8
do need to eat!

ELLEN: Well, there are _____ cans of soup and _____ peanut
9   10
butter in the cupboard. It's not much, but it will keep us going until I get
my check on Monday.

**exercise 6**

In pairs, make short conversations with the following cues and *how much, how many, a few, a little,* and units of measurement. Use the example as a model.

There is only a little sugar left.
How much should we buy?

Let's get three bags.

examples: green onions / two
A: **There are only a few green onions left. How many should we buy?**
B: **Let's get two bunches.**

1. ketchup / one
2. hand soap / five
3. mustard / one
4. eggs / one
5. lettuce / two

6. toothpaste / two
7. cheese / several
8. potato / three
9. laundry detergent / two
10. juice / several

**exercise 7**

With a new partner, make new conversations using the cues in Exercise 6. This time use *not many* and *not much* instead of *a few* and *a little*.

examples: sugar / three
A: **There isn't much sugar left. How much should we buy?**
B: **Let's get three bags.**

green onions / two
A: **There aren't many green onions left. How many should we buy?**
B: **Let's get two bunches.**

exercise 8

Review. Circle the correct answer in each of the sentences here and on the next page.

example: How (much /(many)) apples do you need for the pie?

1. I always put (a few / a little) salt in my soup.

2. We don't have (many / much) potatoes in the house.

3. Is there (much / many) juice in the refrigerator?

4. She eats (lots of / many) candy.

5. We eat (few / little) beef, but we eat (many / a lot of) fish.

6. I bought a (dozen / carton) of eggs.

7. When you go to the store, please buy (some / few) butter.

8. How (much / many) milk should I buy?

9. Jack didn't catch (some / any) fish last night.

10. I forgot to buy a (tube / roll) of toothpaste.

11. There aren't (many / some) Chinese restaurants near here.

12. There isn't (a little / much) ice cream left.

Using What You've Learned

Describing Places.   What's your favorite city? What does it have to offer? Is there a lot of entertainment? Are there good restaurants? Is there public transportation? Are there interesting stores and boutiques? Does it have many problems, such as pollution, traffic, or crime? In a brief presentation, describe your favorite city to your classmates, including both its good points and a few of its bad points.

TOPIC **four**

The *with* Locations and Other Special Uses

Setting the Context

previewing the passage

Which major cities have you lived in or visited? Share your experiences while answering these questions about the picture on the opposite page.

- What city is this? How do you know?*
- Why are major cities often located near water?

---

*The city shown on the opposite page is Rio de Janeiro.

CITIES OF THE WORLD

Most of the greatest cities in the world are located near oceans, rivers, or lakes. New York City, Rio de Janeiro, and Buenos Aires are on the Atlantic Ocean. San Francisco, Tokyo, and Santiago are on the Pacific Ocean. Singapore is located on an island in the South China Sea, and Venice is on an island
5 in the Adriatic Sea. London is on the Thames River, Paris is on the Seine River, Cairo is on the Nile River, and Budapest is on the Danube River. Chicago, Cleveland, and Toronto are all on the Great Lakes—Chicago on Lake Michigan, Cleveland on Lake Erie, and Toronto on Lake Ontario.

Because of their locations, most of these cities have famous landmarks
10 associated with water. New York City has the Statue of Liberty on Liberty Island, San Francisco has the Golden Gate Bridge, and Venice has the Grand Canal, to name only a few.

discussing ideas

What are some other cities that are located on the Atlantic Ocean? On the Pacific Ocean? On major rivers or lakes?

A. *The* with Locations

The appears with many proper names and with other specific locations. The list in the Appendix on pages 400 to 401 gives you examples. Notice the common exceptions in that list.

exercise 1 Underline all the bodies of water listed in the passage "Cities of the World." Which use *the*? Which do not use *the*?

exercise 2 Complete the following passage with *the* or X.

THE OLD AND THE NEW

In cities in ___Ⓧ___ Asia and _____ Europe, the old and the new exist

side by side. In _____ city of Paris, modern factories and department stores
        2
are just around the corner from famous landmarks such as _____ Louvre,
                                                              3
_____ Champs-Elysées, or _____ University of Paris. Similarly, in
    4   5
_____ London, especially along the banks of _____ Thames River,
    6   7
historic buildings like _____ Houses of Parliament and _____ Tower of
                            8   9
London are right in the middle of a busy city full of office buildings and

apartments.

exercise 3 Turn to the map of the United States and Canada on page 216. Use it to help you describe the locations of the following places.

       example: Los Angeles
             Los Angeles is in the West. It's in California.
             It's on the West Coast. It's on the Pacific Ocean.

1. Washington, D.C.
2. Rocky Mountains
3. Miami
4. Hudson Bay
5. St. Louis
6. Vancouver
7. Colorado River
8. Montreal
9. Houston
10. Mackenzie River
11. Boston
12. Honolulu

B. *The* with the Verb *Go*

The use of *to* and *the* with *go* is idiomatic. Compare the following.

with no article or preposition	with *to*	with *to the*
I'm going . . .	**She's going . . .**	**He's going . . .**
downtown	to church	to the beach
home	to class	to the city
there	to school	to the hospital
camping	to town	to the library
shopping	to work	to the mountains
swimming (and other	to New York (or the name	to the museum
-ing words)	of any city)	to the post office
		to the station

 **exercise 4** In pairs, take turns asking and answering questions based on the cues.

> **example:** store
> A: **Where are you going?**
> B: **To the store.**

1. home	**7.** church
2. shopping	**8.** town
3. hospital	**9.** city
4. downtown	**10.** class
5. beach	**11.** there
6. Los Angeles	**12.** work

 **exercise 5** Complete the passage here and on the next page by using *to, to the,* or *X.*

A TRIP TO LONDON

"Good morning, ladies and gentlemen. Welcome to today's tour of Greater London. To start our tour, we're going ___*to*___ Windsor, a suburb of London, where we'll visit famous Windsor Castle. This should take about two hours.

"At 11:00 we'll board the bus again and go _____ downtown. There is
                      1
no tour this afternoon, so you will have some free time to go _____ shop-
                                        2
ping, _____ post office, or _____ British Museum, perhaps. The British
       3   4
Museum is wonderful! Try to go _____ there sometime during your stay in
                                     5
London.

"Remember that tomorrow we are going _____ Brighton, _____
₆   ₇
beach. Bring a bathing suit and a towel, and you can go _____ swimming in
₈
the English Channel."

Review. Complete the following passage with *a, an,* or *X.* Remember: Noncount nouns normally do not take an article, but a word such as *a* or *an* must come before a singular count noun.

THE WINDY CITY

Chicago is ___*an*___ interesting city. It has _____ good museums,
₁
_____ beautiful skyline, _____ first-class entertainment, and _____
₂   ₃   ₄
mixture of people. _____ Chicago's fine restaurants have an international
₅
flavor. You can find _____ Italian, _____ Japanese, or even _____
₆   ₇   ₈
Armenian restaurant there.

Chicago is _____ important commercial and financial center. _____
₉   ₁₀
skyscrapers fill its downtown area, and _____ enormous department stores
₁₁
are located throughout "the Loop," as _____ downtown Chicago is called.
₁₂
Its airport, O'Hare International, is the busiest in the world. _____ airplane
₁₃
lands and _____ airplane takes off every thirty seconds.
₁₄

This busy city is located in _____ beautiful area by Lake Michigan. This
                              15
huge lake plays _____ major role in Chicago's weather. The weather in the
                16
"Windy City" can be unpredictable at any time of year, and the winter can be
especially cold. However, most tourists find Chicago _____ fun place to
                                                     17
visit.

 **Review.** Fill in the blank spaces here and on the next page with *a, an, the, some,*
or *X*. In some cases, there is more than one possible answer.

THE CITY BY THE BAY

San Francisco is in _____ West, in _____ California. This lovely city
                    1   2
is located on _____ Pacific Coast, on _____ beautiful bay. _____
              3   4   5
famous Golden Gate Bridge crosses this bay. Seven highways and two railroad
bridges cross _____ San Francisco Bay. _____ San Francisco is also
              6   7
_____ major seaport. Because of its location, there are _____ wonderful
8   9
views from _____ city. _____ scenery is truly magnificent. In addition,
           10   11
_____ city has _____ good climate. There is _____ little rain most of
12   13   14
the year.

San Francisco is _____ city of many hills. _____ of the world's steep-
est streets go up these hills. In _____ center of _____ city are _____
tall office buildings. Other important landmarks include _____ University of
San Francisco and _____ Palace of Fine Arts.

(Numbers under blanks: 15, 16, 17, 18, 19, 20, 21)

Using What You've Learned

Describing Landmarks.   In pairs, brainstorm a list of "landmarks" or important
places in the town or area you live in. These might include a river, lake, mountain
range, bridge, monument or statue, museum, theater, shopping mall, etc. When
you have a list of places, take turns describing their location.

> example: A: **Where's the art museum?**
> B: **It's on Crest Street, across from the public library.**

Describing Your Hometown.   Work in small groups. What are some of the
important places in your hometown? Does it have any major landmarks? Does
your region or country have major mountains? Is it along an ocean? Are there
many rivers or lakes? Give examples of some of the important features. Using the
example as a model, take turns telling about some of the following.

In the city: museums, bridges, libraries, other important buildings, streets, etc.
In the region or country: forests, rivers, lakes, mountains, oceans, deserts, canals

> example: **I come from Cairo, the largest city in Egypt. Cairo is on the
> Nile River. . . .**

activity 3

Playing a Memory Game. Have you ever played the trivia game "Categories"? To begin, you choose a category: rivers, for example. Going around in a circle, each person must name a river. You can play the game in either of two ways. You can go in alphabetical order—*a*, the Amazon River; *b*, the Brule River, etc. The other way is to use the last letter in one to begin the name of the next—*a*, the Amazon River; *n* (the last letter of Amazon), the Nile River. If you can't think of a name, you are out of the game. The last person in the game wins. You can play as a class or you can divide into teams that will alternate naming rivers. You may use a time limit of thirty seconds or one minute for each answer. Choose a new category each time. Here are some suggestions:

rivers   mountains
lakes   capital cities
countries

Remember: For an answer to be correct, it must include *the*, if it is necessary.

focus on testing

Nouns and Articles

Problems with nouns and articles are usually found on standardized tests of English proficiency. Check your understanding of these by completing the sample items below.

Remember that . . .

- There are two basic noun groups: count nouns and noncount nouns.
- *A* and *an* are not used with noncount nouns.
- When *there* begins a sentence, the verb agrees with the noun that follows it.
- *A little/a few* have a different meaning from *little/few*.

Part 1. Circle the correct completion for the following.

example: There _____ any bridges across the northern rivers.
     a. are
     b. is
     c. aren't
     d. isn't

1. He enjoys traveling on _____ .
    a. a airplane
    b. airplanes
    c. an airplanes
    d. airplane

2. We can't afford to visit London. We have _____ money.
   a. little
   b. a little
   c. few
   d. a few

3. How _____ people were at the museum?
   a. little
   b. much
   c. a little
   d. many

Part 2. Circle the letter below the word(s) containing the error.

example: Ellen has <u>a lot of</u> <u>homeworks</u> <u>to do</u> before <u>the</u> next class.
          A   (B)   C   D

1. It is important to eat food like <u>a fruits</u> instead of <u>too much</u> <u>chocolate</u> or
   <u>A</u>   B   C   D
   fast food.

2. Is <u>there</u> <u>an</u> information about <u>the</u> temperature of <u>the</u> Pacific Ocean?
        A   B   C   D

3. Before we <u>travel</u>, we <u>will</u> <u>go</u> to shopping at <u>the</u> stores near us.
                  A   B   C   D

CHAPTER **three**

Business and Money

Model Auxiliaries and Related Structures

Topic One: Modal Auxiliaries of Request and Permission

Topic Two: Modal Auxiliaries and Related Structures of Ability, Expectation, and Preference

Topic Three: Modal Auxiliaries and Related Structures of Advice and Need

Topic Four: Modal Auxiliaries of Possibility, Impossibility, and Probability

Modal Auxiliaries of Request and Permission

Setting the Context

previewing the passage

Do you have a bank account? What services does your bank offer? Share your ideas by answering these questions about the picture.

- What are some of the services available at this bank?
- What are the various customers probably doing?

BANK ACCOUNTS

MRS. NELSON: Good morning. May I help you?

ALI: Yes, thank you. I would like to open both a savings and a checking account. Could you please tell me about the different kinds of accounts you have?

MRS. NELSON: Certainly. One type of checking account is the NOW account. A NOW account gives you interest on the money in your account. And, if you keep a minimum balance of $500, there is no service charge.

ALI: The NOW account looks good. And would you explain a little about savings accounts, please?

MRS. NELSON: We offer several types. Will you need to make regular deposits and withdrawals?

ALI: Yes, I will.

MRS. NELSON: In that case, I recommend a regular savings account. Our other accounts pay higher interest, but you may not withdraw money without paying a penalty fee.

ALI: I think the regular account will be best. Could I open both a checking and a savings account?

MRS. NELSON: Of course. To begin, would you please fill out these applications?

discussing ideas

What would Ali like to do? What is a NOW account? How is it different from a regular checking account? Why is a regular savings account good for Ali?

A. Introduction to Modal Auxiliaries

The modal auxiliaries *(can, could, may, might, must, ought to, shall, should, will,* and *would)* form a special group because they do not use normal verb tense endings. Instead, they are used *with* verbs to create special meanings. Also, their meanings change according to the context of the sentence. This chapter focuses on simple forms; Chapter 12 includes information on perfect forms.

The simple form of a main verb follows a modal auxiliary. *Not* appears after the modal to form the negative. In a question, the modal appears before the subject. A modal may also be used alone as a short answer. Note that contractions of some modals are very common in conversation.

forms	affirmative statements	negative statements
Long Forms	I **should open** a savings account. You **can open** a bank account now.	I **should not spend** so much money. I **cannot deposit** very much money today.
Contracted Forms	would: **I'd, you'd, he'd, she'd, it'd, we'd, they'd**	**can't, couldn't, shouldn't, won't, wouldn't**

	questions	possible answers
Yes/No Questions and Short Answers	**May** I **help** you? **Would** you **like** more information?	Yes, you **can.** No, I **wouldn't.**

questions		possible answers
Tag Questions and Short Answers	I **could open** an account tomorrow, **couldn't** I? There **won't be** a service charge, **will** there?	Yes, you **could (can).** No, there **won't.**
Information Questions and Short Answers	Where **could** I **get** some information? When **should** we **go** there? What **will happen?**	You **might try** over there. We **should go** soon. I **don't know.**

B. Making Requests and Giving Permission

Requesting Action

		examples	notes
would could can will	Formal ↑ ↓ Informal	**Would** you please help me? **Could** you help me, please? **Can** you help me? **Will** you help me, please?	*Could* and *would* are common in both informal and formal situations. *Can* and *will* are informal; friends or people in the same age group use *can* and *will* in informal conversation. *Please* makes any request more polite.

Requesting and Giving Permission

		examples	notes
may could can	Formal ↑ ↓ Informal	**May** we sit here? No, you **may** not. **May** I help you? Yes, I'd like a soda. **Could** I use your pencil? Yes, you **can.** **Can** I take this chair? Sure. Help yourself.	*May* is rather formal. People of different age groups and people who perform services, such as waiters or salespeople, often use it. *Could* appears in formal or informal requests for permission, but not normally in answers. *Can* is the least formal. It appears in questions and answers.

Note: The following expressions, which do *not* contain modals, are very common both in responding to a request for action and in giving permission:

> *Question:* May I sit here?
>
> *Response:* Of course. Certainly. Surely.
> I'm sorry, but . . . (my friend is sitting here).
>
> Sure. You bet. Okay. No problem.
> Sorry. No way. (very informal)

exercise 1 Underline all modal auxiliaries in the passage "Bank Accounts" at the beginning of the chapter and discuss their meanings.

exercise 2 Mrs. Nelson is helping Ali to open a checking account. Change the commands to polite requests for action.

example: ALI: Help me.
ALI: **Could you help me, please?** *or*
Would you help me, please?

1. ALI: Explain this form to me.
2. MRS. NELSON: Fill out this application.
3. MRS. NELSON: Complete this form.
4. MRS. NELSON: Print your name.
5. MRS. NELSON: Tell me your social security number.
6. MRS. NELSON: Write in ink.
7. ALI: Tell me about savings accounts.
8. MRS. NELSON: Look at this brochure.
9. ALI: Give me a copy to take home.
10. MRS. NELSON: Let me know if you need more information.

In pairs, ask for permission and respond using the following cues. Pay attention to the relationship between the speakers when you ask for permission.

> example: (two strangers in a cafeteria)
> sit down / no / someone else is sitting there
> A: **May I sit here?**
> B: **I'm sorry, but someone else is sitting there.**

1. (customer and a gas station attendant)
   use your phone / no / the phone isn't working
2. (young man applying for a job, speaking to the receptionist)
   speak to the manager / yes
3. (two strangers in a grocery store)
   go ahead of you in line / no / I'm in a hurry
4. (teenager and parent)
   borrow the car tonight / yes
5. (two friends)
   copy your notes from history class / yes
6. (two professional people who meet at a conference)
   have your business card / no / I don't have any right now

C. Making Requests with *Borrow* and *Lend*

Making requests and giving permission often involve borrowing and lending things. The verbs *borrow* and *lend* can be confusing. Compare:

	examples	notes
borrow	May Could }I **borrow** your pen? Can	You ask to borrow something from someone.
lend	Would Could } you **lend** me your pen? Will	You ask someone to lend you something (give it to you for a period of time).

In pairs, form requests and responses by using either *borrow* or *lend* and the cues on the opposite page. Pay attention to the relationship of the speakers when you form your requests. If the response is negative, add an explanation.

examples: (two friends)
borrow $5 / yes
A: **Could I borrow $5 from you?**
B: **Sure.**

lend $5 / no
A: **Could you lend me $5?**
B: **I'm sorry, but I don't have any money right now.**

1. (two students)
lend dictionary / yes
2. (two strangers in a supermarket line)
borrow pen / yes
3. (teenager and parent)
lend $10 / no
4. (student and professor)
borrow calculator / yes
5. (two sisters or brothers)
lend your library card / no
6. (roommates)
borrow your Mercedes tonight / of course

 **exercise 5**

You are at a bank. In pairs, take turns making requests with the following cues and responding to them. These will include both requests for permission and requests for action. Use a variety of modal auxiliaries.

example: explain the charges on my monthly statement
A: **Could you explain the charges on my monthly statement?**
B: **Certainly.**

1. cash a check for me
2. withdraw money from my account
3. explain this loan application
4. describe the bank's policy on bad checks
5. speak with the bank manager
6. take out a $1,000 loan
7. get into my safety deposit box
8. open a savings account with only $10

exercise 6

Complete the conversation here and on the next page with modals of request or permission. Then, in pairs, role-play the conversation. Be sure to ask about currency from your own country, though.

ALI: Excuse me. <u>May (Could)</u> I get some British pounds here?

TELLER: Yes, you _____ . We have a supply of most major currencies.

_____1_____

ALI: _____ you give me $500 worth?

_____2_____

TELLER: You _____ have up to $1,000. Do you want the money in cash or in traveler's checks?

      3

ALI: _____ I have approximately $200 in cash and $300 in traveler's checks?

      4

TELLER: Certainly. _____ you wait for a few minutes until our international clerk is free? She calculates the amount based on today's exchange rate.

      5

ALI: Of course.

TELLER: In the meantime, _____ you please sign here?

      6

Using What You've Learned

activity **1**

Borrowing and Lending Things.   Make a "chain" of requests and responses. Ask *to borrow* something you need from your neighbor. Your neighbor will respond and then will ask his or her neighbor *to lend* something. Continue the chain until everyone has made a request and response. Remember: You must alternate use of *borrow* and *lend*. Here are some suggested items: watch, car, grammar book, class schedule, a dollar, bike.

activity **2**

Making and Responding to Requests.   In pairs or groups of three, make up conversations for these situations. Then role-play your best conversation for the class. Use the vocabulary that follows to help you ask and answer questions as customers and bank officers.

  1. You and your husband (wife) would like to open a joint savings account.
  2. You would like to open a checking account.
  3. You and your friend would like to find out about credit cards.

minimum balance	credit limit	cost for a check that "bounces"
service charge	monthly statement	(goes back to the writer
cost per check	interest	because there's not enough
		money in the account)

TOPIC **two**

Modal Auxiliaries and Related Structures of Ability, Expectation, and Preference

Setting the Context

previewing the passage

What financial services are available to you as a student? What can you do to economize? Share your ideas by answering these questions about the picture.

- Where are these students?
- What services are available for students?

CASH AND CREDIT

JACK: I hear you're almost out of money.

ALI: Well, I'm in a difficult spot. I can't expect much help from home. We have tight currency controls in my country.

JACK: You can get a credit card.

ALI: I don't think I can qualify. Besides, I'm not sure I'll be able to control myself with a credit card. I'd rather get a job and earn the money.

JACK: You're a permanent resident, aren't you? You should be able to get at least a part-time job. But everyone needs a credit card for emergencies. Why don't we go to the bank? The credit manager ought to be there now. We'll just ask for information.

ALI: Okay. There's nothing to lose.

discussing ideas

What is Ali's problem? What are currency controls? Will Ali get help from his parents? Does he have a credit card? Do you have any credit cards? Who is able to get a major credit card?

A. Expressing Ability

	examples	notes
can	Most working people **can** get a credit card, but most high school students **can't (cannot).** **Can** Ali get a credit card? Why **can't** Ali work?	*Can* expresses present ability. It is sometimes difficult to hear the difference between *can* and *can't* in rapid speech. Normally English speakers stress *can* weakly and *can't* more strongly.
could	Last year, I **could** speak English. The year before, I **couldn't.**	*Could* has several meanings, depending on the context of the sentence. When *could* expresses ability, it refers to the past.
be able to + *verb*	A permanent resident **is able to** work. Ali **wasn't able to** find a job. **Will** I **be able to** speak English perfectly?	*Be able to + verb* expresses ability in the past, present, or future. The infinitive *(to + verb)* must come after *be able: be able to find, be able to speak,* etc.

exercise

Your teacher will read the following sentences aloud, using either *can* or *can't*. Listen for the differences in pronunciation and circle the word that you hear. Then, work with a partner and take turns saying the sentences. Be sure to tell each other *which* form you actually said and heard.

1. He (can / can't) open a checking account.
2. She (can / can't) write you a check.
3. You (can / can't) cash a check.
4. (Can / Can't) I get a credit card?
5. I (can / can't) get a job.
6. We (can / can't) take out a loan.

7. They (can / can't) get a credit card here.

8. He (can / can't) pay me today.

9. It (can / can't) work.

10. I (can / can't) understand you.

 Make at least six sentences using *can* and *not be able to*. Use the example and the cues below to help you. If you want, add expressions such as *a little, fairly well, really well, not very well, not at all*. Add your own ideas, also.

example: **I can swim fairly well, but I'm not able to swim long distances.**

change a diaper	ski cross country
cook gourmet food	ski downhill
cut my own hair	speak Chinese (Japanese,
dive off a diving board	Spanish)
do word processing	swim
roller-blade	touch my toes
run	tune a car engine
sew	whistle

 Work in pairs. Prepare at least three suggestions for each of the following questions. Use *can* or *be able to* + *verb*. Use the picture for ideas. Then, share your suggestions with the rest of the class.

examples: **You can eat at the school cafeteria.**
You can buy meal tickets.

1. How can students save money on necessities such as food, housing, and transportation?

2. What fun things can you do free of charge in your city?

3. How can students save money on educational expenses?

4. How can you economize on entertainment (theater tickets, movies, concerts, etc.)?

exercise 4 Think about changes in your life during the past five years. Think about things you couldn't do before that you can do now, and vice versa. Use the chart below to help you. Then create sentences using *could, couldn't, can,* and *can't*.

examples: **Five years ago, I couldn't drive a car.**
Now I can drive a car, but I can't fly an airplane.

could do	couldn't do	can do	can't do
ride a bicycle	drive a car	drive a car	fly an airplane

B. Expressing Expectations

	examples	notes
ought to should	We'll go to the station at 9:00. The train **should (ought to)** be in by then. How long **should** it take us to get to the station? It **shouldn't** take more than twenty minutes.	*Should* and *ought to* sometimes express expectations. They mean "expect to" or "will probably." *Ought to* seldom occurs in questions or negative statements.

exercise 5 The following sentences tell about Ali's expectations. Change each sentence to use *should* or *ought to* instead of the main verb. Then add five original sentences about your own expectations.

example: I expect to find a job soon.
I should find a job soon.

1. I expect to receive a letter from my parents soon.
2. I expect to get a check from my family this week.
3. I'll probably be able to save a little money this month.
4. I expect to have some extra money next month.
5. I'll probably be able to take a short trip.
6. I expect to hear from my friends soon.
7. I expect to get a phone call from home this week.
8. I expect to be able to speak English well within a year.

C. Expressing Preferences

	examples	notes
would like	I**'d like** to visit New York City. I **wouldn't like** to live there, though. **Would** you **like** to go with me? **Would** you **like** me to help you?	*Would like* expresses desires for things that haven't happened yet. A (pro)noun and/or *to + verb* (infinitive) may follow *would like*.
would rather	I**'d rather** travel in the United States than spend a lot of money on clothes. **Would** he **rather** take English? He **would rather** not take history.	*Would rather* expresses preferences or choices. *Than + verb* often follows it. *Not* comes after *rather* in the negative.

 **exercise 6** *Would like* refers to things we want or hope to do in the future. Form sentences from the following cues that tell about things you did and things you would like to do.

I found a job! Now I'd like to save some money.

example: find a job / save some money
I found a job. Now I'd like (would like) to save some money.

1. open a checking account / start a savings account
2. find an apartment / buy a car
3. learn to play tennis / try windsurfing
4. visit New York City / travel to California
5. buy a bicycle / get roller blades
6. take some day hikes / go backpacking
7. learn how to play the piano / try guitar lessons
8. study a lot of English / take some other courses

exercise 7 In pairs, take turns asking and answering questions based on the following cues here and on the next page.

example: go to Las Vegas / not gamble
A: **Would you like to go to Las Vegas?**
B: **Thanks, but I would rather not gamble.**

1. buy a new car / get a used car
2. eat out / cook at home
3. make some investments / keep my money in the bank
4. find a larger apartment / not pay higher rent

5. look at houses for sale / buy a condominium
6. go to the movies / not spend any money
7. use your credit card / pay in cash
8. open a charge account / not have any bills to pay

 **exercise 8**   Using the cues, form sentences with *would rather + than*. Use contractions wherever possible. Follow the example.

> example: Ali / get a job / borrow money
> **Ali would rather get a job than borrow money.**

1. many people / work for themselves / work for a big company
2. I / write a check / use a credit card
3. Kaori / rent an apartment / live in a dorm
4. we / see a movie / go dancing
5. they / cook dinner at home / eat out
6. Carlos / ride his bicycle / go by bus
7. Joe / have a dog / get a cat
8. I / study more grammar / go out tonight

 **exercise 9**   In the following passage, a real estate agent is telling a customer about a house. Circle the modal that best fits the context.

BUYING A HOME

"You know, this is an excellent time to buy real estate. Interest rates are down. Until recently, few people (should /(could))afford the high monthly
                                                                        1
mortgage payments. But now, with the lower interest rates, more people (would like / are able to) afford a house. If you're like most people, you
            2
(would rather / would like) live in your own house than rent from someone
        3
else. So you really (should / can) think about buying now.
                            4

"Now here is a lovely house. It's a real bargain. It has a lot of good features, and you (ought to / would rather) be able to buy it for a good price.
                                5
(Would / Could) you (rather / like) to see the inside? I have the key, so we
    6   7
(would like / can) go in and look around.
        8

"On the right we have a very big living room. You (should / will be able to)
                                                                    9
entertain lots of guests here. . . ."

Underline all examples of modal auxiliaries in the passage "Cash and Credit" and then tell their uses (ability, etc.).

Using What You've Learned

Telling About Things You Can or Can't Do. Students generally do not have much money to spend. Did your financial situation change when you began studying here?

> example: **Before, I could go to restaurants often. Now I can only afford hamburgers.**

Student life does have advantages, however. Often students have much more freedom than working people do. For example, students often have a flexible schedule and wear informal clothing.

> example: **Last year, I couldn't wear blue jeans every day. Now I can. Next year, I won't be able to wear jeans, though, because I'll be working.**

In small groups, discuss the changes you have experienced, and then share them with your class.

Making Plans. Are you the type of person who makes lists of things to do? What does your list for this week look like? In small groups, talk about things you did and then tell what you would like to do before the end of the week.

> example: **I wrote to my family, and I did all my laundry. Before the end of the week, I'd like to finish the next composition for English class. I would also like to visit the art museum.**

Offering Suggestions and Making Excuses. In pairs, take the roles of two students: Student A is very rich and spends a lot of money. A is taking only one class, so he (she) doesn't have to study very much. Student B is on a scholarship and has very little money. B is taking five classes and has to study a lot. B is embarrassed about the situation. B tries to avoid going to expensive places. Use *can, could, should, would, would like,* and *would rather* to create a conversation between the two students.

> example: A: **Could you join me for dinner? Let's go out to that elegant new French restaurant. We can go dancing afterwards or . . .**
>
>   B: **That sounds nice, but we can't go there in blue jeans. Wouldn't you rather have a pizza somewhere? Besides, I can't dance because I hurt my leg . . .**

Modal Auxiliaries and Related Structures of Advice and Need

Setting the Context

previewing the passage

How do you manage your money? Share your ideas and experiences by answering these questions about the picture.

- Describe Ali's room. Is it well-furnished?
- What is Ali planning? Do you have a budget? Does this look like your budget?

MAKING A MONTHLY BUDGET

Do you often run out of money before the end of the month? Then you'd better consider making a budget. To plan a monthly budget, first of all, you should list your fixed expenses. That is, list all the money you *must* spend each month for rent, utilities, phone, food, and so on. If you have to guess at some
5 of your expenses, you should guess higher, rather than lower. Then list large expenses, such as tuition and insurance, and figure out their monthly costs. Subtract all of these from your total monthly income.

Now plan for emergencies, such as medical or dental care. To do this, you ought to add a small amount of your monthly income as fixed expenses for
10 emergencies. The rest is your "spending money" for entertainment, clothing, travel, and so on.

By planning a budget and following it, you won't have to worry about being short of cash each month.

discussing ideas

What are *fixed expenses*? Why should you list all of your fixed expenses first? If some costs change, why should you guess higher, rather than lower? What is *spending money*?

A. Giving Advice

	examples	notes
ought to	You **ought to** attend class regularly.	Both *should* and *ought to* can give advice. *Ought to* is not common in questions or negatives, however.
should	You **should** not be absent.	
had better	You**'d better** hurry or you'll be late to class. **Hadn't** you **better** hurry? You**'d better** not stay here any longer or you'll be late.	*Had better* is stronger than *should* or *ought to.* It does not appear in affirmative questions.

exercise 1

Reread the passage "Making a Monthly Budget" at the beginning of Topic Three. Using *should* or *ought to,* give at least three good pieces of advice for making a budget.

> example: **You should make a list of all of your expenses.**

exercise 2

How can you save money? Change the following commands to negative statements giving advice on how to save more. Use *so much* or *so many* in your sentences.

> examples: Make only a few long-distance phone calls.
> **You shouldn't make so many long-distance phone calls.**
>
> Drink less coffee.
> **You shouldn't drink so much coffee.**

1. Leave fewer lights on.
2. Eat less junk food.
3. Buy fewer things with credit cards.
4. Spend less on groceries.
5. Buy fewer clothes.
6. Take fewer trips.
7. Spend less time on the telephone.
8. Drive less.

exercise 3

In pairs, take turns making suggestions and responses based on the following cues. Use *had better* in your responses.

example: go to the movies / study
   A: **Let's go to the movies.**
   B: **Sorry, but I had better study.**

1. go to the football game / go job hunting
2. visit the art exhibit / clean my apartment
3. go shopping / save money
4. go out to dinner / do my homework
5. stop at the café for coffee / see my professor
6. play a game of tennis / go to the library

**exercise 4**

Change partners and use the cues from Exercise 3 to make new questions and responses. Use the following example as a model and make any necessary changes.

example: go to the movies / study
   MICHAEL: **Why don't we go to the movies?**
   ALI: **Hadn't you better study?**
   MICHAEL: **Yes, but I would rather have some fun.**

**exercise 5**

You are a student who wants to buy or find the following items. In pairs or small groups, take turns asking for and giving advice. Try to share as much information as possible. Use *ought to, should, shouldn't, had better,* and *had better not.*

example: computer
   A: **What kind of computer should I look for?**
      How much should I spend?
      Where should I buy it?
   B: **You should (shouldn't, had better, had better not) . . .**

1. CD player
2. a good apartment

3. inexpensive presents to send home
4. a used bike

B. Expressing Need or Obligation

	examples	notes
must	You **must** have a driver's license in order to drive.	In affirmative statements, *must* expresses need or obligation.
must not	You **must not** drive without a license.	In negative statements, *must not* expresses a strong need not to do something or a prohibition.*
have to	You **have to** take a written test. Does he **have to** take the test in English? Then you **will have to** pass a driving test.	To express present or future need, use *have/has to* or *will have to*.
had to	I **had to** take the written test twice. I only **had to** take the driving test one time.	*Had to* expresses a past need or obligation. In most cases, it means that the speaker completed the action.†

*The opposite of *must not* is *may* or *can,* expressing permission. Compare: *You must not smoke here. You may smoke here.*
†See Chapter Twelve for information on perfect modals that describe past needs that were not completed.

C. Expressing Lack of Need

	examples	notes
not have to	You **don't have to** take the English test if you don't want to. I **didn't have to** study very hard to pass. I **won't have to** study late tonight.	*Not have to* expresses the idea that something is, was, or will not be necessary. It is the opposite of *must* and *have to*.

exercise 6 Complete the following sentences with *must not* or *don't have to*.

example: You <u>must not</u> write a check for more money than you have in your account.

1. You _____ keep your money in a bank, but it's a good idea.

2. You _____ forget to pay your bills on time.

3. At many banks, you _____ pay for your checks if you also have money in a savings account.

4. Today, many banks have automatic teller machines, so

   you _____ go inside a bank at all if you don't want to.

5. You _____ write bad checks.

exercise 7 Complete the following sentences with *must, must not,* or *don't have to*.

examples: If you carry a lot of cash you <u>must</u> be careful.

If you keep your money in the bank, you <u>don't have to</u> worry about losing it.

1. If you open a bank account, you _____ show identification.

2. If you want free checking, you _____ go under the minimum balance.

3. However, if you pay for each check, you _____ keep a minimum balance in your account.

4. If you have a lot of money in the bank, normally you _____ wait very long to get a credit card.

5. If you want to get a credit card, you _____ establish credit with a bank.

exercise 8 Use *had to* to explain how you did the following tasks.

example: open a checking account
            In order to open a checking account, I had to go to the bank and talk to a bank officer. I had to deposit some money and choose some checks . . .

1. get a driver's license
2. get a passport
3. open a savings account
4. find housing in your area
5. be accepted to your school

Using What You've Learned

activity

Explaining Proverbs. A proverb is a wise saying that teaches a lesson. The language of proverbs is often traditional. In small groups, rephrase the following proverbs, keeping the same meanings. Do similar proverbs exist in your language? If so, give your classmates a translation of some of them. After you have finished, choose one member of your group to give a brief report to the class.

example: Don't look a gift horse in the mouth.
Explanation: If someone gives you a gift or does you a favor, you should thank the person. You shouldn't be critical.

1. Early to bed and early to rise makes a man healthy, wealthy, and wise.
2. A penny saved is a penny earned.
3. Neither a borrower nor a lender be.
4. Don't count your chickens before they hatch.
5. Don't put all your eggs in one basket.
6. A bird in the hand is worth two in the bush.

TOPIC **four**

Modal Auxiliaries of Possibility, Impossibility, and Probability

Setting the Context

previewing the passage

What is the best thing to do with your savings? Share your ideas by answering these questions about the picture at the top of the following page.

- What ways of investing are shown in the picture?
- What are *stocks*?
- What can you do in a brokerage office?

INVESTING

You may be one of the fortunate people with plenty of money. In that case, you can save your money or invest it to make more.

If you want a safe investment, banks might be your best choice because they insure your deposits up to $100,000. On the other hand, you could earn
5 much more money by trying alternative investments: jewelry, art, real estate, or a common favorite, stocks.

Investing in the stock market may be either rewarding or disappointing. When a person makes a good investment, we often say, "She must be incredibly lucky!" Or when a person makes a bad investment, we will say, "He must have terrible luck." Yet, most people who successfully invest in the stock market rely on much more than luck. They have a variety of unusual qualities—patience, ability to think independently, flexibility, and self-confidence—in addition to good luck.

discussing ideas

What are some safe ways to invest? Which are the most unpredictable? Why? What qualities do successful investors have? Which quality do you think is the most important? Which ways of investing are the most common in your culture? Have you ever made any investments?

A. Expressing Possibility

	examples	notes
may	He **may** have enough money to pay the bill.	In affirmative statements, *may, might,* and *could* are similar in meaning. They express the idea of "maybe," "perhaps" or "it's possible." *May* never appears in questions about possibilities.

	examples	notes
might	He **might** have to borrow some money.	*Might* rarely appears in questions.
could	It **could** rain tomorrow.	*Could* appears less often than *may* or *might* to express possibility.
may not	He **may not** arrive on time.	*May not* and *might not* mean "maybe not."
might not	I **might not** see you tomorrow.	

 **exercise 1**   In the passage "Investing" on pages 111 and 112, underline all uses of possibility.

 **exercise 2**   You can use *could* or *might* to make suggestions to people. Using the following cues, tell what each person *could* or *might do*. For each situation, try to add one suggestion of your own.

> **example:**   I'm having problems with my math course.
> (talk to your professor)
> (get a tutor)
> **You could talk to your professor.**
> **You might get a tutor.**

1. I don't have enough money to finish school.
   (get a job)
   (apply for a loan)
2. My apartment is very expensive.
   (find a roommate)
   (look for a cheaper apartment)
3. I need to buy an unusual present for a special friend.
   (go to the art fair on Saturday)
   (try the new shopping mall)
4. I just won the lottery!
   (take a long vacation)
   (make some investments)

exercise 3 The following sentences tell about plans and possibilities. Rephrase them with *may* or *might*. Then add your own ideas. Make three statements about things you are hoping or planning to do.

example: It is possible that Ali will open a savings account.
Ali may open a savings account.

1. It is possible that Ali will sell his Persian rug.
2. Perhaps Michael will take Finance 101.
3. Ali has the opportunity to buy a used bike.
4. Maybe Michael will look for a job.
5. It is possible that Michael will try working in real estate.
6. Ali has a chance to sell his car.
7. Michael has a chance to vacation in Mexico.
8. Ali will possibly go along on the trip.

exercise 4 In pairs, take turns responding to the following statements. Using the cues, tell what *may* or *might* happen as a result of each situation. Then add your own ideas or opinions in each case.

example: There are problems in the Middle East.
(some oil countries / not be able to export oil)
(price of gas / go up)
Some oil countries might not be able to export oil.
The price of gas may go up.

1. That factory is going bankrupt.
(many people / lose their jobs)
2. The banks have just raised interest rates.
(people / put more money in the bank)
(some people / not be able to afford new homes)
3. A new company is opening in town.
(there / be a lot of new jobs soon)
4. That airline always has delays and mechanical problems.
(the government / investigate the situation)
(people / not fly on that airline anymore)

 B. Expressing Impossibility or Disbelief

	examples	notes
can't couldn't	It **can't** be five o'clock! That **couldn't** be Irene! She's out of town.	*Can't* and *couldn't* often express the idea of impossibility. They show surprise or shock.

exercise 5 Respond to the following situations with exclamations using *can't* or *couldn't*. Then explain why you are surprised.

> example: The thermometer outside your window says it's 80°F.
> **That can't be right! It's the middle of winter!**

1. The sign at your local gas station says that gas costs $6.85 a gallon.
2. You see a woman on the street who looks exactly like your mother.
3. Your digital clock says 2:00 P.M., but it's dark outside.
4. The bill at a hamburger place for you and a friend comes to $68.92.
5. The movie you are watching stops after twenty minutes.
6. Your telephone bill arrived, and it shows forty-five different phone calls to Australia and New Zealand.
7. A travel agent tells you that a week's stay at the Plaza Hotel in New York will cost you $85.00.
8. A letter arrived for you saying that you got the highest score in history on the TOEFL test.

C. Expressing Probability

	examples	notes
must	John walks five miles a day. He **must** enjoy walking.	*Must* expresses the same idea as "probably."
must not	He **must not** have enough money to ride the bus.	*Must* does not appear in questions about probabilities.

exercise 6  In pairs, take turns responding to the following statements. Use *must* and the verbs *be* or *feel* with the cue to form your responses.

> example: I just bought a new house. (broke)
> **You must be broke.**

1. Prices on the stock market are falling. (nervous)
2. My bank is bankrupt. (worried)
3. I just inherited a lot of money. (thrilled)
4. I just lost $500 at the horse races. (upset)
5. My investments are doing extremely well. (rich)
6. Someone stole my son's wallet. (furious)
7. My wife just found a job. (relieved)
8. My friend didn't get a job with our company. (disappointed)

exercise 7  Read each sentence and then try to come to a conclusion about the reason for each decision or situation. Use *must* in your conclusions. Several conclusions may be possible for each sentence.

example: Michael has decided to get a job.
He must need money.

1. Ali has decided to move closer to campus.
2. Michael has decided to drop Finance 101.
3. Ali has decided to wait for a while before he opens a savings account.
4. Michael has decided not to invest in the stock market.
5. Ali's father has decided not to come to visit Ali this year.

exercise 8 **Review.** In small groups, rewrite the following conversation by changing the words in italics. Add a modal auxiliary or use a different modal but try to keep the same meaning.

example: What *can* I do for you today?
What could (may) I do for you today?
or
May I help you?

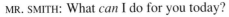

NEW ACCOUNTS

OPENING AN ACCOUNT

MR. SMITH: What *can* I do for you today?

NELLA: I'*d like to* open up a savings account and a checking account.

MR. SMITH: Will there be just one name on the accounts? You look very young.
You *can't* be married.

NELLA: Actually, I am married, but I *would prefer to* have the accounts in my
name only.

MR. SMITH: I see. *Could* you please fill out these two applications? You *should* fill
in both the front and the back.

NELLA: *May* I use your pen?

MR. SMITH: Certainly. We *prefer* everything in ink. How much *do you want* to
deposit in the accounts?

NELLA: It will be $325,700 altogether.

MR. SMITH: *Could* you repeat that? You *probably* mean $3,257.

NELLA: No, I meant $325,700.

MR. SMITH: My goodness!

NELLA: *Please let me* explain. We *might* buy a condominium. We *should* know
more about it by the end of the month.
₁₂ ₁₃ ₁₄

MR. SMITH: Please let us know if we *can* be of help to you. We *may* be able to give
you a loan, for example.

NELLA: Thanks for your help.

Using What You've Learned

Problem Solving.   In small groups, try to think of at least three possible
solutions for the following problems. Discuss the advantages and
disadvantages of each solution and then decide which one is best. Present your
conclusion to the class.

1. An American family has invited you to dinner and you would like to take
   them a gift. What can you take?
2. Suppose that the public transportation system in your city stopped working
   tomorrow. How could you get to school?
3. Your family sends you money each month, but this month the money didn't
   arrive. How can you get money to pay your rent?

Responding to Good or Bad News.   How did you do on the last test? Did you
get an A (or an F)? Have you had an interesting date recently? In pairs, take turns
telling your news and responding to your partner's news. Use your own ideas or
choose some of the following.

get an A (F)   meet a new boyfriend
get a new apartment   (girlfriend)
break up with a boyfriend   lose your job
    (girlfriend)

Giving Advice.   Congratulations! You have just won $2,500,000, the grand prize
in the state lottery! What will you do with all that money?

The first thing is to contact an investment counselor who will give you advice
on various possibilities: gold, precious gems, real estate, the stock market, savings
banks, art, antiques, etc.

Because you've never been to an investment counselor before, you decide to
get friends' and financial counselors' advice before making your decisions.

One-third of the class can set up office as investment counselors with various
specialties. The rest of the students are investors. Afterwards, take turns role-
playing some of your conversations about investing.

Modals and Related Structures

Problems with modals are usually found on standardized tests of English proficiency. Check your understanding of these by completing the sample items below.

Remember that . . .

- Modals do not use normal verb tense endings.
- The meaning of a modal can change according to the context of the sentence.
- Sometimes *must* means "probably."

Part 1. Circle the correct completion for the following.

    example: The bank _____ give him an account with free checking.
          a. wouldn't able to
          b. was not able
          c. wouldn't to
          d. wouldn't

1. The bank _____ his account.
    a. might closing
    b. might to close
    c. might close
    d. close

2. I don't see Ali. He _____ here today.
    a. must be not
    b. must not be
    c. must to be not
    d. must not to be

3. You_____. You'll make a mistake.
    a. 'd better not hurry
    b. better not hurrying
    c. 'd better not to hurry
    d. 'd better don't hurry

Part 2. Circle the letter below the word(s) containing the error.

    example: Yuki would rather to work at the bank than work at the
                 A   (B) C   D
            factory.

1. Jack didn't have to pay back the loan last year, but he will have pay it
         A   B   C   D
    this year.

2. Not many people must afford a high mortgage payment, so they
        A   B
    should not make that mistake.
       C   D

3. Lots of people would like a big house, but they would not afford it and
              A   B
    could not make the payments.
      C   D

CHAPTER four

Jobs and Professions

The Perfect Tenses

Topic One: The Present Perfect Tense

Topic Two: The Present Perfect Continuous Tense; The Present Perfect Tense (2)

Topic Three: The Past Perfect Tense

Topic Four: Review

The Present Perfect Tense

Setting the Context

What is the best way to find a job? Share your experiences while answering the following questions about the picture.

- Where are these people and what are they looking for?
- What information is on the bulletin board?

JOB HUNTING, BUT HAVEN'T HAD ANY LUCK?

Does this describe your situation?

- You're in school, or you've just graduated.
- You've never had a job, so you don't have any "work experience."
- You've already visited "the other" employment agencies, but they still haven't found a job for you.

If you haven't found a job yet, call us or stop by for a free consultation. We specialize in finding jobs for people like you.

HEADHUNTERS LIMITED
70 East Second Street
555-0160

What kind of company is Headhunters Limited? What types of people do they try to help?

A. The Present Perfect Tense (1)

The present perfect tense has different meanings. It can describe actions or situations that occurred at an *unspecified* time in the past. It also refers to *repeated past* actions. With specific past times *(yesterday, in 1985)*, the simple past tense is used.

uses	examples	notes
Actions or Situations at an Unspecified Time in the Past	I**'ve been** to Madrid. My sister **has** just **returned** from there. **Have** you ever **been** there?	Time expressions often used with this meaning of the present perfect tense include *already, ever, just, recently, still, yet, so far, up to now, once, twice, three (four, etc.) times.*
Repeated Past Actions at Unspecified Times	I**'ve gone** there five times. My sister **has visited** Spain many times.	

forms	affirmative statements	negative statements
Long Forms	I **have worked** there. She **has worked** there.	I **have not worked** there. He **has not worked** there.
Contracted Forms	I**'ve worked** there. She**'s worked** there.	I **haven't worked** there. He **hasn't worked** there.

	questions	possible answers
Yes/No Questions and Short Answers	**Have** you **gone** there? **Has** he **gone** there?	Yes, I **have**. No, I **haven't**. Yes, he **has**. No, he **hasn't**.
Tag Questions and Short Answers	You've called them, **haven't you**? He hasn't called them, **has he**?	Yes, I **have**. No, he **hasn't**.
Information Questions and Short Answers	When **have** you **written** them? Why **has** he **written** them? Who **has called**? What **has happened**?	Many times. Because of some problems. No one. Nothing important.

Note: See Appendix pages 396 to 397 for spelling rules for the *-ed* ending. See Appendix pages 394 to 395 for a list of irregular past participles.

 **exercise 1** Underline all uses of the present perfect tense in the advertisement at the beginning of the chapter.

 **exercise 2** As your teacher reads the following irregular verbs, give the three forms of each verb. Pay attention to the pronunciation of each form.

1. be	**10.** fight	**18.** mean
2. begin	**11.** find	**19.** read
3. bring	**12.** fly	**20.** ring
4. choose	**13.** go	**21.** spend
5. catch	**14.** have	**22.** steal
6. come	**15.** know	**23.** take
7. drink	**16.** lay	**24.** think
8. eat	**17.** lie	**25.** write
9. feel		

exercise 3 A retired physician visits an employment agency to look for part-time work. Complete the following, using regular verbs in the present perfect tense. Pay attention to the spelling and pronunciation of the past participles.

CHARLES: I _have worked_ (work) for many years as a physician and I _____
                                                              1
(enjoy) it very much. I am retired now, but I would like to work part-time.

AGENT: _____ you _____ (decide) what kind of work you would
                                                              2
like to do?

CHARLES: I _____ (not decide) yet. I would prefer outdoor work. I like
                                    3
gardening and forestry. Two of my former patients _____ (try)
                                                                                        4
landscaping jobs. One of them, John Thomas, recently _____ (start)
                                                                                                        5
working with city golf courses. Do you have anything like that?

AGENT: I don't think we have any job openings with landscaping companies. However, we _____ (receive) a notice from the City Parks Department
₆
about a gardening job at the Children's Zoo. _____ you

_____ (consider) working as a gardener?
₇

CHARLES: That might be perfect for me. I _____ (garden) all my life, and I'm
₈

pretty good at it!

AGENT: I think we can get this job for you unless the zoo _____ (hire)

someone else. I'll let you know.
₉

exercise 4

In pairs, practice interviewing for a job. Take turns as "employer" and "job applicant." Ask and answer questions about your previous work experience by forming complete sentences with the present perfect tense. Add additional information, if you can.

example: Applicant: Thomas Woo
Job title: Auto mechanic
EMPLOYER: Have you worked as a mechanic before?
APPLICANT: **I have changed tires. (I have filled them with air, and I have repaired flat tires.)**

1. Applicant: Thomas Woo
Job title: Auto mechanic
Previous experience:
  a. tune engines
  b. replace mufflers
  c. clean radiators
  d. repair brakes

2. Applicant: Christina Barragan
Job title: Architect
Previous experience:
  a. design apartment buildings
  b. help with designs for offices
  c. plan a park
  d. develop plans for a convention center

3. Applicant: Alex Gutierrez
Job title: Chef
Previous experience:
  a. work as assistant chef in a large restaurant
  b. manage a small restaurant
  c. prepare special parties
  d. create several new recipes

4. Applicant: Sara Albrecht
Job title: Clothing store manager
Previous experience:
  a. manage a small clothing store
  b. hire new employees
  c. place orders
  d. organize special sales

exercise 5 Complete the following with the present perfect form of the irregular verbs in parentheses. Use contractions when possible.

1. I _'ve had_____ (have) a bad day. So far, I

_____ (bring) several customers the wrong

food, I _____ (break) a lot of dishes, and no

one _____ (leave) me tips!

2. What a terrible day! So far, I _____ (give)

the wrong change three times, I _____

(make) a $1,000 error, and someone _____

(steal) my keys.

3. I quit! So far today, I _____ (lose) three

brushes, I _____ (fall) off the ladder, and I

_____ (put) my foot in a paint can.

4. What else can go wrong? Tonight so far, I

_____ (sleep) through the alarm twice,

and the guard dog _____ (bite) me.

5. Things _____ (not go) very well today . . .

So far, I _____ (not sell) any daisies, I

_____ (send) customers the wrong flowers,

and I _____ (freeze) the roses.

6. I'm the worst driving instructor in town! So far, I

_____ (run) a red light, I _____

(hit) a tree, I _____ (drive) down a one-way

street, and a policeman _____ (give) me a

ticket.

Interactions Two • Grammar

exercise 6 Work in pairs. One of you is an office manager, and the other is an applicant for an office job. The office manager should ask questions based on the following cues. The applicant should reply with short answers.

> example: work in an office
> A: **You've worked in an office, haven't you?**
> B: **Yes, I have,** *or*
> **No, I haven't.**

1. type reports
2. take dictation
3. file letters
4. use an adding machine
5. do bookkeeping

6. work on a word processor
7. study data processing
8. send bills to customers
9. record payments
10. sort mail

B. *Ever, Never, Already, Just, Recently, Still,* and *Yet*

These adverbs are frequently used with the present perfect tense. Questions and affirmative statements with *already, just,* and *recently* refer to actions or situations that occurred at an unspecified time in the past. *Ever, never, still,* and *yet* refer to past actions or situations that also include the present.

	examples	**notes**
Questions	Have you **ever** had a job?	*Ever* means "at any time." It must come before the past participle.
	Have you **already** started work? Have you started work **already**?	*Already* means "before now." It may come before the past participle or at the end of a question.
	Have you started work **yet**?	*Yet* means "up to now." It is normally at the end of a question.

examples		notes
Affirmative Statements	Yes, I've **just** started work.	*Just* refers to the recent past— a few minutes, hours, or days ago. It must come before the past participle.
	Yes, I've **already** started work. Yes, I've **recently** started work. Yes, I've started work **recently.**	*Already* and *recently* normally come before the past participle or at the end of a statement.
Negative Statements	No, I have **never** worked. *or* No, I have**n't ever** worked. No, I haven't started work **yet.**	*Never* and *not ever* mean "not at any time." They must come before the past participle. *Yet* normally comes at the end of a negative statement.
	No, I **still** haven't started work.	*Still* also means "up to now." It emphasizes the continuous nature of the situation. *Still* must come before *has* or *have*.

exercise 7   John is having a hard time finding a job. He is telling Caroline about his job search. In pairs, use the example as a model to form short conversations.

example: try all the computer companies
CAROLINE: **Have you tried all the computer companies yet?**
JOHN: **Yes, I've already tried the computer companies.** *or*
Yes, I've tried the computer companies already.

1. look in the want ads
2. put an ad on the bulletin board
3. talk to the manager of the insurance company
4. apply for jobs at the phone company
5. check all the banks
6. buy an answering machine for the replies
7. get a job interview with the city employment office
8. send your resume to all the big companies in the area

exercise 8

With a new partner, do Exercise 7 again. Ask the questions with *yet* but give original responses with *still*.

exercise 9

Find out something interesting about your classmates. In pairs, use the following model and cues to make short conversations. Use *ever* in your questions. The responses are up to you. You may want to use *never* in your responses.

> **examples:** work in a hospital
>> A: **Have you ever worked in a hospital?**
>> B: **No, I've never worked in a hospital, but I have worked in a nursing home.**
>
>> work for your government
>> A: **Have you ever worked for your government?**
>> B: **Yes, I've worked for the Ministry of Agriculture as a chemist.**

1. write a newspaper article
2. sell tickets for a sports event
3. live in another country
4. build or remodel a house
5. plow a field
6. have an unusual job
7. be in a very interesting place
8. do something very embarrassing
9. see a bad accident
10. experience something thrilling like skydiving

exercise 10

Circle the correct answers in the following conversation between a demanding boss and his secretary.

AL: Have you started the report (just / yet)? The boss has (just / yet) asked for it.
           1   2

MARY: No, I haven't. I (already / still) haven't finished all the letters you dictated this
                                      3
morning.

AL: I have (already / still) told the boss that she can have the report today.
                      4

MARY: I'll try, but I have (yet / just) finished talking to one of our customers on the
                                        5
phone, and I'm a little behind.

AL: I don't think we've (never / ever) had such a busy day!
                                        6

MARY: Don't worry. I haven't finished (already / yet), but I'm sure I will. If you have
                                                            7
time, you could give me some help.

AL: What would be best? I've (just / never) typed a business letter before, but I
                                        8
could address the envelopes and answer the phone.

MARY: That will help a lot.

Using What You've Learned

 **Complaining.** Write a dialogue using the present perfect tense and the adverbs *ever, never, still, yet, already, just.* You may want to consider a dialogue between complaining roommates, a student and his or her advisor, a parent and a child.

> example: ANN: I have washed the dishes three times this week. It's your
> turn. I've already done my share.
> KEESIA: But I've just finished cleaning the bathroom. Do you think
> it's fair if I do the dishes, too?

Work with a partner. Practice your dialogues. If you like, perform your dialogues for the class.

 **A Guessing Game.** In small groups, choose one person to pretend he or she has had an unusual job, such as an astronaut, snake charmer, or lion tamer. That person will answer questions and give a few hints to the rest of the group as they try to guess the job title. Use the present perfect in your questions or responses.

> examples: **Have you ever worked with animals?**
> **Yes. I have worked with dangerous animals.**
> **Have you worked in a zoo?**
> **No, I haven't, but I have worked with animals that you can
> find in a zoo.**

Have you ever worked as an animal trainer?
Yes, you guessed it!

TOPIC two

The Present Perfect Continuous Tense; The Present Perfect Tense (2)

Setting the Context

previewing the passage

What is it like to work in a restaurant? Have you ever worked in one? Share your experiences while answering these questions about the picture.

- Where are these young people working?
- What job is each of the employees doing?
- Why does someone write a letter to a local newspaper?

Editor
Morning News
Martin, Ohio

Dear Editor:

5   My 21-year-old son, Bill, is mentally handicapped. Earlier this year, a
pizza parlor hired him, and he has worked there since March. According to his
boss, he has been doing very well. The management has made a special effort
to help Bill feel comfortable. Because of this, Bill has learned to fit in with the
other employees. In fact, everyone at the pizza parlor has been trying to help.
10   This is the first chance that Bill has had to earn his own living. It has made
a strong impression on him. He has seemed so happy during this time. Above
all, he is proud of himself because he feels useful, and he is financially
independent.
    The public school special education program prepared Bill for this job.
15 When he was in school, he had several training jobs. These taught him the
skills for his work.
    I would like to say thank you to the pizza parlor and the Martin Public
Schools! We appreciate your help so much!

Sincerely,

Mickey Duke

**discussing
ideas**   What are several reasons Bill has been successful at this job? What is a *special
education* program?

A. The Present Perfect Continuous Tense

The present perfect continuous tense describes actions or situations that began
in the past and have continued to the present or are still true in the present.
This tense emphasizes the continuous nature of the activity. It does not
normally occur with repeated actions.

uses	examples	notes
Activities That Began in the Past and Have Continued to the Present	I **have been working** for the company since 1982. My boss **has been working** here for ten years. This week, we**'ve been training** some new employees.	Time expressions often used with this tense include *for* (+ period of time), *since* (+ beginning time), *so far, to date, up to now. How long* is frequently used in questions.

forms	affirmative statements	negative statements
Long Forms	We **have been working** hard. He **has been working** hard.	I **have not been working** hard. She **has not been working**.
Contracted Forms	I**'ve been working** too much. She**'s been working**.	We **haven't been working** hard. He **hasn't been working**.

	questions	possible answers
Yes/No Questions and Short Answers	**Have** we **been making** mistakes? **Has** it **been causing** problems?	Yes, you **have**. No, you **haven't**. Yes, it **has**. No, it **hasn't**.
Tag Questions and Short Answers	You've been working a lot, **haven't you**? He hasn't been leaving early, **has he**?	Yes, I **have**. No, he **hasn't**.
Information Questions and Short Answers	Where **have** you **been working**? How long **has** she **been working** there? Who **has been helping** her? What **has been happening** here?	At the bank. For two months. Mary has. Nothing new.

Note: See Appendix pages 396–397 for spelling rules for the *-ing* ending. See pages 13–14 for a list of verbs that are not normally used in the continuous tenses. Remember, however, that *hear, mean, need, see,* and *want* sometimes do appear in the present perfect continuous tense.

exercise 1  These people have been working all day, and they are tired. Tell why by forming complete sentences with the present perfect continuous tense.

example: bank teller / count money
He's a bank teller, and he's tired. He's been counting money all day.

1. cab driver / drive a taxi
2. airplane pilot / fly
3. mechanic / tune engines
4. gym teacher / run
5. secretary / file papers
6. dentist / fill cavities
7. surgeon / operate
8. policeman / direct traffic

**exercise 2**

Imagine that you are telling a friend about your work this week. In pairs, take turns asking and answering questions, using the cues that follow.

> **example:**   office / fun / learn to use the new computer
>> A: **How has work at the office been going?**
>> B: **It's been fun this week. We've been learning to use the new computer.**

1. travel agency / exciting / plan a tour to China
2. restaurant / busy / prepare for a large party
3. laboratory / interesting / experiment with different chemicals
4. law office / difficult / work on a new case
5. newspaper / enjoyable / write some good stories
6. hospital / confusing / try out a different schedule
7. university / challenging / teach too many classes
8. doctor's office / hard / see a lot of new patients

**exercise 3**

Complete the following letter with either the simple present or present perfect continuous form of the verbs in parentheses. In some cases, more than one form is correct. Try to explain those cases.

Dear Laurel,

You are so lucky you _do not work_____ (not work) here now! As you

know, in a small office everyone _____ (need) to do her share,

                                                             1

but that _____ (not happen) here!

                        2

We _____ (work) so hard because Caroline

              3

_____ (be) either sick or on a coffee break. She even

        4

_____ (come) to work late for two weeks. Can you believe it?

      5

She used to do such a good job, but she _____ (do) a
terrible job lately. Also, she _____ (make) a lot of mistakes
and _____ (complain) a lot.

    Enough of that. Let's hope Caroline changes soon and that she
_____ (have) a good excuse for her behavior.

Love,

Gwynne

 B. # The Present Perfect Tense (2): The Present Perfect Versus the Present Perfect Continuous

The present perfect continuous tense describes actions or situations that began in the past and have continued to the present or are still true in the present. To express the same meaning with a nonaction verb, use the present perfect tense.

    Time expressions such as *for* + period of time and *since* + beginning time usually appear in these sentences to give the past-to-present meaning. A few verbs, such as *live, work,* and *study,* are used with the present perfect continuous or the present perfect tense with little difference in meaning when a time expression is used. Compare:

uses	examples with action verbs	examples with nonaction verbs
Actions or Situations Still True in the Present	**I've worked** at IBM for five years. *or* **I've been working** at IBM for five years. We**'ve lived** here since 1981. *or* We**'ve been living** here since 1981.	**I've known** John for five years. We **haven't heard** any news since yesterday.
Actions or Situations at an Unspecified Time in the Past	**I've worked** at IBM. **I've lived** in Boston. He**'s studied** at several different schools.	**I've owned** several cars. She**'s been** there four times.

Notes: See pages 13–14 for a list of verbs that do not normally appear in the continuous tenses. Remember that *mean, need, want, hear,* and *see* sometimes appear in the present perfect continuous tense.

exercise 4 Reread the opening passage. Underline all the verbs in the present perfect or present perfect continuous tenses. Discuss which verbs could appear in either tense.

exercise 5 The following sentences use the present perfect tense. Tell which actions or situations are still true now and which occurred at an unspecified time in the past.

examples: I've worked at that bank. → **unspecified time in the past**
I've worked at that bank for five years. → **still true now**

1. Lately I've felt bored with my job.
2. So I've applied for a job at another company.
3. I've wanted to work there ever since I finished school.
4. I've had a job interview there.
5. I've called the manager several times.
6. She's been on vacation since the first of the month.
7. The company has had several different managers.
8. I have never failed to get the job I want.

exercise 6 Form complete sentences from the following cues by adding *for* or *since*.

example: Bill has had a job / several months
Bill has had a job for several months.

1. Bill has worked at the pizza parlor / last spring
2. Bill has been at work / 7:30
3. Jane has been working here / seven years
4. She has been supporting herself / six months
5. Mr. Johnson has been unemployed / March
6. He has been searching for a job / a long time
7. Margaret has had four interviews / the beginning of the month
8. She's gotten two jobs offers / Monday

activity 7 Petros is telling about his lab job. Complete the passage with the present perfect or present perfect continuous form of the verbs in parentheses. Give both forms when possible, and explain any difference in meaning.

"I _'ve wanted (have been wanting)_ (want) to work in a lab for a long time,

and finally I _'ve gotten_____ (get) the opportunity to try. I

_____ (start / just) working, and so far it
      1

_____ (be) a very interesting experience. My employer
      2

_____ (own) the lab since 1972. He _____
      3   4

(have) a lot of different employees since then. One person

_____ (work) for him for fifteen years, but most of the
5
employees now _____ (not work) there for very long.

"So far, the work _____ (not seem) very difficult. Of
7
course, I _____ (not understand) everything, but I
8
_____ (learn) a lot. At night, I _____ (study)
9   10
some of the manuals at home, and everyone at the lab _____
11
(help) me during the day. I _____ (appreciate / really) their
12
help."

exercise In pairs, take turns asking and answering questions about Sandy's work schedule.
Use the following cues.

> Sandy's work schedule at General Hospital:
>
> | | |
> |---|---|
> | 6:30 | take temperatures |
> | 7:30 | check vital signs (pulses, blood pressure) |
> | 7:45 | serve breakfast |
> | 8:00 | give the patients medicine |
> | 9:00 | help with bathing |
> | 9:30 | make beds |
> | 10:00 | write notes on the charts |
> | 10:30 | have a conference with doctors |
> | 11:00 | explain procedures to patients |

examples: 8:00 / check the patients' pulses
A: **Has Sandy checked the patients' pulses yet?**
B: **Yes, she has. She checked them a half hour ago.**

7:00 / check the patients' pulses
A: **Has Sandy checked the patients' pulses yet?**
B: **No, she hasn't checked them yet.**

1. 10:00 / help with bathing the patients
2. 9:00 / make beds
3. 7:00 / take temperatures
4. 11:00 / have a conference with the doctor
5. 9:30 / write notes on the chart
6. 7:30 / give the patients medicine
7. 11:30 / finish her morning work

Complete the following with the simple present, simple past, present perfect, or present perfect continuous form of the verbs in parentheses. In some cases, more than one form is correct. Try to explain those cases.

A NEW LIFE FOR BILL

Bill _____ (start) working at the pizza parlor in March. He _____ (work) there successfully for several months. Since the begin-
1
ning, the owners of the pizza parlor _____ (make) a special effort to
2
help Bill feel comfortable. Because of this, Bill _____ (learn) to get
3
along well with the other employees and the customers. In fact, everyone at the
pizza parlor _____ (help) Bill in every way they can.
4

For the first time in his life, Bill _____ (be) able to earn his own
5
living. This _____ (make) a strong impression on him. He
6
_____ (receive / already) several paychecks, and he
_____ (open / just) his own savings account. But paychecks
7
_____ (not be) the most important part of the job. Most
8
importantly, Bill _____ (be) proud of himself because he
9
_____ (feel) useful. Now he _____ (have) a good reason
10   11
to get up in the morning.

Last year, the public school special education program _____
12
(train) Bill for this job. It _____ (teach) him the skills he
13
_____ (need) to find and keep a job. Both Bill and his parents
14
_____ (be) hopeful about his future.
15

Using What You've Learned

Panel Discussion.   Divide the class into groups of four or five. Each group will prepare a panel discussion on recent changes in one of the following areas: the workplace, community health, international sports, or education. Use time expressions such as *normally, usually, lately, recently,* and *since* with the present perfect or present perfect continuous tense.

> **example:** LUCAS: **We're going to talk about sports. There's been a lot of activity in international sports lately. We're going to look at soccer, skiing, and tennis. Since Julian has read a lot about soccer, we will start with him.**
> JULIAN: **In South America recently, . . .**

activity 2   **Interviewing.**   Have you ever applied for a job? Have you ever had a job interview? In pairs, role-play interviews for a variety of jobs, using the following format as a guide.

INTERVIEWER	INTERVIEWEE
Good morning (afternoon).	. . .
To begin, what is your name?	My name is . . .
And . . . ?	I live . . .
Have you finished high school	
(university) studies?	. . .
Why are you applying for this job?	Well, I haven't . . . ,
Have you ever . . . ?	but I have . . .
Oh, really? When was that?	. . .
Since then, how long (often,	
many times) have you . . . ?	. . .
Is there anything else you would	
like to tell me about yourself?	. . .

activity 3   **Complaining.**   Is there anything that you would like to complain about? Has your landlord been promising to fix the kitchen sink for weeks but still hasn't done it? Have your roomates been promising to clean the apartment but still haven't cleaned it? Take this opportunity to practice complaining! Each person should make at least one complaint.

> example: **My roommate has been promising to clean out the refrigerator since Christmas. Here it's February and he still hasn't done it!**

activity 4   **Discussing Changes.**   Have there been important changes in the economic life of your country or city? How has the economy changed? Why have these changes taken place? Did the economy of your country rely on one crop like coffee? Did your city have one major industry like the auto industry in Detroit?

In small groups, choose a country, a city, an industry, or a profession and compare the past situation with the present situation. Discuss what changes have taken place and the reasons for them. Make notes about the most interesting changes and report them to the class.

The Past Perfect Tense

Setting the Context

Have you looked through the want ads in your local newspaper? Share your information while answering the following questions about newspaper ads.

- What kind of newspaper is this (for example, a city daily or a student newspaper)?
- What kinds of jobs are available for students?

Help Wanted

POSITION AVAILABLE—
Childcare providing care to children from families in crisis. Requirements: Three credits in early childhood education, six months experience in childcare. Hours: 20–40 hours/week; $7.80/hour. Call The Respite Center. 555-2350.

POSITION AVAILABLE—
Family Service Worker: To work with parents and families in crisis. Duties: Take incoming calls, assess needs, provide counseling, arrange childcare, provide information to parents. Requirements: B.A. Social Work plus relevant experience. Master's candidates preferred. Hours: 20 hours/week. $10.40/hour. Call The Respite Center: 555-2350.

WORK IN COLORADO: If you would like to work at a ski resort this winter, Telluride, Colorado might be the place for you. See our slide presentation. May 8 at 7 p.m. in the Union. Watch for our recruiters on campus May 9 & 10. For more information about Telluride Ski Corp., contact the office of Financial Aid.

RENTAL AGENTS: Must be personable and dedicated. Full- and part-time positions available. Offering opportunities for advancement. Must have transportation. Send resume and salary requirements to P.O. Box 7214, Milwaukee, WI 53202.

SUMMER WORK: Time is running out. Have you got your summer job lined up? We still have openings. Write Summer Opportunities, P.O. Box 421, Madison, WI 53701.

SEEKING aggressive graduate skier, salesperson with car, to market travel programs in an interstate area. Immediate need. Salary with commission. European travel and work within 1 year. Call Sue at Adventure Travel, Milwaukee, WI (414) 555–1448.

FINDING A JOB

MANUEL: I lost my job two weeks ago, and it's been very difficult to find a new one. I've spent the last few days job hunting. Before this, I had always spent my free time with my girlfriend, Sandy. She must think that I'm not interested in her anymore.

JOHN: Job hunting has been very difficult for me, too. I need a job, but like most students, I haven't ever had one. I don't have the work experience most employers want.

MANUEL: Last week I found out that a friend of mine had just quit her job in the physics lab. Why don't you apply for it?

JOHN: That sounds great! I'll do that right away. I haven't ever worked in a lab, but I did well in my science courses last year. You know, I'd considered being a dishwasher, but this sounds much better!

MANUEL: Well, I think I've just taken care of your employment problem! Now I've got to concentrate on mine.

How had Manuel spent his free time before he lost his job? What did Manuel find out last week? What had John considered doing?

The Past Perfect Tense

The past perfect tense refers to an activity or situation completed *before* another event or time in the past. It is more common in written English than in spoken English. Chapter 7 covers sentence types that often use this tense.

forms	affirmative statements	negative statements
Activities Completed Before Another Time in the Past	John **had arrived** at work long before 8:30. By 9:15, his boss still **had not arrived**. **Had** his boss **arrived** by 9:30? It was the first time that his boss **had** ever **been** late.	Time expressions often used with this tense include *before (1950), by (May 1), by then, by that time, already, ever, never, still, yet*. Adverbs of frequency have the same placement as with the present perfect tense.

forms	affirmative statements	negative statements
Long Forms	She **had arrived** by noon.	It **had not arrived** by noon.
Contracted Forms	I**'d arrived**.	You **hadn't arrived**.

	questions	possible answers
Yes/No Questions and Short Answers	**Had** she **arrived**?	Yes, she **had**. No, she **hadn't**.
Tag Questions and Short Answers	You had gone there, **hadn't you**? She hadn't already left, **had she**?	Yes, I **had**. No, she **hadn't**.
Information Questions and Short Answers	When **had** you last **seen** Mary? Where **had** he last **seen** Mary? Who **had** last **seen** her? What **had happened** to her?	Two weeks before the accident. At school. John. We don't know.

Note: See Appendix pages 396 to 397 for spelling rules for the *-ed* ending. See pages 394 to 395 for a list of irregular past participles.

exercise 1

Underline all past perfect verbs in the passage "Finding a Job." Can you explain why that tense was used in each case?

exercise 2

On Wednesday, John finally got a job. He began work the following Monday. Use the information in John's calendar and the past perfect tense to discuss John's preparations for his new job and his future.

example: **By Tuesday, John had had a job interview.**

Monday		Monday	
22	*Interview*	**29**	*Start working*
Tuesday		Tuesday	
23		**30**	
Wednesday	*Got a job!*	Wednesday	
24 ● New Moon	*Call Emily*	**31** ◖ First Quarter	
Thursday	*Buy work clothes/*	Thursday	
25	*new shoes*	**1**	
Friday		Friday	
26	*haircut / bus pass*	**2**	*First paycheck*
Saturday		Saturday	*Buy engagement*
27	*do laundry / movies*	**3**	*ring for Emily*
Sunday		Sunday	*Dinner with Emily*
28	*write parents*	**4**	*and her parents*

exercise 3

In pairs, take turns asking and answering questions about John. To check your answers, refer to the calendar above.

example: get a haircut / Thursday
A: **Had John gotten a haircut by Thursday?**
B: **No, he hadn't. He got a haircut Friday.**

exercise 4

Using the following cues, form sentences with the past perfect and *ever*.

example: as a taxi driver / drive a taxi
When I got a job as a taxi driver, it was the first time that I had ever driven a taxi.

1. as a bank teller / wear a suit
2. in an office / carry a briefcase
3. in a hospital / see an operation
4. in a bank / use a computer
5. as a secretary / take dictation
6. in a gas station / repair an engine
7. in a restaurant / clear tables
8. as a painter / work on a scaffold

First, read the following passage for meaning. Then complete the passage with appropriate tenses of the verbs in parentheses. Choose from the simple past, past continuous, past perfect, simple present, and future tenses.

ELEPHANT WINS IN COURT

Rampyari _____is_____ (be) an unusual female. She _____had been_____ (be) a working woman for many years, but after an accident she

_____ (lose) the ability to make money. Until that time, she
      1

_____ (work) loyally for her employer, without bonuses or over-
      2

time pay. Then, she _____ (go) to court about her job.
                          3

During her trial, Rampyari _____ (come / never) to the court-
                                4

room. Because of her large stomach, she _____ (not be) able to
                                              5

climb the stairs to the courthouse. Also, she _____ (be) very upset
                                                  6

and emotional because she _____ (not work) anymore. She
                              7

_____ (retire) early, long before the normal age, but it
      8

_____ (not be) by choice.
      9

Finally, after two years in court, Rampyari _____ (receive)
                                                10

$2,300 in damages. She _____ (become) wealthy. And she
                          11

_____ (become) the first elephant in Indian history to win in the
      12

courtroom!

Before 1981, this lovable circus performer _____ (entertain)
                                                13

audiences for sixteen years. Then one winter night, she _____
                                                            14

(walk) down an Indian highway when a truck _____ (hit) her.
                                                15

Because of the injury, now she _____ (walk) with difficulty. She
                                    16

_____ (be) still young for an elephant, and perhaps she
17

_____ (go) back to work sometime in the future, but not in the
18

circus. That would be too difficult for her now.

If she goes back to work in the future, the defense lawyers will ask for a

retrial. No one _____ (want) to pay $2,300 to a working elephant.
19

Adapted from *The Christian Science Monitor*

Using What You've Learned

activity 1

Making a Survey. Talk to five or more of your classmates to find out how their career or educational plans have changed. After you fill in the chart, discuss your findings in small groups. Use the past perfect tense whenever possible.

example: **Ms. Mitchell had planned to teach, but she got a job as a library assistant instead.**

Name	Career Plans	First Job	Second Job
M. Mitchell	Teacher	Librarian Assistant	Typist

activity 2

Discussing Employment Possibilities. In pairs or in small groups, discuss one or more of the following. Then give a summary of your discussion to the entire class.

1. Is unemployment a major problem in your area or country? What has caused it? Has your government tried to improve the situation? Which jobs have the best future? Which jobs have no future?
2. Do you think jobs in the field you have chosen will change very much in the future? Have they changed very much in the last twenty years? What has caused these changes? What may cause future changes?

The Present and Past Perfect Tenses

Problems with the present and past perfect tenses are usually found on standardized tests of English proficiency. After you review these verb tenses, check your understanding by completing the sample items below.

Remember that . . .

- The present perfect tense can refer to an action occurring at some time before the present, but the time is unspecified.
- Time expressions can be a guide to understanding the meaning of a sentence.
- The perfect tenses are formed using *has, have,* or *had* + past participle.

Part 1. Circle the correct completion for the following.

example: John _____ with the employment office twice since last week.
- **a.** has been checking
- **b.** has checked
- **c.** is checked
- **d.** have checked

1. Alex and Tom _____ at the supermarket for five months.
   - **a.** have been worked
   - **b.** have worked
   - **c.** has worked
   - **d.** have working

2. Caroline _____ a reduction in her salary.
   - **a.** have taken
   - **b.** has taken
   - **c.** taken
   - **d.** has took

3. The employment office _____ me since I moved to Los Angeles.
   - **a.** never been calling
   - **b.** has been calling
   - **c.** have called
   - **d.** has been called

TOPIC **four**
Review

Setting the Context

How has the medical profession changed much in the last hundred years? Share your ideas and experiences while answering the following questions about the picture, which shows a scene from the 1800s.

- Where are these customers?
- What kinds of operations are taking place?
- What is the profession of the men who are standing?

In North America many professionals, particularly those in health care, practice differently from the way they used to. As an example, doctors took care of everyone in a family, and they went to a patient's home when there was a problem. Now doctors are specialists; they practice in large clinics, and
5 technicians do many of the doctors' former duties.

Strange as it may seem now, barbers were also surgeons. They cut hair *and* performed operations. They did not do operations in the stomach or the chest, however. Most people avoided those operations, anyway.

People also avoided dentists if at all possible. A person who was going to
10 see the dentist was an unhappy person. In the days before anesthesia, those visits were often extremely painful. Dentists had one solution to almost every tooth problem: pull the tooth.

Fortunately, much has changed. Health care today is often quite painless— except when the bill arrives.

discussing ideas

How has health care changed in North America? Around the world? What did barbers do in the past that they no longer do?

exercise 1

Review. Add *a, an, the, some,* or *x* to the following list. Give all possibilities for each.

1. _a, the_ house

2. _____ hour

3. _____ ear

4. _____ potatoes

5. _____ tea

6. _____ Nile

7. _____ elephant

8. _____ Rocky Mountains

9. _____ love

10. _____ Russia

11. _____ person

12. _____ homework

13. _____ White House

14. _____ Pacific Ocean

15. _____ Mexico City

16. _____ Queen of England

exercise 2

Review. Divide into four or five teams. How many different sentences can you make using the nouns and prepositions that you find in the photo?

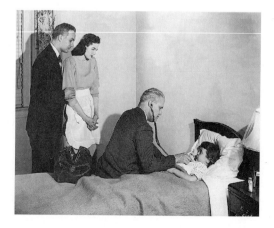

Review. Follow the model and make sentences about what people used to do. Then add information of your own about what we do today. Use the simple present and present perfect tenses.

example: people / send messages by telegraph
People haven't sent messages by telegraph for a long time. Today we send messages by computer.

1. doctors / make house calls
2. dentists / clean teeth
3. milkmen / deliver milk
4. businessmen / travel by train

5. pharmacists / make their own medicine
6. housewives / wash the clothes by hand
7. farmers / plow with horses
8. firemen / shovel coal on trains

Review. Complete the passage using appropriate forms of the verbs in parentheses. Choose from all tenses.

CHANGES IN MEDICINE

Modern medicine _began_____ (begin) in the nineteenth century. At

that time, French physicians _____ (develop) methods of clinical

medicine that we _____ (use) ever since.
         2

There _____ (be) many important landmarks from that time to
         3

the present. A French physician, René Laennec, _____ (invent) the
                                                         4

stethoscope in the early 1800s. Later, in 1842, a U.S. physician, Crawford

Long, _____ (anesthetize) a patient with ether. Painless operations
         5

_____ (be) possible since that day. This _____ (be) the
         6   7

beginning of modern surgery.

The science of how the body fights disease and infection _____
(interest) many medical scientists for hundreds of years. Louis Pasteur first

clearly _____ (show) that bacteria cause disease, and Joseph Lister
_____9_____

_____ (discover) that bacteria enter a patient during surgery,
_____10_____

explaining why so many surgical patients _____ (die). These men
_____11_____

and scores of other scientists since that time _____ (revolution)
_____12_____

medicine and medical treatment.

exercise 5 **Review.** Complete the sentences using appropriate forms of the verbs in parentheses. Choose from all tenses covered in the book.

TEMPORARY JOBS

The temporary work industry _____*grew*_____ (grow) from 21

billion (in revenues) in 1991 to 34 billion in 1994. In recent years, employment

agencies _____ (have) great success finding temporary
_____1_____

workers for employers. These agencies _____ (be) usually
_____2_____

able to locate jobs for all types of people, including accountants.

People want temporary jobs for different reasons. Some people

_____ (take) temporary work because the job market
_____3_____

_____ (be) poor, because they _____ (need)
_____4_____   _____5_____

_____ the flexibility of short-term work, or because they
_____6_____

_____ (want) to get their foot in the door in a certain business
_____7_____

or industry.

Companies _____ (rely) on temporary workers lately
_____8_____

because they _____ (find) that it can be less expensive for
_____9_____

them. For example, today temporary workers sometimes

_____ (not receive) benefits, such as health insurance.
_____10_____

Employment agencies can help by providing benefits, but most employees

hope that in the near future businesses _____ (provide)
_____11_____

benefits once again.

Review. Complete the following passage by using the appropriate present, past, and future tenses.

COMMUTERS, BEWARE

NY Sept. 17   In a one-minute stop, five masked men _____
(push) their way onto a commuter train and _____ (announce) a
                                                          2
robbery. One masked man _____ (fire) a shot into the air, while the
                                        3
others _____ (put) wallets and purses into a large bag. The robbers
              4
_____ (not go) up and down the aisles. Their victims
        5
_____ (be) the ones closest to them.
        6

   After one minute, the masked men _____ (run) as the train
                                                     7
doors _____ (close) and the train _____ (leave) the
            8   9
station.

   "Usually you just _____ (fall) asleep on the train and you
                                10
_____ (feel) safe. Now I _____ (be) more careful when
        11   12
the train _____ (be) in the station," said Tom Brown of Beacon,
                13
N.Y. Another commuter, Ralph Jackson, said, "From now on, I

_____ (stay / just) in the city rather than _____ (take)
        14   15
the train home late at night."

Using What You've Learned

activity **1**

Discussing Changes.   In groups of four or five, discuss the answers to the following questions. Use *can*, *could*, and *be able to* in your discussion.

1. What could you do in your country that you can't do now?
2. What could you do as a child that you can't do now?
3. What can women do now that they couldn't do years ago?

activity **2**

Giving Advice.   In groups, discuss the following situations. Try to use *should*, *ought to*, *must*, *have to*, and *had better* in your discussion.

What do you say to a friend if. . . ?

a. his room looks terrible—messy and dusty
b. he spends too much time calling long distance
c. you think he is too thin
d. he plays computer games every possible minute

activity **3**

Debate.   Use the modals *have to, ought to, should, could,* and *must* to debate these questions:

1. Should all high school students attend one high school or should students attend academic, comprehensive, or technical schools according to their interests and abilities?
2. What should a school system do with violent or unmotivated students?
3. What should a society do with adults who have committed violent acts and do not show the ability to reform themselves?

activity **4**

One-Upmanship.   What have you done to outdo your classmates? Someone begins by explaining what he or she has done that no one else has. Everyone in the class tries to find something better. Use the present perfect tense in your statements.

example: number of languages
        A: **I have learned to speak three languages: Spanish, Aymara, and English.**
        B: **I can top that! I have learned four languages: Hmong, Thai, Lao, and English.**

Whoops!   What had you forgotten to do and what were the consequences? Use the past perfect tense and share your experiences.

example: bring a passport to the airport
Luckily, I left early for the airport. As the Greyhound bus took me from my home to the nearest airport, I remembered that I had forgotten my passport.
Consequences: $20 bus ticket home and back to the airport

CHAPTER **five**

Lifestyles

Phrasal Verbs and Related Structures

Topic One: Inseparable Phrasal Verbs

Topic Two: Separable Phrasal Verbs

Topic Three: Separable and Inseparable Phrasal Verbs

Topic Four: Participles and Adjectives Followed by Prepositions

Inseparable Phrasal Verbs

Setting the Context

What was a typical American family like forty years ago? Share your ideas and opinions by answering these questions about the picture.

- Who are the people in this picture? What is each person doing?
- What time of day is it? How do you know?

THE "TYPICAL" AMERICAN FAMILY

   In the 1950s, according to popular television shows, the American family (let's call them the Smiths) consisted of a mother, a father, and two or three children. The Smiths were a very happy family. Their problems were not serious; the children got along with each other, and Mr. and Mrs. Smith
5 obviously cared about each other very much.
   Mr. Smith (Dick) was a businessman, and Mrs. Smith (Susie) was a housewife. She spent most of her time at home, where she took care of the house and the children (Billy and Mary). In the morning, she usually got up before the rest of the family, went into the kitchen, and made breakfast. Soon
10 Dick, Billy, and Mary sat down to eat. The children talked about their plans for the rest of the day while Dick looked at the newspaper and thought about his day's work. Susie, of course, cheerfully served everybody.
   When breakfast was over, the children left for school and Dick went to work. Then Susie Smith sat down with a cup of coffee and the morning

15 newspaper. She had the whole day to herself, until the children came back from school. At that time, she listened to them patiently as they talked about their day at school, and she helped them with their homework.

According to television, this was the "typical" scene in family after family, all across the United States. Nowadays, we laugh when we look at those old
20 1950s television programs because we know how very much they differed from real life.

discussing ideas

What did each person in the "typical" American family use to do in the mornings? Do you think this family was really typical? Why or why not? Can you describe the "typical" American family of today?

A. Inseparable Phrasal Verbs (1)

Certain prepositions customarily follow certain verbs. These prepositions are sometimes called *particles*. The following is a short list of some common verb + particle combinations in English. These phrasal verbs are "inseparable" because the particle has only one possible position in the sentence. In most cases, it immediately follows the verb. With the phrasal verbs in this group, the particle does not change the basic meaning of the verb.

verbs	examples
agree (disagree) with	Mary doesn't **agree with** her mother.
belong to	That toy **belongs to** Billy.
care about	Mrs. Smith **cares about** her children.
consist of	The family **consists of** four people.
depend on	Children **depend on** their parents.
differ from	Your opinion **differs from** mine.
dream about (of)	Mary **dreams about** getting married someday.
laugh at	Everybody **laughed at** the dog's tricks.
leave for	The children **leave for** school at 7:45 A.M.
listen to	The mother **listened to** the child's story.
live with	She **lives with** her daughter.
look at	Last night we **looked at** old photographs.
look for	She **looked for** her keys for an hour.
sit down	Everyone **sat down** at the table.
talk about	We **talked about** our plans for the summer.
talk to	My teacher **talked to** me about my homework.
think about (of)	Mr. Smith is **thinking about** his work.
wait for	Mrs. Smith **waited for** Mary at the bus stop.

Some phrasal verbs can have a noun or pronoun between the verb and the particle. Here are some examples.

verbs	examples
ask (someone) about	Mrs. Smith **asked** the children **about** their day.
ask (someone) for	Dick **asked** Susie **for** a second cup of coffee.
borrow something from someone	Susie **borrowed** some milk **from** her neighbor.
help (someone) with	Dick **helped** Susie **with** the dishes.
lend something to someone	The neighbor **lent** some milk **to** Susie.
remind someone about	Billy **reminded** his mother **about** the football game.
remind someone of	You **remind** me **of** your grandmother.

 **exercise 1** Underline all the verb + particle combinations in the passage "The 'Typical' American Family" on pages 152 and 153. Discuss the meanings of the verbs with your classmates.

 **exercise 2** Fill in the blanks with the correct particle.

example: During breakfast, Mrs. Smith reminded her husband

_about_____ the parents' meeting that evening.

1. Billy spent fifteen minutes looking _____ his geography book.

2. During the day, Susie Smith listened _____ the radio while she worked in the house.

3. She borrowed some sugar _____ her neighbor.

4. At school, the children laughed _____ a funny story.

5. Mary lent her red pencil _____ a classmate.

6. During class, Billy dreamed _____ going outside and playing.

7. This reading book belongs _____ Mary.

8. At work, Dick Smith asked his boss _____ a raise.

9. Susie waited _____ the children to come home from school.

10. Then Susie helped them _____ their homework.

11. During dinner, the family members talked _____ their day.

12. Mrs. Smith almost always agrees _____ Mr. Smith.

exercise 3 In pairs, ask and answer the following questions about your life as a high school student. Use the phrasal verbs in italics in your answers.

> **example:** A: Was it easy for you to *talk about* your problems with your teachers?
>
> B: **No, it wasn't easy for me to talk about my problems with my teachers.**

1. At what time did you use to *leave for* school?
2. Did someone *help* you *with* your homework?
3. Did you ever *disagree with* your teachers?
4. Did your teachers *care about* your opinions?
5. What did you sometimes *dream about* while you were sitting in class?
6. When you were a teenager, whom did you *talk to* about your future?
7. As a teenager, did you *belong to* any clubs or sports teams?
8. When you were a teenager, what did you *think about* English?

 B. Inseparable Phrasal Verbs (2)

There are many verb + particle combinations in which the particle changes the meaning of the verb. That is, the meaning of the two words together is different from the meanings of the verb and the preposition by themselves. These verb + particle combinations have an *idiomatic* meaning. They are different from sentences with prepositional phrases. Compare the following:

	examples	**notes**
Verb + Prepositional Phrase	Jim **lives on Middleton Street.** (The house where Jim lives is located on Middleton Street.) Jim **ran into his house.** (Jim entered his house, running.)	In these sentences the verb keeps its basic meaning.
Verb + Particle (Phrasal Verb)	Jim **lives on** $500 a month. (Jim spends $500 a month.) Jim **ran into** an old friend. (Jim met an old friend by chance.)	In these sentences, the verb has an idiomatic meaning.

On the next page is a short list of inseparable phrasal verbs with their idiomatic meanings.

verbs	examples	meanings
come back	Are you going to **come back** early?	return
drop (stop) by	My neighbor **dropped by** this afternoon.	visit
get along with	The Smiths **get along with** their neighbors.	be friendly with
get together with	Let's **get together with** the Nelsons this weekend.	meet socially
get up	On weekends, everybody **gets up** late.	leave one's bed after sleeping
go over	Let's **go over** the homework.	review; correct
grow up	I **grew up** in Wisconsin.	become an adult
live on	Can you **live on** $500 a month?	exist; support oneself financially
look after	Will you **look after** the boys while I'm out?	supervise; watch
look like	You **look like** your father.	resemble
move out of (move into)	When are you **moving out of** your apartment? When are you **moving into** your new house?	leave; relocate
run into	I **ran into** an old friend yesterday.	meet accidentally
stay up	How late did you **stay up** last night?	remain awake
take care of	Will you **take care of** my plants while I'm gone?	watch; supervise

 **exercise** *4*

In pairs, ask and answer the following questions about your life with your family. Use the phrasal verbs in italics in your answers.

example: A: Do you ever *run into* friends when you are shopping?
             B: **Yes, sometimes I run into friends when I am shopping.**

1. Where did you *grow up*?
2. When you were very small, who *looked after* you?
3. When you were a child in school, did you *come back* home for lunch?
4. Did someone *go over* your homework with you?
5. How late did you *stay up* on school nights?

6. Do you *look like* your father or your mother?
7. Do you *get along with* everyone in your family?
8. In your family, who usually *gets up* first?
9. Who *takes care of* the house?
10. Do relatives and neighbors *drop by* your house very often?

Replace the verbs in italics with phrasal verbs from the Inseparable Phrasal Verbs (2) chart on page 156.

> example: When Susie and Dick go out in the evening, a babysitter *watches* the children.
> **When Susie and Dick go out in the evening, a babysitter *looks after* the children.**

1. That child doesn't *resemble* either of her parents.
2. When are you going to *return*?
3. I *meet* my best friend for dinner once a week.
4. Yesterday, I *accidentally met* my college roommate on the street.
5. I need to *review* my notes before the test tomorrow.
6. Please feel free to *visit* us any time you're in the area.
7. I have only a part-time job, so it's hard for me to *exist on* my salary.
8. We are going to *leave* this apartment next month.

exercise 6

The letter here and on the next page, from Susie Smith to her friend Nancy, contains many particle errors. Cross out the errors and correct them as in the examples. Use the lists on pages 153 to 156 to help you. Note the date!

March 18, 1957

Dear Nancy,

    I have been thinking ~~over~~ *about* you a lot lately. I'm sorry for not writing sooner, but I've been so busy with the children.

    I ran ~~through~~ *into* your mother at the market the other day, and we talked with your life in the BIG CITY! It's interesting how much your life differs in your

5 mother's—and mine.

    You asked me for my life as a "typical American housewife." My life consists in my children, my husband, and my home. As you know, we recently moved on this big, expensive new house, so we don't have much money these days. I thought in trying to find a part-time job because it's not easy to live

10 with Dick's salary. Dick doesn't want me to work, though, and I think it's more important for me to take care to the house and kids. Anyway, I know I can depend for Dick to support us all.

The kids are wonderful. They are growing in so fast! Every afternoon, when they come to from school, we talk with their day, and I go under their homework with them. I really enjoy listening on them.

What else can I tell you, Nancy? Sometimes I get together from other mothers in my neighborhood and we talk on our kids and husbands. I think I'm lucky because Dick helps me for the housework more than most other husbands do. Occasionally, I go to my neighbor Julie's house and ask her about some advice, or I borrow some sugar or something of her. Now and then I run around some old friends from high school.

And that's my life, Nancy. Sure, sometimes I dream for doing something different and exciting, and I think on you in the city. But really—I am very happy.

Love,

Susie

Using What You've Learned

Describing a Traditional Family. In small groups, discuss the following questions. Then use this information as the basis for a brief presentation to the class.

1. In your country, how many people does a traditional family consist of? How many people work outside the home?
2. Who usually takes care of small children?
3. Do young couples in your country live with their parents, or do they live by themselves?
4. The "typical" family in the United States has changed a lot in the last thirty years. Has the "typical" family in your country also changed? In what ways?

Separable Phrasal Verbs

Setting the Context

previewing the passage

Do you know the meaning of the terms *nuclear family* and *extended family*? In American society, which one is more important these days? How about in your culture? Share your opinions by answering these questions about the picture.

- Who are the people in the pictures? What is the relationship between them?
- What do the pictures tell about their lifestyles?

Last week my oldest son, Bob, called me up. He said, "Mom, Jean and I had a great idea: For your birthday, we'd like to take a family photograph. What do you think?" I thought it over and decided it would be nice to have a photograph of all my children and grandchildren together.

5 The photo was ready yesterday, so Bob picked it up. And here it is! I must say, it's beautiful. That's me, sitting in the center. Over on the left are Jean and Bob and their teenage son, Alan. Next to Bob, the woman with the baby is my daughter Dawn. She and her husband separated recently; I had hoped that they would work out their differences, but it didn't happen that way. Now Dawn is

10 trying to bring up two children by herself. It's not easy, so I help her out whenever I can.

Behind me in the picture are my daughter Patty, her husband Steve, and their two kids. Such a happy family; they enjoy doing things together, and they always talk over their problems without arguing.

15 And on the right you see my youngest son, Michael. He always wears such strange clothes . . . I really can't figure him out. But he's young; he's still trying out different ideas and lifestyles. He'll be all right.

My husband and I worked hard to bring our kids up well. They're very different from one another, but they're fine people and I love them all. They

20 make me very happy.

discussing ideas Using the information in the passage, can you identify each person in the photograph? How do the woman's four children differ from one another? Is this a "typical" North American extended family? In what ways?

A. Introduction to Separable Phrasal Verbs

With *inseparable* verbs, the verb and particle are a unit; they must be together. However, English also has *separable* phrasal verbs. With these verb + particle combinations, *noun* objects may come after the verb + particle or between them. *Pronoun* objects must come between the verb and particle. Compare:

	examples	**meanings**
Inseparable	*noun* My mother **ran into** Laurie. *pronoun* My mother **ran into** her.	My mother saw Laurie. My mother saw her.

	examples	meanings
Separable	*noun* I **called up** my ⌢mother.	I telephoned my mother.
	noun I **called** my ⌢mother **up.**	I telephoned my mother.
	pronoun I **called** ⌢her **up.**	I telephoned her.

Common Separable Phrasal Verbs

verbs	examples	meanings
bring up	Dawn **is bringing** her kids **up** by her-self.	raise (a family)
call up	Yesterday my son **called** me **up.**	telephone (verb)
drop off	Could you **drop** me **off** downtown?	take someone or something (on the way somewhere, often by car)
figure out	I can't **figure out** this problem.	understand, solve (a problem); decide
find out	Did you **find out** her phone number?	learn, discover
help out	My mother often **helps** me **out** with the kids.	assist, help
look over	Please **look over** your paper before you give it to me.	read quickly; review
pick out	Did you **pick out** a present?	choose, select
pick up	I **picked** her **up** after class.	go (often by car) to get someone
take out	Please **take out** the garbage.	take outside
talk over	We **talked** the situation **over.**	discuss
think over	I'll **think over** your advice.	think about something carefully
throw away	Did you **throw** yesterday's paper **away**?	discard; put in the garbage
try out	Let's **try out** these new skis.	test, experiment with
wake up	The phone **woke** me **up.**	cause someone to stop sleeping
work out	I hope we can **work** it **out.**	find a solution, resolve something

**exercise 1**   Underline all the separable phrasal verbs in the passage "Family Photograph" on page 160, and circle the noun or pronoun object of the verb. In each case, change the word order of the verb, particle, and object *if possible*.

> **example:** My son <u>called me up</u>. → *no change possible*
> I had hoped that they would <u>work out their differences.</u> → *work their differences out*

exercise 2   Fill in the blanks with the correct particle.

> **example:** I would like to look __over__ the plans. → *look the plans over*

1. I threw _____ my mother's letter by accident.

2. Please think my suggestion _____ and give me your opinion.

3. I can't figure _____ the answer to this math problem.

4. These days it's really hard to bring kids _____ .

5. I need to drop _____ a package at the post office.

6. Every day, Mrs. Smith picks her children _____ at the bus stop.

7. We tried _____ a new computer system, but we didn't like it.

8. I call my mother _____ every Sunday.

9. The noise from the birds woke Mr. Smith _____ at 5:00 A.M.

10. Let's talk _____ your idea with the boss.

exercise 3   Change all the noun objects in Exercise 2 to pronouns. Pay attention to word order.

> **example:** I would like to look over the plans.
> I would like to **look them over.**

B. Phrasal Verbs Related to Clothing, Cleaning, and Household Items

There are a few groups of related phrasal verbs in English. Some examples follow.

verbs	examples	meanings
have on	She **has on** a new hat.	*Have on* means "wear"; *on* means "on one's body."
put on	I always **put** my socks **on** first.	
try on	Did you **try** it **on** before you bought it?	
take off	Please **take off** your coat.	*Off* means "remove from the surface of something."
clean off	**Clean off** the table, please.	
dust off	I **dusted off** the bookshelves.	
wash off	I **washed** the grease **off** my hands.	
clean out	We need to **clean out** this closet.	*Out* means "remove from the inside of something."
sweep out	Please **sweep out** the garage.	
clean up	Don't go into the kitchen until I **clean** it **up.**	*Up* means "lift or remove something that dropped or fell." It also means "completely."
pick up	Please **pick up** your toys.	
sweep up	I have to **sweep up** the floor.	
wash up	It's time to **wash up** for dinner.	
turn off	Could you **turn** the TV **off**?	*Off* means "stop something" such as water or an electrical appliance.
turn on	Please **turn** the light **on.**	*On* means "start something" such as water or an electrical appliance.
turn down	**Turn down** that stereo!	*Down* and *up* refer to sound levels.
turn up	Could you **turn** the TV **up**?	

 **exercise 4**   First, complete the following phrases with appropriate particles. Then substitute a pronoun for the noun. Some phrases may have more than one correct answer.

> **example:** turn _down (up, on, off)_ the stereo→ turn it down

1. sweep _____ the closet

2. clean _____ the bathroom

3. turn _____ the lights

4. clean _____ the table

5. turn _____ the sound

6. clean _____ the house

7. dust _____ the lamp

8. take _____ your hat

exercise 5   Patty, Steve, and their two children are a happy family. In pairs, take turns asking and answering questions about them, using the separable phrasal verbs in this section. Use the example as a model.

Patty and Steve share everything....

> **example:** drop off the children at school / Steve
> A: **Who drops the children off at school?**
> B: **Steve drops them off at school.**

1. clean up the kitchen / Steve
2. pick up the kids' toys / the kids
3. take out the garbage / the son
4. wake up the children / Patty
5. help the kids out with homework / Patty and Steve
6. sweep out the garage / Patty

7. clean off the table before dinner / the daughter
8. call up Grandma on Saturdays / the kids
9. pick out new living room furniture / Patty and Steve
10. help out around the house sometimes / Patty's mother

exercise 6   Complete the following sentences with the correct verb, pronoun, and particle. Some will have more than one correct answer.

> example: Oh, no! I've just spilled orange juice on the floor. I'd better <u>clean it up</u> .

1. Before you pay for a new shirt in a department store, you should _____ .

2. The music in the restaurant was so loud that we couldn't talk to each other. We asked the manager to _____ .

3. This sweater is too hot; I'm going to _____ .

4. My car is full of papers, bottles, and other junk. It's time to _____ .

5. Mary's toys were all over the floor. Her mother asked her to _____ .

6. Yesterday I noticed that our bookshelves are covered with dust. Today I'm going to _____ .

7. Sometimes Mr. Jones cannot find his reading glasses. He forgets that he already _____ .

8. The TV wasn't loud enough, so I _____ .

9. We don't need that light over there; please _____ .

10. The table is covered with newspapers and letters. Please _____ so that we can eat dinner.

 C. Phrasal Verbs Related to School or Studies

verbs	examples	meanings
add up	Your answer is wrong because you forgot to **add up** the last group of numbers.	total

verbs	examples	meanings
finish up	Class is over; please **finish up** your tests.	*Up* can mean "completely" or "thoroughly." In some cases it does not change the basic meaning of the verb.
write up	Please **write up** this report for Monday.	
check in	A librarian **checks** books **in.**	receive
check out	I **checked out** three books.	take (books or movies from the library, etc.)
do over	You did this assignment incorrectly; please **do** it **over.**	repeat, do again
look over	I have to **look over** my notes before the next class.	read or look at quickly
fill in	Please **fill in** all the answers.	give (information on a form)
fill out	You need to **fill out** this application.	complete (a form)
hand in / turn in	I **turned in** my composition late.	give (for example, to the teacher)
hand out	The teacher **handed out** some exercises.	give (for example, to the students)
hand back	The teacher **handed back** our essays.	return (for example, to students, after correction)

exercise 7 In pairs, take turns asking and answering questions based on the following cues. Use the pronoun form in your answer. Pay attention to verb tenses.

example: finish up your homework / yes, an hour ago
A: **Have you finished up your homework?**
B: **Yes, I finished it up an hour ago.**

1. check the books out of the library yet / yes, two days ago
2. write up your lab report / no, tomorrow
3. look over your report to check for mistakes / yes, before I typed it
4. turn in the final copy yet / yes, the day before yesterday
5. your teacher hand back the tests / yes, yesterday afternoon
6. fill out the scholarship application yet / no, later
7. add up the monthly expenses yet / no, this evening
8. do your chemistry assignment over / yes, this morning

Using What You've Learned

 *activity*   **Interviewing.**   Using the following cues, ask your partner about his or her activities this week. Indicate your partner's answer in the chart. Use the examples as models.

> examples: sweep up the kitchen
> A: **Have you swept up the kitchen yet (this week)?**
> B: **Yes, I swept it up on Sunday.**
>
> hand in your composition
> A: **Have you handed in your composition yet (this week)?**
> B: **No, I haven't.**

activity	yes, when?	no
sweep up the kitchen	Sunday	
hand in your composition		X
call up your parents		
take out the garbage		
clean up your room (apartment, house)		
throw away yesterday's newspaper		
think over your plans for the summer (winter, etc.)		
finish up your homework for tomorrow		
clean out your car		
pick out a birthday present for your friend (sister, mother, etc.)		

Separable and Inseparable Phrasal Verbs

Setting the Context

What choices do young people have after they finish high school? Share your ideas and opinions by answering these questions about the pictures.

- What is this young man doing in each picture?
- Did this young man work *before* he went to college? Why do you think he did this?

GOING BACK TO SCHOOL

    I was a terrible student in high school. Studying and learning were hard for me. I had to do many assignments over. I couldn't keep up with my class-mates. Naturally, I didn't have a very good attitude; I wanted to get through with school as quickly as possible and get a job. And that's exactly what I did.

5 As soon as I graduated, I moved out of my parents' house. I spent the next five years working as a carpenter and living on $300 a month. It was hard.

    I went through a lot during those five years, and my experiences really helped me to grow up. Finally, at age twenty-four, I felt ready to go back to school. After looking into lots of professional possibilities, I decided to study

10 accounting. Math had always been pretty easy for me; I could add up numbers in my head.

    I thought I'd be the oldest person in all my classes, but I've come across lots of people who took a few years off before starting college. Most of us are glad that we waited until now to begin our studies.

What kind of student was the young man in high school? How has he changed? Do young people in your country ever take time off between high school and college? What do they do with this time? In your opinion, is it a good idea to work for a few years before starting college?

A. More Separable Phrasal Verbs

verbs	examples	meanings
call back	Did Charles **call** you **back**?	telephone again
cut out	Save the newspaper. I want to **cut** an article **out.**	cut, remove
get back	Did you **get** your stolen wallet **back**?	receive
give back	Did you **give** the money **back**?	return
look up	I **looked** the word **up** in the dictionary.	search for information (in a book)
point out	He **pointed out** several problems.	mention, indicate
put away	He **put away** his toys at bedtime.	put something in its proper place
start over	Let's **start** the song **over** from the beginning.	begin again
take off	Yesterday I **took** a day **off.**	take a vacation

Note: Take off has several meanings. As a separable verb, it can mean "take a vacation," as shown above or "remove," as shown on page 163. *Take off* can also be an inseparable phrasal verb meaning "leave": *The plane took off on time.*

B. More Inseparable Phrasal Verbs

verbs	examples	meanings
check into check out of	We **checked into** a first-class motel.	enter, register; leave
come across	Did you **come across** that letter?	find (something); meet (someone)
get through with	I want to **get through with** this job as quickly as possible.	finish
go over to	Let's **go over to** Miki's house.	go to visit
go through	I don't want to **go through** that again!	experience
keep up with	I can't **keep up with** the class.	stay equal to (in time, distance, money, work, etc.)
look into	We should **look into** the cost before we rent that house.	get information on
put up with	How do you **put up with** all this noise?	tolerate, live with

 **exercise 1**   Underline all the separable and inseparable phrasal verbs in the passage "Going Back to School" on page 168. Discuss the meanings of the verbs.

 **exercise 2**   Replace the verbs in italics with phrasal verbs from the preceding lists. Use either separable or inseparable phrasal verbs. Pay attention to the placement of noun and pronoun objects.

> **example:**   After I used my neighbor's camera, I ~~returned it~~ *gave it back* to him.

1. Yesterday I *found* some old photographs while I was cleaning.
2. I have to *finish* this assignment before I can go out.
3. We *registered* at the most expensive hotel in town.
4. I am tired of your rude behavior. I'm not going to *tolerate* it anymore.
5. I *searched for* information about India in an encyclopedia.
6. This composition is no good. I'll have to *begin* it again.
7. She *experienced* some difficult times while she was in college.
8. The tour guide *indicated* the most interesting museums to visit.

exercise 3   In pairs, ask and answer the following questions.

1. Is it difficult for you to *keep up with* the other students in this class?
2. Did you *look into* other English classes before you decided to take this one?
3. When was the last time you *took* a day *off* from work or school? What did you do?
4. Has your teacher ever told you to *do* a composition *over*? Did you do it?
5. Are you planning to *go over to* a friend's house tonight?
6. Have you *come across* any good restaurants lately?
7. Would you like to *start* your education *over* again? What would you like to study?
8. What is the worst experience that you have *gone through* since you have been in this city?

exercise 4   **Review.**   Replace the italicized verbs with phrasal verbs. Choose from the following list and pay attention to word order in your sentences.

add up	live on
call up	look for
drop by	look into
figure out	move out of
get along with	run into
help out	work out

MIKE: Boy, it's great to be finished with school. What are your plans now?

JOHN: I'm trying to *decide* where to live. I have to *leave* the dorm this weekend.
^{1} ^{2}

MIKE: You know, I *met* my friend Bruce on campus yesterday. He has a big apartment
^{3}
near the lake, and he's *trying to find* some roommates. He's a nice guy. I think
^{4}
you would *be on good terms with* him.
^{5}

JOHN: Do you know if it's expensive? I don't have much money to *exist on*. When-
^{6}
ever I *total* my bills, I realize how poor I am.
^{7}

MIKE: I'll *get information about* it. I'll *telephone* him this evening. Maybe we can
^{8} ^{9}
visit there tomorrow to see it.
^{10}

JOHN: It's really nice of you to *assist* me this way.
^{11}

MIKE: I'm happy to do it. I'm sure we can *resolve* your problem.
^{12}

exercise 5   **Review.**   Replace the italicized verbs with phrasal verbs. Choose from the following list, and pay attention to word order in your sentences.

figure out	start over
get up	take care of
give back	take out
look like	talk over
move out (of)	think over
put away	throw away
put up with	work out

LINDA: You know, Marge, I can't *understand* how you can live this way. Look at this place! It *resembles* a disaster area. Your papers are all over the floor. Why don't you ever *return* them *to their proper place*? And why is the kitchen full of trash? Why don't you *put* anything *in the garbage*? I'm telling you, I don't think I can *tolerate* this mess much longer! I'm thinking about *leaving this apartment*!

MARGE: Let's *discuss* the situation. Maybe we can *find a solution to* the problems. What else is bothering you?

LINDA: Lots of things. You never *take* the garbage *outside*. You borrow my things and then you forget to *return* them. You never *take responsibility for* the plants. And that's not all . . .

MARGE: Okay, okay. Look, I'll try to be neater. I'll *get out of bed* a little earlier in the morning and do some housework before I go to work. Let's *begin again*, okay? I don't want you to *leave*.

LINDA: Well, I'll *think about* it *carefully*.

exercise 6   **Review.**   Circle the correct answer in each sentence below.

1. When I'm at the beach, I enjoy looking (over / at / like) the birds and the waves.
2. I don't know the answer to your question. However, I will look (at / into / after) it and give you an answer tomorrow.
3. The bathtub is full. Turn (off / down / up) the water.
4. I made a lot of mistakes on my composition. I need to go (through / over to / over) them with my teacher.
5. My sister and I are good friends. I get (along with / together with / through with) her very well.
6. After Mr. Smith washes the dishes, he puts (them away / them on / up with them).
7. When Mr. and Mrs. Broder go out for the evening, their neighbor takes (out / off / care of) their baby girl.
8. Suzy's toys are all over the floor. Now she has to pick them (out / up / on).
9. Last week Joe was sick, so he had to take a couple of days (out / off / in) from work.
10. Last year I had a bad car accident, and I spent two weeks in the hospital. It was a terrible experience, and I hope I never go (over / through / for) anything like it again.

Using What You've Learned

activity    **Role-Playing.**   Pretend that you are one of the following people. While shopping at the supermarket, you are very surprised to meet an old high school classmate whom you haven't seen in ten years. Naturally, you stop and talk to each other for a few minutes. Tell your old friend about your lifestyle: your marital status, social life, job, etc. Use as many phrasal verbs as possible in your role play.

1. You are thirty years old and still in college because you love to learn. You tried out five majors and finished two. Then you got a master's degree, and now you are beginning a Ph.D. program. You are happy being a "professional student."
2. You have recently gotten married, and you are staying at home while your husband/wife works. You like housework and enjoy being at home.
3. You are beginning a business and don't have much money. You are single, but you have little time to go out or meet people because you are always working.

TOPIC **four**

Participles and Adjectives Followed by Prepositions

Setting the Context

previewing the passage

Is adventure something that only young people look for? Share your ideas and opinions by answering these questions about the picture.

- Describe the picture. Where do you think this is?
- Does this woman have a traditional lifestyle? What kind of person is she, probably?
- Do you know people like her? Describe them.

THE ELDERLY

The elderly is a phrase that used to cause a lot of negative feelings in older people. It made them feel that they were finished with the best part of their lives; their days of discovery and excitement were over.

No longer. The elderly today are often very healthy and adventurous. Many
5 of them continue working well into their seventies or even eighties. Those who

quit working are excited about their hobbies and interests. Retirement is not boring or frightening for them.

Helen Broomell of Minocqua, Wisconsin, is a perfect example. For forty-three years, she had been accustomed to the traditional life of a housewife and
10 mother. During that time, she brought up six children.

When her last child moved out, she was not sad about it. On the contrary, she was thrilled about the opportunity to be completely on her own. Helen began to make preparations for the adventure of a lifetime. "And then," she says simply, "I took off."

discussing ideas
How are the elderly today different from older people in the past? Describe Helen Broomell. What do you think she means when she says, "I took off"?

A. Participles Followed by Prepositions

Many present and past participles may be used as adjectives to describe feelings. As an adjective, the *present* participle (the *-ing* form) appears alone or is followed by a phrase with *to* or *for*. The *past* participle may be followed by a variety of prepositions, however. Chapter Eight includes more information on the uses of participles.

	examples	notes
Verb	Traveling **interests** me. Wild animals **frighten** me. Hiking **tires** me.	Below is a list of common verbs of emotion that follow these patterns.
Present Participle	Traveling is **interesting** (to me). Wild animals are **frightening** (to me).	The present participle as an adjective describes the effect of someone or something on someone else.
Past Participle	I am **interested in** traveling. I am **frightened by** wild animals. I am **tired of** hiking.	The past participle as an adjective describes someone's feelings, opinions, or reactions. In addition to other prepositions, *by* can follow many participles.

Common Participles Used as Adjectives of Emotion

Be is used with all of the following past participles of emotion. They may also appear after the verbs *get (become)*, *feel*, and *seem*.

> You **seem** tired.
> I **am (feel)** tired.
> I **get** tired easily when I don't eat well.

If you use a verb after one of these participle + preposition combinations, it must be in the *-ing* form. Compare:

> I'm tired of **school.**
> I'm tired of **studying.**

past participles	examples
amazed at (by)	We were **amazed at** the beauty of Alaska.
annoyed at (with, by) something;	We became **annoyed by** the travel delays.
annoyed with a person	We became **annoyed with** the bus driver.
bored with (by)	I got **bored with** the tour guide's descriptions.
confused about (with, by)	We were **confused about** the schedule.
excited about (by)	Everyone got **excited about** the boat trip.
frightened of (by)	Jim seemed **frightened of** the animals.
inspired by	We were **inspired by** the scenery.
interested in	I was **interested in** everything I saw.
pleased about (with, by)	We were **pleased about** our decision to go to Alaska.
satisfied with (by)	We felt **satisfied with** most of the arrangements.
thrilled about an action thrilled with a person or thing	We were **thrilled about** seeing a glacier. I was **thrilled with** the pictures I took.
tired of	By the end of the trip, we were **tired of** traveling.
worried about	Now, I'm **worried about** paying the bills.

exercise 1   Underline all the present and past participles that act as adjectives in the passage "The Elderly" on pages 174 and 175. Circle the prepositions used with the participles.

> **example:**   Those who quit working are <u>excited</u> (about) their hobbies and interests.

exercise 2   Complete the following passage with the missing prepositions. In some cases more than one preposition may be correct.

TRAVELS IN THE WILDERNESS

Helen Broomell had always been interested _____in_____ Alaska's great wilderness. Although she had been satisfied _____ her life as

₁ a housewife, she was thrilled _____ the opportunity to take off by

₂ herself. At age 66, she traveled 600 miles of the Yukon River alone by canoe.

There were many problems and inconveniences during Helen's trip, but they were not annoying _____ her. On the contrary, she was so

₃ excited _____ her experiences that the following summer, at age 67,

₄ she canoed another 700 miles.

On her trip, Helen came across a few Eskimos, but for the most part, she was by herself. Helen never got bored _____ traveling alone,

₅ but occasionally she was frightened _____ the dangers of the

₆ wilderness (a bear once joined her for dinner!).

Some older people (and many younger ones), who are worried

_____ the problems of daily living, are amazed _____

₇   ₈
Helen's story. Yet her experiences can be inspiring _____ people

₉ who never want to get tired _____ life.

₁₀

exercise 3   Choosing from the following verbs, make sentences with past participles.

    bore   confuse   frighten   inspire   tire   worry

example: At first Helen's family was ____confused____ by her decision to leave; they didn't understand it.

1. Helen's family was _____ about her plan to travel alone.

2. She told them she wasn't _____ with her life as a housewife, but she did want a change.

3. She didn't get _____ of her life on the road; she loved every minute of it.

4. Helen was _____ by the beautiful, high mountains of Alaska; she plans to return.

5. She was _____ by a bear once, though.

B. Adjectives Followed by Prepositions

Many adjectives are customarily followed by certain prepositions. The following is a short list of some common combinations in English.

adjectives + prepositions	examples
absent from	Joanne is **absent from** her first class several times a week.
accustomed (used) to	She is not **accustomed to** getting up early.
afraid of	She's **afraid of** her teacher.
angry about (something) angry at (with) someone	Joanne was **angry about** waking up late. The teacher was **angry at** Joanne.
different from	This new clock is **different from** my old one.
happy about (an action) happy with (a person or thing)	I'm **happy about** moving there. I'm not **happy with** this car.
nervous about	I am **nervous about** the exam.
responsible for	I felt **responsible for** the problem.
sad about	We all felt **sad about** her decision to leave.
sorry about (a thing) sorry for a (person or thing)	She felt **sorry about** her rude remark. I felt **sorry for** the lost dog.
sure about (of)	Are you **sure about** your decision?

exercise 4

Take a look at the picture on page 178 and imagine that this is where you live. Tell about "your home" and "your lifestyle" by completing the sentences below. Add appropriate prepositions.

example: I'm not sorry _____about_____ moving away from the city.

1. I'm not afraid _____ living alone in the woods. In fact, I love it.

2. I don't need help from other people. I'm accustomed _____ doing everything by myself.

3. I like being alone. I am responsible _____ myself, and no one else.

4. I feel very sure _____ my decision to live in the wilderness.

5. Sometimes in the winter, I get a little nervous _____ the cold temperatures, though.

6. Occasionally, I feel a little sad _____ not seeing my parents often.

7. In general, I'm very happy _____ the life I have here.

8. I sometimes feel sorry _____ people who live in cities.

exercise 5

Now, imagine that you are eighty years old. Tell about "your lifestyle." Complete the following sentences using participles and adjective + preposition combinations. Remember, if you use a verb after these expressions, it must be in the *-ing* form.

example: At eighty years old, I'm accustomed . . . **to a slow pace.**
to lots of sleep.
to forgetting some things.

At eighty years old . . .

1. I'm not used . . .
2. At times I am afraid . . .
3. And I get worried . . .
4. But I'm still excited . . .
5. I rarely get angry . . .
6. Sometimes I feel sad . . .
7. I get tired . . .
8. Some days I'm not sure . . .
9. I get nervous . . .
10. I am not sorry . . .

 **exercise 6**   **Review.** Complete the passage with one of these prepositions, as in the example.

about	on	to
for	out	up
of	over	with

HOUSING OR LIVING?

At 84, Nathan Saperstein is accustomed _____*to*_____ living with lots

of people. He's the oldest resident in "The Shared Living House" in Boston.

Saperstein lives _____1_____ fifteen others, aged 23 to 84. Everyone has a

private bedroom, but the five bathrooms and the kitchen belong

_____2_____ everyone.

Everyone helps take care _____3_____ the house. Each person is

responsible _____4_____ certain jobs. Saperstein's job is "security guard."

He explains, "At 11:00 P.M. I turn the lights _____5_____ and make sure

that everything is okay." Others take _____6_____ the garbage, clean

_____7_____ the kitchen and bathrooms, or figure _____8_____ the

bills. Although the jobs are divided, the housemates help each other

_____9_____ whenever possible. The success of the house depends

_____10_____ cooperation.

Saperstein is very satisfied _____11_____ his situation. He gets along

well _____12_____ all of his housemates. In other places, he says, a person

might never find _____13_____ his neighbor's name. "Here I am part of a

family. I know people care _____14_____ me." Saperstein is pleased

_____15_____ the atmosphere of the house. The housemates always make

time to talk _____16_____ each other.

Of course, living with a large group means that everyone sometimes has to

put _____17_____ _____18_____ some inconveniences. When there is a

problem, the housemates have a meeting to talk it _____19_____ . In this

way, they are usually able to work the problem _____20_____ .

A few people are unable to get used _____21_____ living with such a

large group, and they move _____22_____ of the house. But most of the

housemates are thrilled _____23_____ the opportunity to have such a home.

As Saperstein's 65-year-old housemate Christine Spurgeon says, "This isn't

housing; it's *living*."

exercise 7

Review. In pairs, take turns quizzing each other on phrasal combinations. Using the clues that follow, form true sentences based on your knowledge and experiences. If the combination is separable, also give the separated form.

> **example:** A: bring . . . a family
> B: **It's expensive to bring up a family.** *or*
> **It's expensive to bring a family up.**

1. call . . . a friend
2. be excited . . . a trip
3. get accustomed . . . speaking English
4. check . . . a hotel
5. clean . . . the house
6. feel nervous . . . a test
7. get together . . . friends
8. go . . . a bad experience
9. hand . . . a composition late
10. stay . . . late studying
11. put . . . your coat
12. pick . . . a friend at his or her apartment
13. do . . . a grammar exercise
14. be interested . . . sports
15. talk . . . a problem with your parents
16. dust . . . the bookshelves
17. add . . . your monthly expenses
18. think . . . a decision
19. take . . . your shoes
20. run . . . an old friend
21. have . . . a new shirt
22. look . . . a friend's cat while she is on vacation
23. borrow five dollars . . . a friend
24. grow . . . in California
25. try . . . a new grammar book

Using What You've Learned

Expressing Feelings and Opinions. How do you feel about living in a new culture? Are you still excited about it, or do you get sad or homesick? First, write ten questions to ask a classmate about his or her feelings. Use preposition combinations from the lists in this section. After your teacher has checked your questions, separate into pairs or small groups. Take turns asking and answering your questions.

Describing People. What is it like to grow old in your culture? How are the elderly treated? Where do older people live? What is their role in family life? Do many older people keep on working?

Individually or in small groups, prepare a brief presentation on the elderly in your society. As you prepare your presentation, try to include as many phrasal verbs or other preposition constructions as possible.

Phrasal Verbs and Related Structures

Items with phrasal verbs are usually found on standardized tests of English proficiency. After you review the verb tenses, check your understanding by completing the sample items below.

Remember that . . .

- Phrasal verbs can be both separable and inseparable.
- Usually the preposition or *particle* immediately follows the verb.
- The *particle* can change the meaning of the verb.

Part 1. Circle the correct completion for the following.

> example: The Smiths _____ .
>   **a.** depended their daughter on
>   **b.** cared their daughter about
>   **c.** disagreed with their daughter
>   **d.** grew their daughter up

1. Mr. and Mrs. Smith are able to _____ a lot of noise.
    a. get together with   **c.** put away
    b. put up   **d.** put up with

2. The Smiths _____ a small amount of money each month.
    a. live with   **c.** live on
    b. run into   **d.** get through with

3. They _____ from Chicago yesterday.
    a. called me up   **c.** called to
    b. called up me   **d.** called for

Part 2. Circle the letter below the word(s) containing the error.

> example: Mr. Smith <u>is interested</u> <u>in</u> going to Alaska, but he is <u>afraid</u>
>   A   B   C
>   <u>about</u> the Alaskan polar bear.
>   (D)

1. He is <u>thrilled</u> <u>about</u> the trip, frightened <u>by</u> the bears, and worried <u>on</u>
          A   B   C   D
    the cost of the trip.

2. The tourists are usually inspired <u>at</u> the mountains, amazed <u>at</u> the
                                       A   B
    weather, and <u>pleased</u> <u>with</u> the trip.
                 C   D

3. At the end of the trip, they are <u>tired</u> <u>of</u> traveling, <u>sad of</u> leaving their
                                      A B   C
    new friends, and <u>excited about</u> going home.
                      D

CHAPTER **six**

The Global Village

Compound and Complex Sentences (1)

Topic One: Compound Sentences

Topic Two: Complex Sentences

Topic Three: Clauses of Contrast (Concession), Reason, and Purpose

Topic Four: Clauses of Time and Condition: Present and Future Time

in this chapter

Compound Sentences

Setting the Context

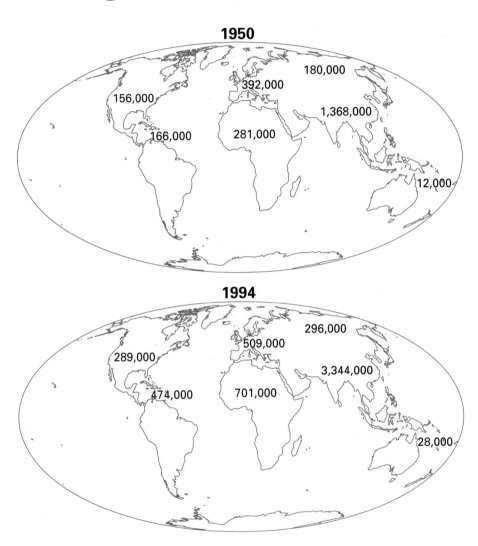

1950

1994

previewing the passage

What is the population of the earth today? How quickly is it growing? Share your ideas and opinions by answering these questions about the picture.

- Which continents have the most population today?
- Which areas have grown the fastest in recent years?

Is the world getting smaller, or are we filling more of it? In many ways, our world seems so much smaller. In the last one hundred years, major improvements in communications and transportation have made it possible for us to go more places faster and to communicate with more people more easily.

5   The world may seem smaller, yet it is the same size, of course. A primary reason for the difference is population growth. The world's population has changed tremendously, and this has made it feel smaller. In 1974, the population of the world was 4 billion, but today it is approaching 6 billion.

We can communicate faster, and we can travel faster, but above all, there
10 are many more of us. We are rapidly filling the spaces.

discussing ideas

What population trends are occurring in your native city or country? What trends are occurring where you live now? Is the population growing? Rapidly? Is it declining? Why?

A. Basic Sentence Structure

Every complete sentence in English has at least one subject and verb. The subject is usually the most important person, place, thing, or idea in the sentence. The subject may be a word, a phrase (a group of words), or a clause (a group of words with a subject/verb combination). The verb tells what the subject is or does. Of course, sentences may have more than one subject, more than one verb, or more than one subject/verb combination.

		examples
Subjects	**Noun**	**Population** is a serious issue.
	Pronoun	**It** increased by 87 million people worldwide in 1993.
	Phrase	**The population of the world** is a serious issue.
		Birth rates and life expectancy are higher.
	Clause	**What will happen** is a serious question.
Verbs		The world population **is growing** rapidly.
		Birth rates **are** higher.
		Today, more babies **are born** and **can live** longer.

 Identify the subject(s) and verb(s) in the following sentences. Put one line under each subject and two lines under each verb.

> **example:** In the last 150 years, <u>world population</u> <u><u>has grown</u></u> tremendously.

1. Throughout most of history, our earth had huge, unpopulated areas.

2. Until the 1800s, world population growth was very slow.

3. Mothers frequently died during childbirth, and babies often could not survive the first year after birth.

4. Medical discoveries and agricultural improvements have caused great changes in the world population.

5. In 1920, the average life expectancy in the U.S. was 54 years for men and 55 years for women.

6. Today, the average baby girl in the U.S. will probably live 79 years, and the average baby boy may live 73.

7. Infant mortality is also decreasing around the world.

8. We now have better nutrition and medical care, so fewer babies die before or after birth.

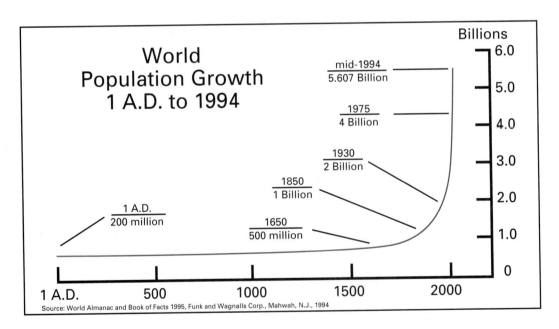

World Population Growth 1 A.D. to 1994

Source: World Almanac and Book of Facts 1995, Funk and Wagnalls Corp., Mahwah, N.J., 1994

exercise 2 Identify the subject(s) and verb(s) in the following 10 items. Put one line under each subject and two lines under each verb. Then tell whether the sentence is complete (C) or incomplete (I).

example: __C__ The world is becoming smaller.

__I__ Today is possible to travel everywhere faster.

1. _____ The United States has a population of about 260,000,000.

2. _____ The population of the United States is increasing slowly.

3. _____ Some European countries unchanging or declining populations.

4. _____ France, for example, is encouraging families to have more children.

5. _____ In Africa, are gaining population at an alarming rate.

6. _____ Is a major problem.

7. _____ Kenya 3.3 percent each year.

8. _____ Lagos, Nigeria, one of the densest[*] cities in the world.

9. _____ The population growth of the world will affect all of us.

10. _____ We all concerned about it.

B. Introduction to Compound Sentences

A simple sentence has one subject/verb combination. A compound sentence is two or more simple sentences joined together by a comma and a coordinating conjunction. The coordinating conjunctions are *and, but, for, nor, or, so,* and *yet*. A semicolon (;) may sometimes be used *instead of* one of these conjunctions.

examples	
Simple Sentences	India has 900 million people. It is expected to reach one billion by 2000.
Compound Sentences	India has 900 million people, **and** it is expected to reach one billion by 2000. India has 900 million people; it is expected to reach one billion by 2000.

[*]*density* number of people per square mile or square kilometer

C. Coordinating Conjunctions

Coordinating conjunctions can join words, phrases, and clauses. When these conjunctions join clauses, they form compound sentences. A comma generally comes before the conjunction in a compound sentence.

examples	notes
China has a huge population, **and** it is growing.	*And* shows additional information.
Argentina is a large country, **but (yet)** it has a small population.	Both *but* and *yet* show contrast. *But* is more common in spoken English.
Population growth is a problem, **for** the earth has limited resources.	As a conjunction, *for* means "because." *For* is formal; it is more common in writing than in speaking.
Norway is not large, **nor** does it have a large population. Norway is not large, **nor** is it overpopulated.	*Nor* joins two negative statements. The word order of the clause with *nor* changes: The appropriate auxiliary verb must come *before* the subject.
Governments can ignore the problem, **or** they can help to solve it.	*Or* shows a choice between two possibilities.
China is trying to slow its population growth, **so** it has put limits on family size.	As a conjunction, *so* means "as a result" or "therefore."

 **exercise 3**   Underline all the compound sentences in "People, People, and More People" on page 185. Circle the coordinating conjunctions.

exercise 4   Which of the following are compound sentences? Which are simple sentences? Underline the subject(s) with one line and verb(s) with two lines. Label each sentence simple (S) or compound (C). Then, circle the connecting words and/or punctuation.

example: __C__ All people on earth <u>are</u> of the same species, *Homo sapiens,*

⸨but⸩numerous different cultural and ethnic <u>groups</u> <u>exist</u>.

1. _____ In the past, people talked about different races, and they divided the human population according to race.

2. _____ In the past, scientists divided the world population into different groups; traditionally, the groups were Caucasoid, Mongoloid, and Negroid.

3. _____ Today, people talk about different races, but the word *race* has little meaning.

4. _____ The word *race* does not have much meaning nowadays, nor will it in the future.

5. _____ Very few "pure" races exist today, for people worldwide have migrated and intermarried.

6. _____ Today, human differences are only partly biological.

7. _____ Our differences are often cultural, economic, political, or religious.

8. _____ Humans have differences, of course, yet we have more similarities.

9. _____ In what ways are all people similar?

10. _____ We can speak of similarities such as use of language, or we can look at social structures such as government and family.

 **exercise 5** Combine the following sentences with *and, but, or, so, yet,* or *nor.* If a noun is repeated, change it to a pronoun in the second clause. Use each conjunction at least once. Pay attention to punctuation as you write your new sentences, and change nouns to pronouns when necessary.

example: The population of the world has increased throughout history. In this century, the population of the world has grown the fastest.
The population of the world has increased throughout history, but in this century, it has grown the fastest.

1. The population of the world is increasing.
   The populations of some countries in Africa are increasing the fastest.
2. A growing population has many needs.
   Some countries are unable to meet these needs.
3. A larger population needs more water.
   A larger population requires more energy and food.
4. Ethiopia, for example, must increase its agricultural production.
   Many young Ethiopians may not get the food they need.
5. These countries cannot change farming methods rapidly.
   These countries cannot change other traditions easily.
6. Many parents want their children to help them and take care of them in later years.
   Many parents have large families.
7. Parents know large families are expensive.
   Parents prefer to have lots of children.
8. Some governments are trying to slow the population growth.
   These governments limit the number of babies for each family.

D. Coordinating Conjunctions with Words and Phrases

Coordinating conjunctions can also join words, phrases, and clauses within one sentence. *And, but, yet,* and *or* are often used to join two or more verbs, nouns, adjectives, and so on. No commas are used with two words, phrases, or clauses.

examples

Verbs	Today, the world **produces** enough food **and can nourish** every human.
Nouns	Problems with food involve **distribution and diet.**
Adjectives	People everywhere are eating beef, which is **harder and more expensive** to produce than other foods.
Adverbs	We can eat **simply but adequately.**
Phrases	Today, hunger is not caused **by scarcity or by overpopulation.**
Clauses	In the future, hunger will be worse **because the population is growing and because diets are changing.**

 **exercise 6** Shorten the following sentences as you learn some facts about population today. Eliminate the unnecessary words. Also eliminate commas when necessary.

example: Worldwide, more babies are born each year, and more babies survive their first twelve months.
Worldwide, more babies are born each year and survive their first twelve months.

1. Our population grows because more people are born, and our population grows because fewer people die at a young age.
2. The population of the U.S. increased by 121 percent from 1805 to 1926, and it increased by 200 percent from 1926 to 1974.
3. The population of Europe has grown only a little in recent years, and the population of Europe will grow only slightly in the future.
4. Some areas of the world will increase greatly by the year 2020, or they will double their population by the year 2020.
5. In Europe, the birth rate from 1985–1990 was 14.7 percent, yet it will be approximately 13 percent from 2020 to 2025.
6. On average, in Asia, women live two years longer than men, but in Russia, women live ten years longer than men.

exercise 7 Reread your sentences from Exercise 5. Are there any sentences that you can shorten by eliminating repetition? Rewrite those sentences.

Using What You've Learned

activity 1 **Explaining Population Changes.**   What is the population of your native country, region, province, or state? What was it fifty years ago? Have there been many changes in the population? Has it grown? Has it declined? Have people migrated to or from this area?

Prepare a brief report for your classmates. Include as many facts and figures as you can find. Then give your report in small groups or for the entire class. Later, you may want to combine the information researched by your group or by the class as a whole. You can do this in written form, or you can create graphics (charts or graphs) comparing cities, regions, or countries.

activity 2 **Talking about Ethnic Groups.**   What ethnic or religious groups live in your hometown or area? What changes have they brought, or what special contributions have they made? Choose one particular part of the population of your hometown, region, or country, and tell about it. You can do so in a composition, or you can prepare an informal talk to give in small groups or for the class.

TOPIC **two**

Complex Sentences

Setting the Context

previewing the passage

How many countries are there in the world today? Share your ideas and opinions by answering these questions about the picture.

- What is happening in the cartoon?
- What changes have occurred in the world map in the past ten years?

Some of the larger countries of the world are breaking up into smaller units. The former Soviet Union is now a collection of smaller states or countries less formally tied together. Dozens of new nations have been created since the end of the 1980s. Currently, over 180 countries are
5   members of the United Nations. The U.N. began with only 50 countries when it was founded in 1945.

This trend toward more and smaller nations does not tell the whole story, however. Although many nations now exist, in some ways our borders are disappearing. Independent countries are joining together so that they can
10 improve trade, discuss regional and world issues, and share technology. Some of the important alliances* today are NAFTA, E.U., and Mercosur.

discussing
ideas

Was your native country once part of a larger country? Has your native country joined another country? Has it made any economic or political agreements with other countries?

A. Introduction to Complex Sentences

Complex sentences are sentences that have a main (independent) clause and at least one dependent clause. A main clause has a subject and verb and can stand alone. It is a complete sentence. A dependent clause also has a subject and verb, but alone, it is *not* complete: it depends on the main clause.

main clause   dependent clause

example: The U.N. was created because world leaders wanted to meet.

examples	
Simple Sentences	The U.N. was created in 1945. World leaders wanted to discuss major problems.
Complex Sentences	The U.N. was created in 1945 **because** world leaders wanted a place to discuss global problems. **Because** world leaders wanted a way to discuss global problems, they helped to create the U.N. The U.N. was created **so that** world leaders could meet to discuss global problems.

---

alliance   connection or union between individuals, states, or countries, for example.

	examples
Incomplete Sentences **(Dependent Clauses)**	When the U.N. was created. Because leaders wanted to meet. So that leaders could meet to discuss problems. Although the U.N. began with only 50 countries.

exercise Tell whether the following are complete (C) or incomplete (I) sentences.

example: __I__ Because international trade is important.

1. _____ People worldwide make money by buying and selling.

2. _____ Because people want to buy and sell internationally.

3. _____ International trade is a major source of income for many countries.

4. _____ Although some countries have high imports and low exports.

5. _____ When a government taxes imports.

6. _____ Governments often tax imports to protect their own industries.

7. _____ Taxes on imports are called tariffs.

8. _____ Today, different countries are joining together so that they can trade more easily.

9. _____ Many countries are trying to avoid more taxes and bureaucracy.

10. _____ Because government bureaucracy often makes trade very difficult.

B. Types of Adverb Clauses

In a complex sentence, the dependent clause is connected to the main clause by a subordinating conjunction, such as *when, because, although, if*. English has numerous subordinating conjunctions; each shows a different relationship between the two clauses. In this chapter, you will study some clauses of condition, contrast, purpose, reason, and time. In Chapter Seven, you will study more clauses of time.

types of dependent clauses	common subordinating conjunctions	examples
Condition	if unless	**If** a country doesn't have a resource such as oil, it must import the resource.
Contrast (Concession)	although even though	Sometimes imported goods are very inexpensive **even though** they are taxed.
Purpose	so that	Countries often tax imports **so that** they can protect national industries.
Reason	because	Some imported goods are very expensive **because** the taxes on them are high.
Time	after, before, until since when, whenever while, as	Some countries tax imports only **until** their own industries are strong. **When** a country imports more than it exports, it has a trade deficit.

 **exercise 2** Circle all the subordinating conjunctions in "A World Without Borders" on page 192. What does each express (condition, contrast, purpose, reason, result, time)?

 **exercise 3** Tell whether the following are simple, compound, or complex sentences. Find the subject(s) and verb(s) of each. Put one line under subjects, and two lines under verbs. Circle any connecting words.

  example: <u>Simple</u>   Many <u>countries</u> <u><u>are forming</u></u> economic unions today.

  <u>Compound</u> Many <u>countries</u> <u><u>are forming</u></u> economic unions today (so that) <u>they</u> <u><u>can trade</u></u> more easily.

  1. _____ Several economic unions exist today.

  2. _____ The European Union is facing several difficult challenges, so its effectiveness is still not clear.

  3. _____ Members of the E.U. are trying to resolve the challenges so that the alliance can be successful.

  4. _____ The North American Alliance was created when Canada, Mexico, and the United States signed a trade agreement: NAFTA.

5. _____ Mercosur is an economic alliance among several Latin American countries including Argentina and Brazil.

6. _____ Someday, all of the Americas may join together economically.

7. _____ Although defense alliances were important in the past, today economic alliances are perhaps even more necessary.

exercise 4   Underline the dependent (adverb) clause and circle the connecting word in each of the sentences here and on the next page. Then tell what relationship the connecting words express (condition, contrast, purpose, reason, result, time).

example:　(Although) economic alliances can help countries, certain parts of the population may suffer.　_Contrast_

1. The European Union will be difficult to achieve because some members do not want to lose certain rights.

2. Even though the members know the importance of cooperation, each country has its own special interests.

3. Government leaders are continuing to meet so that they can resolve their differences.

4. When E.U. members began to discuss a common currency,[*] they found a lot of opposition to this idea.

5. If a member nation cannot control its own money, it can no longer make certain important decisions.

6. Although the E.U. is facing difficulty, it is a beginning point for discussion of common interests.

7. It also provides a common forum so that Europeans can discuss issues involving all the countries.

8. If nations can meet to discuss important issues, there may be a greater chance for world peace.

Using What You've Learned

Describing Economic Conditions.   Prepare a brief talk for your classmates about the economics of your native country. If there are several students from one country, you may want to form a panel. Choose an area to talk about such as imports, exports, natural resources, primary industries, or unions with other countries. Don't try to explain everything about the economy. Prepare for a maximum of five minutes.

Give your talk in small groups or for the whole class. Then answer questions that your classmates may have for you.

Describing Political Changes.   During the major changes of the last ten years, what has happened in your native country? Has it separated from another country? Has it joined another country? Has it formed economic alliances? Share your information in small groups, or you may form a panel of students from the same country or region to answer questions your classmates have.

---

*currency   form of money of a country

Clauses of Contrast (Concession), Reason, and Purpose

Setting the Context

What changes have occurred in technology to make our world seem smaller or at least more accessible? Share your ideas and information while answering these questions about the picture.

- What methods of communication are in the picture?
- What means of travel are shown?

A SMALLER WORLD

Although population growth certainly makes our world seem smaller it is not the only factor in this change. Our world *is* smaller because technology has made communication and travel easier and faster. It no longer takes months to go from one place to another, and a letter is only a fax or an e-mail away.

5 Cable systems and satellites now link the world so that we can have live
   coverage of anything and everything. We can see news as it happens and watch
   sports events while they are taking place.
        Because technology has shortened the distance through time and space, we
   can communicate and travel easily to even the farthest places. So, although the
10 circumference of the earth at the equator continues to be 24,901 miles, we can
   see, talk to, or be almost any place within minutes or hours, not weeks or
   months.

**discussing
ideas**

What technologies are mentioned in the passage? What experience have you had
with each? What other technologies do you know of that have changed either
travel or communications?

A. Clauses of Contrast (Concession) and Reason

Clauses of contrast (with *although* and *even though*) and clauses of reason
(with *because*) can begin or end sentences. A comma is generally used after a
dependent clause that begins a sentence.

uses	conjunctions	examples
Contrast	although even though	**Although computers are still expensive today,** they are much cheaper than several years ago.
Reason	because	Many people buy laptop computers **because they are portable.**

exercise 1

Quickly reread the passage "A Smaller World" on pages 197 and 198. Find any
complex sentences with adverb clauses of contrast and reason. Underline the
dependent clause and circle the connecting word.

exercise 2

Complete the following sentences with *because* or *although*.

   example: Cable television became possible *because*_____ new
   technologies were developed.

   1. Cable television was originally created _____ people in rural

   areas couldn't get good broadcasts.

   2. _____ cable TV began in rural areas of the U.S., today it exists

   all over the world.

3. _____ many cable networks now exist, the most famous are perhaps CNN* and ESPN.*

4. Ted Turner created CNN _____ he saw a need for 24-hour news broadcasting.

5. None of the major U.S. networks was interested in Turner's idea _____ they thought people would not watch news all day.

6. _____ the major networks were not interested in Turner's idea, he did not give up.

7. Turner kept on pursuing his idea _____ many people told him to forget about it.

8. Today, Turner and others in the cable industry have become millionaires _____ they developed cable programming.

B. Clauses of Purpose

> Clauses of purpose are formed with *so that*, meaning "in order to" or "for the purpose of." Clauses with *so that* do not begin sentences. A modal auxiliary or *(not) have to* must follow *so that*. *Can, may,* or *will* are used in a present or future time frame, and *could, might,* or *would* are used in a past time frame. Commas are not usually used with these clauses.

use	conjunction	examples
Purpose	so that	I am saving my money **so that I can buy some new equipment.** I opened a savings account **so that I could earn some interest.**

Note: Do not confuse *so that* with the coordinating conjunction *so,* meaning "therefore" or "as a result." Compare:
  I needed milk, *so I went to the store.*
  I went to the store *so that I could get some milk.*

 Find any clauses of purpose in the passage "A Smaller World" on pages 197 and 198. What verb forms are used in the dependent clause? What punctuation is or is not used?

---

*CNN = Cable News Network; ESPN = Entertainment and Sports Programming Network

 **exercise 4**

Use *so that* to combine the following pairs of sentences. Remember that you must use a modal auxiliary *(can, could, will,* or *would)* in the dependent clause. Make other necessary changes in the dependent clause.

> example: I applied for a loan at the bank. I wanted to buy new computer hardware and software.
>
> **I applied for a loan at the bank so that I could buy new computer hardware and software.**

1. People use computers. They want to communicate in a variety of ways.
2. People buy modems. They want to send computer messages by telephone.
3. In large offices, computers are often linked on a network. Users can share expensive programs.
4. Muirhead, Ltd., of England created the first fax machine. It wanted to send all types of documents via cable.
5. Cities are replacing copper cables with fiber optics. They want to have fast, reliable communication systems.
6. Telephone companies have special phone lines. They can move computer data at very high speeds.
7. Frederick Smith started Federal Express in 1973. He wanted to offer overnight mail service.
8. Smith bought his own trucks and planes. He didn't want to have to rely on other companies.

exercise 5

First read the following passage to get the general meaning. Then complete it with *although, because,* or *so that.*

E-MAIL AND THE INTERNET

Electronic mail is the fastest growing way of communicating in the world.

Actually, e-mail is many computer networks connected to each other. Today,

dozens of networks exist ____so that____ almost thirty million people from

all continents can communicate with each other. _____ e-mail is
1
so fast, convenient, and inexpensive, many people prefer it to regular mail
services.

The original network was set up by the U.S. government in the 1970s
_____ researchers could communicate with each other.
2
_____ the U.S. was in a "cold war" against the former Soviet
3
Union, it wanted researchers in military projects to have fast and easy
communication.

_____ the Internet was originally for military purposes, today
4
it is used for anything and everything. People use it _____ they
5
can share information and computer programs. They use the Internet
_____ they want to exchange ideas. They even use it
6
_____ they can "meet" new friends—all "on-line."
7
Now, the Internet has been expanded _____ people can send not
8
only written text but also sound and video. In the future, it may be possible for
the whole world to be connected via computer. Just imagine the possibilities!

 **exercise 6** Complete the following sentences. If possible, form *true* statements about your own life.

1. I would like to buy a (better) computer because . . .
2. I want a (better) computer so that . . .
3. Although some computer hardware is expensive, . . .
4. I like . . . software because . . .
5. I like . . . software although . . .
6. I (want to) use e-mail so that . . .
7. Fax machines are great because . . .
8. Fax machines are great although . . .
9. I'm saving my money so that . . .
10. I'm saving my money because . . .

Using What You've Learned

Playing a Guessing Game.   In small groups, take turns telling about one item of technology that has made your life easier. It may be as simple as a paper clip or as complex as a mainframe computer. Describe the item or process but *don't* say the name. Let your partner(s) guess. If your description is too clear, they'll guess immediately, so give your clues one at a time.

example: **There's a great invention that has made my life simpler. It was invented by a Swiss named de Mestral in 1948. Although it has many uses, for me the most important is with little children. Children's shoes are often made with this so that even little children can fasten them without help. What is it?**[*]

TOPIC four

Clauses of Time and Condition: Present and Future Time

Setting the Context

previewing the passage

What kinds of travel opportunities do people have today? Share your ideas by answering these questions about the pictures.

- What is the scene in each poster?
- Which of these vacations would you like to take?

[*]Answer: velcro

In the past, it took months or even years to travel to faraway places, but today you can get to almost any corner of the world in a matter of hours or days. For example, if you want, you can catch a boat to Antarctica, lie on a beach in Tahiti, visit the Eiffel Tower, or trek in the Himalayas. After you have
5 made those trips, you can head off to Buenos Aires or Montreal for a quick getaway. And when you visit many places like these, you will be able to choose from camping or rustic accommodations to the most elegant luxury hotels in the world. So, if you're ready, we'll leave today!

discussing ideas

Have you traveled to any of the places mentioned above? Have you taken any exotic trips? If not, where do you hope to go someday?

A. Introduction to Clauses of Time and Condition

There are a variety of connecting words to express time relationships in English. These include *when, whenever, after, before,* and *until.* Some describe things that happen at different times; others describe things that happen at the same time. You will study several uses of these connecting words in this chapter and others in Chapter 7.

Clauses of condition, with *if* and *unless,* can be similar to clauses of time, but they also express cause and effect. You will study some of these clauses in this chapter. You will study other clauses of condition in Chapter 12.

B. Clauses of Time and Condition: Present or Unspecified Time

When and *whenever* can relate two actions or situations that exist at the same time or that immediately follow each other. *Whenever* is similar to *when,* but it is used to emphasize the idea of "any time" or "every time."

If may relate two actions or situations by time and by cause and effect. Sentences with *if* are similar to sentences with *when* or *whenever,* but *if* gives added meaning: The main clause is the effect or result of the *if* clause.

	examples	notes
when	**When** I **plan** a trip, I always **get** as much information as possible. I **ask** a lot of questions **when** I **visit** the travel agent.	The simple present tense is usually used in both clauses in these sentences. Modal auxiliaries may also be used. The dependent clause may begin or end the sentence. Use a comma after a dependent clause that begins the sentence.
whenever	**Whenever** I **travel**, I **get** very excited.	
if	**If** it's possible, we **make** our travel plans in advance. You **should plan** ahead **if** you **want** discount prices.	*It* has the same basic meaning as *when*, but it also emphasizes cause and effect.

exercise 1 Test your knowledge of geography. Match the following locations and landmarks. Then form complete sentences with *if*. Use the example as a model.

example: **1.** *e* Paris—The Eiffel Tower
If you visit Paris, you can see the Eiffel Tower.

1. Paris
2. Cairo
3. Bangkok
4. San Francisco
5. Buenos Aires
6. Tokyo
7. Moscow
8. Hong Kong
9. London
10. Bogotá

a. Westminster Cathedral
b. The Golden Gate Bridge
c. The Ginza
d. The Gold Museum
e. The Eiffel Tower
f. The Pyramids
g. The Floating Market
h. The Tiger Balm Gardens
i. The Teatro Colon
j. Red Square

exercise 2 Use the map showing time zones on page 205 to help you answer the following questions.

1. If you travel between the following cities, how many time lines do you cross?

example: from Stockholm to New York
If you travel from Stockholm to New York, you cross six time lines.

a. from Berlin to New York
b. from Rio de Janeiro to Chicago
c. from Bangkok to Los Angeles
d. from Cairo to Miami

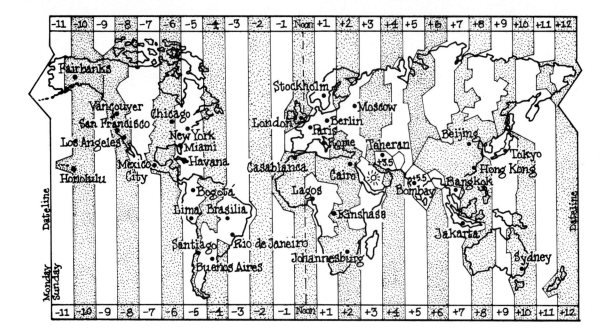

2. If you travel between the following cities, do you gain time or lose time?

> **example:** from Paris to Moscow
> **If you travel from Paris to Moscow, you lose time.**

a. from Paris to Beijing
b. from Rome to Mexico City
c. from Honolulu to Tokyo
d. from San Francisco to Buenos Aires

3. What are the relative times in the following cities? For example, when it's 6:00 A.M. in Chicago, what time is it in Honolulu? (To convert Greenwich Mean Time—GMT—to local time, add or subtract the value at the top of the chart.)

> **example:** 6:00 P.M.—Chicago / Honolulu
> **When it's 6:00 in the evening in Chicago, it's 2:00 in the afternoon in Honolulu.**

a. 6:00 A.M.—Chicago / Paris
b. 7:00 A.M.—New York / Teheran
c. 6:00 A.M.—Los Angeles / Tokyo
d. 9:00 A.M.—Santiago / Kinshasa
e. 12:00 noon—Mexico City / Bogotá

f. 7:00 A.M.—Vancouver / Jakarta
g. 6:00 A.M.—Chicago / Buenos Aires
h. 8:00 A.M.—your current town / your hometown

 **exercise 3**   Complete the following sentences in your own words.

> **example:**   Whenever I telephone my parents (friends, girlfriend, or
> boyfriend), . . .
> **I forget about the time difference!**

1. Whenever I call my parents (friends, etc.), . . .
2. I call them if . . .
3. When we talk, . . .
4. I try to call whenever . . .
5. If I forget to call, . . .
6. When I get the telephone bill, . . .

exercise 4   Answer the following questions in your own words.

1. What happens when you try to read in a moving car?
2. Do you get seasick if you travel by boat?
3. What is *jet lag*? When do people get jet lag? (Do people get jet lag when
   they travel north-south? East-west?)
4. Many people recommend special diets or exercises before long-distance
   travel. How should you prepare yourself (physically) if you plan to take a
   very long trip by plane?
5. Many people have a terrible fear of flying. How do you feel whenever you
   get on an airplane? What do you think about when you are on a plane?

 # C. Clauses of Time and Condition: Future Time

Time clauses can relate statements about future plans or possibilities. Sentences with *if* and *unless* show a direct cause-effect relationship. The action or
situation in the main clause is the effect or result of the action or situation in
the dependent clause.

examples	notes
after	**After I complete** this project, I **am going to take** a long vacation.	The verb in the dependent clause is usually in the simple present tense. It may *not* be in a future tense. The verb in the main clause is usually in a future tense, but a modal auxiliary may also be used. In some cases, the present perfect tense may be used in the dependent clause to stress that the action has been completed. The dependent clause may begin or end the sentence. Use a comma after a dependent clause that begins the sentence.
before	It **will be** a week **before I complete** it.	
until	I **can't leave until I've finished** everything.	
when	**When** I **finish** this project, I **will take** some time off.	
if	**If** the weather **is** nice, I **will go** to the beach. I **am going to stay** home **if** the weather **isn't** nice.	
unless	**Unless** it**'s cold**, I **will go** to the beach. I **am going to stay** home **unless** the weather **is** nice.	

 **exercise 5** Complete the sentences here and on the next page with appropriate present, present perfect, or future forms of the verbs in parentheses, as in the example.

1. Before we _____*reach*_____ (reach) the year 2050, Americans _____ (have) many new forms of public transportation.

2. In many places, when you _____ (leave) your house in the morning, you _____ (not get) into your own car because you _____ (not have) one.

3. If you _____ (need) to use a car, you _____ (request) one on your computer.

4. After your computer _____ (process) your request, it _____ (arrange) to deliver a car to your door.

5. If you _____ (live) in an area with good weather, you _____ (not take / probably) a car. Instead, you _____ (go) by bicycle to a train just minutes from your house.

6. You _____ (not need) to buy your own bicycle unless you _____ (want) a special type, because neighborhoods _____ (have) a collection of bicycles to share.

7. When you _____ (travel) long-distance, you _____

(be) able to go by train or plane.

8. You _____ (make) all your travel plans from your home

computer before you _____ (leave).

Change the appropriate clauses in the following sentences from *if* to *unless* or from *unless* to *if*.

example: If people don't stop driving cars, traffic and pollution will be even greater problems in the future.
Unless people stop driving cars, traffic and pollution will be even greater problems in the future.

1. If people don't use mass transit more often, our streets and highways will become even more crowded.
2. If cities don't offer more mass transit, traffic will get even worse.
3. Unless everyone starts using smog control devices, cities like Los Angeles will become unsafe to live in.
4. If we don't develop a new kind of car, air pollution will become even more dangerous.
5. Unless we find an alternative to gasoline engines, we will add even more pollution to the air.
6. Unless we begin to make changes now, air pollution will cause more and more serious health problems.

Cars are still here today, though, and Nadia's going to buy her first used car. She's a little nervous about it, so she's making careful plans. These are some of the things she is going to do. Using *before, after,* and *until,* form complete sentences from the following cues. Use each subordinating conjunction at least once.

examples: take the car to an auto mechanic
Before she buys her car, she's going to take the car [to an] auto mechanic.

get insurance
After she has bought her car, she's going to get insurance.

1. look at several different cars
2. read about cars in consumer magazines
3. compare prices
4. borrow her parents' car
5. test drive the car
6. ask her friends for advice
7. register the car at the Department of Motor Vehicles
8. not use public transportation

**exercise** ⟪**8**⟫   In pairs, take turns making additional questions and answers based on the cues. Use *if* in your responses.

example: Are you taking the car? (stop at a gas station)
   A: **Are you taking the car? Would you mind stopping at a gas station?**
   B: **If I take the car, I'll stop at a gas station.**

1. Are you going near a gas station? (fill up the tank)
2. Are you planning to stop at a gas station? (add some oil)
3. Are you going to add oil? (check the water in the radiator, too)
4. Are you going to have extra time? (put air in the tires)
5. Are you going to have enough money? (buy new windshield wipers)
6. Are you planning to talk to the mechanic? (make an appointment for a tune-up)
7. Are you planning to go to a post office? (mail the payment for the car insurance)
8. Are you going near a police station? (pay this traffic ticket)

Review. Complete the following sentences in your own words. Try to make *true* statements.

example: If you come to visit my country, **I'll take you to see all the great sights!**

1. In my country, tourists usually visit . . . because . . .
2. When tourists visit my native country, . . .
3. If they want to visit museums, . . .
4. If they want to explore the countryside, . . .
5. You should try to visit . . . unless . . . .
6. Before you go to . . . , ...
7. You should check with a travel agent so that . . .
8. When people come to my hometown, . . .
9. If you want a comfortable hotel, . . .
10. Campers and hikers often go to . . . so that . . .
11. The most interesting excursions are to . . . because . . .
12. Unless you have lots of time / money, . . .

exercise 10 **Review.** Complete the following passage about energy and movement by circling the appropriate connecting words. Be prepared to explain your choices.

ENERGY CONSUMED TO TRAVEL ONE KILOMETER
(in calories of energy per gram)

bicyclist	0.15	car	0.75–0.85
horse	0.50–0.70	cow	0.82
jet aircraft	0.60	pigeon	0.92
person, walking	0.75	dog	1.40

(Although)/ Because) cars seem necessary to many people, bicycles are still one of the best means of transportation. Cars are convenient, (because / but) bicycles are more efficient. (Although / When) people ride bicycles, they move using the least amount of energy possible.
        1
        2

According to a Duke University study, (when / yet) a mouse walks one kilometer, it uses more than 50 calories of energy per gram of body weight. A rabbit uses only 5 calories. (When / Because) the average cyclist travels one kilometer on a good bicycle, he or she uses much less energy. In fact, a normal bicyclist is almost three times more energy-efficient than any other traveler.
        3
        4

Bicycles are very efficient (because / so) they use the leg muscles perfectly. (If / Although) you study the leg muscles, you can see that the bicycle is designed (so that / when) you can pedal very easily. This is unfortunate for some people, who ride bicycles (or / so that) they can get in shape.
        5
        6
        7
        8

(Because / Although) bicycling takes very little energy, it does not help most

people lose weight. You must bicycle long distances or very fast (so that / if)

you want to burn energy.

exercise 11   **Review.**   Combine the following sentences about air travel with *if, when,*
whenever, because, although, or *so that.* Change verb tenses and change nouns to
pronouns when necessary. Be sure to use correct punctuation when you form your
new sentences.

> example: People think about long-distance travel. People think about planes.
> **When (whenever) people think about long-distance travel,**
> **they think about planes.**

1. Planes are fast and relatively economical.
   Long-distance travelers often choose planes over trains or boats.
2. Planes seem very much a part of our lives.
   Planes have been in existence only about 100 years.
3. Companies are constantly doing research on planes.
   Companies want to develop faster and more efficient planes.*
4. Many of this century's greatest inventors have worked on planes.
   Tremendous advances have taken place in flight technology.
5. Engineers compare older planes with those of today.
   Engineers tell us that today's planes are safer.
6. Many airlines offer bargain fares to major cities.
   Airports today are full of vacationers and business people.
7. We will look into the future.
   We will find many new varieties of air transportation.
8. Inventors are working on new ideas.
   Inventors want to develop faster and cheaper methods of transportation.*
9. Inventors will probably develop faster and cheaper methods of
   transportation.
   New methods of air travel may replace airplanes.
10. We will enter the twenty-first century.
    We will have many different kinds of high-speed travel.

---

*Write 3 and 8 two ways, using two different connecting words.

Using What You've Learned

Explaining a Process. Do you have any good ideas for some breakthrough technology? It may be a new robot, a new communication device, a non-polluting energy producer, an all-in-one refrigerator-food preparer / server and dishwasher, or whatever. Don't worry about technological complications. Just let your imagination go and draw up plans for an invention that will make your life simpler, easier, or happier. Draw a sketch of your invention and prepare to explain how it works.

Then, in pairs or small groups, tell why you created this invention and give directions on how your great invention works. Explain it step by step, using connecting words such as *because, if, so that,* and *when* whenever possible.

example: **If you're homesick and want to see your family but you don't have the time or the money to go by plane, try my "transporter." It's designed so that you can stop by your home for lunch and be back here for your afternoon classes. Now, how does this marvelous machine work? Well, when you push Button A, . . .**

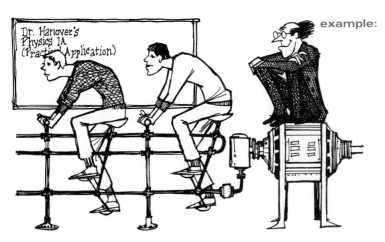

example: **If you want to lower your energy costs at school and get more work out of the students, you can use my "student generator." Every morning when the students arrive, they sit on bicycles instead of at desks. During the class, each student pedals and produces energy for the electricity and heat. If a student doesn't do the homework, he or she has to pedal an extra hour. . . .**

activity 2

Making Decisions. Making decisions is always a complicated process because we never know what may happen in the future. One way to make the choices clearer is to complete a decision tree such as the one below. A decision tree helps you see the effects of each choice.

Decision:
I can go to Mexico on our break, or I can stay home.

If I go to Mexico — I won't have any money next term.
I'll practice my Spanish.
I'll have an exciting time.

If I stay home — I'll be bored.
I'll save money.
I'll have time to study for the TOEFL.

In pairs or in small groups, consider a decision that you are facing. It may be a general problem, such as how to study for an upcoming test or how to learn English faster, or it may be a specific problem you have now. Together work out a decision tree for each problem. Later, tell the class what you decided to do. Did the decision tree help you?

focus on testing

Use of Compound and Complex Sentences

Compound and complex sentences are frequently tested on standardized English proficiency exams. Review these commonly tested structures and check your understanding by completing the sample items below.

Remember that . . .

- Two sentences written together must have a connecting word or appropriate punctuation.
- Only certain verb tenses can be used in clauses of time or condition.
- _So_ and _so that_ have different meanings.
- A modal auxiliary generally follows _so that._

Part 1. Circle the correct completion for the following.

example: _____ I go to France, I plan to visit my friend.
  a. So that
  (b.) When
  c. So
  d. Yet

1. When you _____ to Europe, you should see the Swiss Alps.
  a. will travel
  b. traveling
  c. travel
  d. travels

2. I don't drive my car into town _____ the weather is bad.
  a. unless
  b. if not
  c. so that
  d. but

3. She _____ her visit more if she comes here during the summer.
  a. enjoy
  b. is enjoying
  c. will enjoy
  d. will be enjoy

Part 2. Circle the letter below the word(s) containing an error.

example: U.N. organizers <u>will decide</u> to erect a building in New York
                          (A)

so that world leaders could <u>meet</u> <u>regularly</u>.
B   C   D

1. <u>Because</u> the Internet <u>was</u> originally created <u>so that</u> military researchers
      A   B   C

<u>could communicate</u> with each other.
      D

2. <u>When</u> you <u>will take</u> the *Concorde* from New York to London, you
      A   B

<u>will arrive</u> in less than <u>three and one-half</u> hours.
      C   D

3. <u>Probably</u> the population of the world <u>will continue</u> to grow rapidly, but
      A   B

<u>although</u> in some countries the rate of growth <u>has decreased</u>
      C   D

significantly.

CHAPTER **seven**

North America: The Land and the People

Compound and Complex Sentences (2)

Topic One: Compound Sentences and Transitions

Topic Two: The Past Perfect Continuous Tense; Time Clauses (1)

Topic Three: Time Clauses (2)

Topic Four: Contrast of Simple, Compound, and Complex
                  Sentences

Compound Sentences and Transitions

Setting the Context

previewing the passage

The term *North America* includes Mexico, Canada, and the United States, but this chapter focuses on Canada and the United States, where most people speak English. What do you know about the people and the geography of this area? Share your information and experiences while answering these questions about the map.

- What is the capital of the United States? Of Canada?
- What are the most important geographical features of Canada and the United States?

Quebec City, Quebec, Canada

LAND OF CONTRASTS

Canada and the United States occupy a huge land area, and there are many differences from region to region. One difference lies in the climate, which varies from the extreme cold of Alaska and the Yukon to the lovely, warm climate of Hawaii. You can see the influence of the climate in the faces of
5 the strong, tough Alaskan, on the one hand, and the relaxed, smiling Hawaiian on the other hand.

In addition to differences in geography and climate, the United States and Canada have many different types of people. For example, along the East Coast you will see the influence of British, Dutch, French, Italian, German,
10 Scandinavian, and Hispanic culture—in the architecture, the food, the language, the customs, and the appearance of the people. The Midwest is a combination of Irish, German, Polish, and Scandinavian people, mainly. In contrast, the people of the Southwest have mixed Indian, Spanish, and northern European blood. In Canada, most immigrants were French or
15 British; for this reason, Canada has two official languages: French and English.

Vancouver, British Columbia, Canada

discussing ideas   What three reasons are given for the regional differences in North America? How are the people different in the U.S. East, Midwest, and Southwest?

A. Compound Sentences (Review)

If necessary, see Chapter Six, page 187 for an explanation of compound sentences.

exercise 1

Review.   Combine the following pairs of sentences with *and, but, or, so,* or *yet.* Use each conjunction at least once. Pay attention to punctuation.

1. Canada's border on the north is the Arctic Ocean. Its border on the south is the United States.
2. Canada is the second-largest country in the world (after Russia). It has a smaller population than Korea or Italy.
3. Much of Canada is covered by ice and forests. Eighty-nine percent of the land area has no people.
4. Forests cover much of Canada's land area. Canada is a world leader in the production of paper and wood products.
5. Most Canadians speak English as their first language. Some people speak French.
6. Immigrants to Canada can choose to learn English. They can learn French instead.

B. Transitions

Transitions are words or phrases that connect two related ideas. In written English, they often appear in compound sentences joined by a semicolon. In most cases, a comma follows the transition. English has many transitions. The following list includes some of the most common ones.

uses	transitions	examples
Giving Examples	for example for instance	Canada is a land of diversity; **for example,** it has two national languages.
Adding Information	in addition furthermore moreover besides	Canada has large deposits of many valuable minerals such as gold, silver, and copper; **in addition,** it is very rich in farmland, fish, and lumber.
Emphasizing	in fact	Canada has thousands of streams, rivers, and lakes; **in fact,** one third of the world's fresh water is in Canada.
Showing Similarity	likewise similarly	Canada produces many minerals; **likewise,** some parts of the United States are rich in mineral resources.
Showing Contrast (Opposition)	in contrast on (the) one hand/ on the other hand	Quebec is a very old city with buildings from the 1700s; **in contrast,** Toronto is a newer city with highrises and skyscrapers.
Showing Contrast (Concession)	however nevertheless still as a result	French is the main language in Quebec; **however,** many people there also speak English. The Canadian Arctic receives only ten inches of rain or snow each year; **nevertheless,** it has thousands of lakes and rivers.

uses	transitions	examples
Giving Reasons or Results	consequently for this (that) reason therefore	South-central Canada has wide, flat, fertile plains; **as a result,** many farmers moved to this area to grow wheat.
Giving Sequences	now, next, then first, second, etc. earlier, later meanwhile finally	European settlers moved into Canada gradually. **First,** the English and French came to the eastern part of the country. **Later,** more English moved to the western coast. **Finally,** settlers began farming the central plains.

Note: Most transitions come at the beginning of a sentence. Except for transitions of sequence, transitions may also be used with a semicolon (;) in compound sentences. In both cases, a comma normally follows the transition.

However may also be used at other points within a sentence. Commas are almost always used at each point. Compare:

I enjoyed the dinner. **However,** I did not like the dessert.
I did not, **however,** like the dessert.
I did not like the dessert, **however.**

exercise 2 Rewrite the following sentences about Canada and use each of the following transitions once: *in addition, nevertheless, for example, similarly, however, in contrast, as a result, later.*

example: Canada is rich in history and culture. It also has great natural resources.
   Canada is rich in history and culture; in addition, it has great natural resources.

1. Canada has ten provinces, and it has two territories: the Northwest Territories and the Yukon Territory.
2. Eastern Canada has many historical places. Visitors can see walled cities, forts, and bridges from the early 1700s.
3. Central Canada has very fertile plains, so many farmers settled in the provinces of Manitoba, Saskatchewan, and Alberta.
4. Large prairies cover central Canada. Much of western Canada is mountainous.
5. Many people visit the mountains of western Canada, but there are few roads into these wild areas.
6. Northern Canada is a cold, treeless region, but many people consider it extremely beautiful.

7. The French were the first Europeans to settle in Canada. The British came and conquered them.
8. Eastern Canada is famous for its tourist attractions. Western Canada has fascinating places to visit.

exercise 3

Choose the best transition, and combine the following pairs of sentences about North America. Use correct punctuation.

example: New England has large wooded areas. (however / similarly / for example) The Great Lakes region has great areas of forestland.
New England has large wooded areas; similarly, the Great Lakes region has great areas of forestland

1. Canada produces many wood products. (therefore / for example / likewise) Canada is the world's largest exporter of newsprint.
2. The land in the U.S. Midwest is rich, wide, and flat. (for this reason / on the other hand / in addition) Many farmers settled there.
3. The Rocky Mountains are high and dangerous. (as a result / meanwhile / nevertheless) Early settlers crossed them and reached the Pacific Ocean.
4. Rivers on the east side of the Rockies flow to the Atlantic Ocean. On the west side they flow to the Pacific. (for instance / moreover / for this reason) The Rocky Mountains are called the "Continental Divide."
5. Death Valley, California, receives less than 2 inches of rain per year. (consequently / finally / on the other hand) The state of Washington gets up to 150 inches per year.
6. In the 16th century, the French were exploring Canada. (meanwhile / still / for instance) Europeans were also settling farther south along the Atlantic coast.

exercise 4

First, look at the map of North and South America on the next page. Then complete the following five paragraphs with appropriate transitions. Indicate where several choices are possible.

1. The Americas reach from the North Pole to the South Pole; _____, they have every sort of climate. The area near the equator is closest to the sun; _____, it has very warm temperatures._____, the areas near the poles are terribly cold all year. Between the poles and the equator, both continents have a range of temperatures; _____, South America has more areas with tropical climate.

2. Both North and South America resemble triangles; _____ , the South American triangle is farther east. _____, it is farther from the South Pole than North America is from the North Pole.

3. Both continents have major north-south mountain ranges in their western areas. _____, both continents have smaller mountain ranges on their eastern sides. _____, the Andes in South America are much higher than the Rockies in North America. Seventeen mountains in the Andes are over 20,000 feet; _____, only one peak in North America, Mt. McKinley, reaches that height.

4. North America has a huge, flat, grassy area called the Great Plains. _____, in South America there is a flat, grassy region in Argentina called the Pampas.

5. Both North and South America have tremendous rivers. The Mississippi River in North America runs from north to south. _____, the Amazon in South America runs from west to east.

Interactions Two • Grammar

Write sentences using the cues below.

1. The weather in (one area of North America that you know) is . . .
   In contrast, the weather in (your native country or area) is . . .
   Therefore, . . .
2. Both Canada and the United States have immigrants from all over the world.
   Therefore, they . . .
   However, they . . .
3. (Many) people in (your native area or country) originally came from . . .
   As a result, . . .
   Moreover . . .
4. When I first came to (the place where you are studying), I had many feelings about living in a new culture.
   First, . . .
   Then, . . .
   Later, . . .
   Now, . . .

Now choose one set of sentences to use as the basis for a short composition. Ask your teacher or consult an encyclopedia if you need more information.

Using What You've Learned

 **activity**

Comparing Regions or Countries. Prepare a composition or an oral report in which you compare one of the following:

- a region of the U.S. or Canada to the region (country) where you grew up
- a region of the U.S. to a region in Canada
- the area where you live now to another area in the U.S. or Canada

In your description, use as many conjunctions and transitions as possible. You can talk about the following topics:

climate	natural resources
geography	cities
types of people	animals
language	industries

examples: Norway is like Canada because we have a lot of forests. In addition, we have very cold winters.
About 27% of the people in Canada speak French. Similarly, in the southern United States there are people whose first language is French. They are called "Cajuns."

The Past Perfect Continuous Tense; Time Clauses (1)

Setting the Context

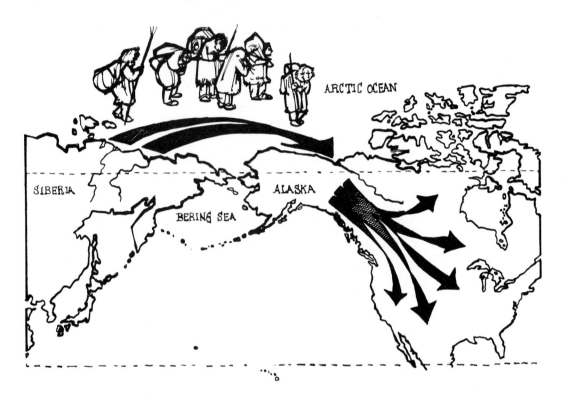

previewing the passage

What do you know about the settling of the Americas? Share your information and ideas while answering the following questions about the picture:

- Where did America's first immigrants come from?
- When did these people come?
- Who are the descendants of these people today?

AMERICA'S FIRST IMMIGRANTS

Although we call American Indians "Native Americans," their ancestors actually came to America from Asia. A land bridge had developed between Siberia and Alaska thousands of years ago. Sometime before 13000 B.C.,

Asians who had been looking for new hunting and fishing places and warmer
5 weather crossed the bridge from Asia to Alaska and continued southward.
Many moved on to Central and South America to begin new societies and
cultures. Approximately one million Native Americans were living in today's
United States when the first Europeans arrived. Because the Europeans had
been searching for a passage to India, they mistakenly called the Americans
10 "Indians."

***discussing
ideas***

Are there any "real" Native Americans? How did American Indians reach North
America? Why did they come to North America?

A. The Past Perfect Continuous Tense

The past perfect continuous tense expresses a past activity in progress *before*
another event or time in the past. Like the past perfect tense, it occurs more often
in written English than in spoken English. These time expressions often appear
with the past perfect continuous: *before 1492, by last week, by then, by that time,*
for + a period of time.

forms	examples	notes
Statements	Long before 1492, Indians **had been living** in the Americas. However, Indians **had not been living** in all areas of North and South America.	Use *had been* + present participle for all forms.
Yes/No Questions	**Had** Indians **been living** there for a long time?	Short answers are: "Yes, they **had**." "No, they **hadn't**."
Information Questions	**How long had** Indians **been living** there before 1492? **Who had been living** there?	*Had* comes before the subject in most information questions.

exercise 1

Reread the opening passage, "America's First Immigrants," on page 224. Underline the past perfect continuous verbs. Discuss their relationship to the other verbs
or time expressions in the sentences.

exercise 2 Look at the five pictures on pages 226 to 228 and the cues below them. Using the past perfect continuous tense, make statements about the lifestyles of the Indians long before the arrival of Columbus.

example: Wichita / construct homes of grass

Long before the arrival of Columbus, the Wichita Indians had

been constructing homes of grass.

1. Choctaws / play sophisticated ball games

_____

_____

2. Ojibwa / gather wild rice

_____

_____

3. Mandan / live in complex villages around central plazas

_____

_____

_____

4. Comanche / make clothing from skins and preserve meat by drying it

_____

_____

_____

5. Caddo / weave baskets and use animals in their work

_____

_____

_____

B. Time Clauses with the Past Perfect and Past Perfect Continuous Tenses

	examples	**notes**
when	**When** Columbus arrived Indians had been living in the Americas for thousands of years.	In sentences with time clauses, the dependent clause may begin or end the sentence. Use a comma after a time clause that begins a sentence. In sentences with *when, before, by the time (that)*, and *until*, the verb in the dependent clause is in the simple past tense. The verb in the main clause is in the past perfect (continuous) tense.
before	**Before** many years passed, thousands of these Indians had died.	
by the time (that)	Many tribes had been friendly **until** the Europeans began to take their land.	
until	**By the time (that)** the American Revolution began, most Indians had moved west.	
after	**After** the Europeans had settled the Atlantic Coast, they began to move west.	In sentences with *after*, the verb in the dependent clause is often in the past perfect (continuous) tense and the verb in the main clause is in the simple past.

Note: *After, before, by,* and *until* are also prepositions of time and may begin phrases:
The American Revolution began in 1776. *By then,* most Indians had moved west. *Until the 1750s,* many Indians had been living along the East Coast.

exercise 3  Change the following sentences to include the past perfect continuous tense by adding *By the time the Europeans arrived . . . for centuries.*

example: Some North American Indians used sophisticated farming methods.
By the time the Europeans arrived, some North American Indians had been using sophisticated farming methods for centuries.

1. Indians grew tobacco, potatoes, and corn.
2. Hopi Indians raised cotton and used it to make cloth.
3. Indians throughout the Americas made pots, jars, and baskets.
4. Indians in the Southwest and Mexico created beautiful gold and silver objects.
5. Pueblo Indians in the Southwest constructed large, apartment-style buildings.

 **exercise 4**
Combine the following pairs of sentences. Use the connecting word in parentheses, and punctuate your sentences correctly.

> **example:** The Europeans arrived. Indians in the Southwest had been irrigating their farmland for centuries. (when)
> *When the Europeans arrived, the Indians in the Southwest had been irrigating their farmland for centuries.*

1. Columbus landed in the New World. Many Indians had never heard a European language. (until)
2. Tribes with different languages had been using a common sign language to communicate. The Europeans arrived. (before)
3. The Europeans had settled on the Atlantic Coast. They began trading with the Indians. (after)
4. The Indians had been using seashells as money for a long time. The Europeans discovered the New World. (when)
5. They began to intermarry with the Indians. The Europeans had been in America for only a short time. (after)

 **exercise 5**
Combine the following pairs of sentences, adding *when, before, until, by the time (that)*, or *after*. (In some cases, more than one word may be correct.) Pay attention to punctuation.

> **example:** The Aztecs had already built many sophisticated cities. The Europeans arrived in Mexico.
> *By the time the Europeans arrived in Mexico, the Aztecs had already built many sophisticated cities.*

1. The Europeans had settled in the Americas. They learned new farming and building methods from the Indians.
2. The Incas had been constructing excellent roads for a long time. The Europeans arrived in South America.
3. Columbus and his men landed on the Atlantic Coast of America. They had never tasted corn.
4. Europeans destroyed the great buffalo herds. Many Indian tribes had depended on the buffalo for their existence.
5. The Indians met the white settlers. They had never suffered from smallpox or other European diseases.

 **exercise 6**
Complete the paragraphs on the opposite page about the discovery of the Americas with simple past, past perfect, or past perfect continuous forms of the verbs in parentheses.

Historians believe that Europeans _____ (live) in the Americas
1
long before the time of Columbus. By the ninth century, Scandinavian adventurers _____ (make / already) long ocean voyages. Some of them
2
_____ (reach) North America and apparently _____ (visit)
3   4
Canada more than six centuries before Columbus _____ (travel) to the
5
New World. Furthermore, it seems that they _____ (live) in Canada
6
for a short time before the twelfth century. These adventurers _____
7
(construct) grass houses, _____ (build) a steam bath, and
8
_____ (make) nails from local iron.
9

As far as we know, no one _____ (cross) the Atlantic Ocean from
10
Southern Europe before 1492, when Christopher Columbus _____
11
(sail) to the coasts of Cuba and Hispaniola. According to his journal, he
_____ (see) "mountains that _____ (seem) to reach the sky"
12   13
and palm trees that _____ (be) "wondrous to see for their beautiful
14
variety." After Columbus _____ (return) to the Old World, he
15
_____ (tell) incredible stories about what he _____ (see)
16   17
during his voyages.

Using What You've Learned

Describing Historical Events.   Choose an important event in the history of your
country. Imagine that you were alive at that time. Write a paragraph or tell your
classmates about your life before that event. Write in the first person, and use the
past, past perfect (continuous), or past continuous tenses.

> example: Before the Europeans came to North America, we had been
> living peacefully in our villages for many generations. We had
> learned how to farm and how to hunt. We had invented a
> system of money, and we used it for trading with other villages.
> We had many unique holidays and traditions. For example, . . .
> After the Europeans arrived, everything changed . . .

TOPIC three

Time Clauses (2)

Setting the Context

previewing the passage

What do you know about the immigrants who came to the Americas? Share your information and ideas while answering the following questions about the picture.

- What ethnic groups do you recognize in the picture?
- When did the various groups arrive in North America?

AMERICA: "A NATION OF NATIONS"

In the late 1800s, when Walt Whitman said that America was not just a nation, but a "nation of nations," he was living at a time of major immigration to the United States. Immigration had begun long before then, and it has continued steadily ever since. America is a nation of immigrants: today, one
5 of every five Americans is either foreign born or a child of foreign-born parents.

Since the English founded the colony of Jamestown, Virginia, in 1607, more than 50 million people have begun new lives in the United States. When the first immigrants arrived during the 1600s, they settled along
10 the Atlantic coast. Later immigrants moved west to the Allegheny Mountains. In the nineteenth century, immigrants eventually reached the West Coast.

America's immigrants are of all races, religions, cultures, customs, and traditions. Although each group has had difficulties, most immigrants have chosen to stay. The United States is one of the few countries in the world
15 where so many different groups live side by side.

*discussing
ideas*

In your opinion, who has an easier time adjusting to a new life: immigrants today or immigrants a hundred years ago? Why?

A. Time Clauses with the Simple Past and Past Continuous Tenses

When and *while* can relate two activities or situations that happened (or were happening) at the same time in the past. *When* can also relate events that occurred in a sequence.

	examples	notes
when	**When** Columbus **discovered** America, he **believed** he was in the Orient.	Clauses with *when* are normally in the simple past tense. *When* means "at the time that" or "after."
while	**While** Columbus **was exploring** the Americas, Portuguese sailors **were exploring** the coast of Africa. Columbus **was exploring** the Americas **while** Portuguese sailors **were exploring** the coast of Africa.	Clauses with *while* are normally in the past continuous tense. If both verbs in a sentence are in the past continuous, it means that the two actions were in progress at the same time. In such sentences, *while* can go at the beginning or in the middle.
when or while	Columbus **was looking** for India when he **discovered** the Americas. Columbus **discovered** the Americas **while** he **was looking** for India.	The simple past and the past continuous may appear in the same sentence. In these cases, *while* begins clauses with the past continuous and *when* begins clauses with the simple past. One event began before the other one and was in progress when the second event interrupted it.

   Combine the following sentences with *when*. Make any other necessary changes and use correct punctuation.

> example: Columbus arrived in the Americas.
> Columbus believed he was in the Orient.
> *When Columbus arrived in the Americas, he believed he was in the Orient.*

1. Europeans first arrived in the Americas.
   They knew nothing about the land or its inhabitants.
2. Over fourteen million Indians were in Central and South America.
   European explorers reached the New World.
3. There were only about a million Indians in today's United States.
   Europeans began to colonize North America.
4. People in Europe heard about the new continent.
   Many left their homes to begin a new life in the New World.
5. Some colonists bought land from the Indians.
   Some colonists arrived.
6. Other colonists arrived.
   Other colonists took the land from the Indians.

exercise 2   Use the following chronology of immigration to America to form sentences with *while*. Form as many sentences as possible for each time period. Pay attention to your use of verb tenses and punctuation.

> example: 1619–1630
> British Puritans settled in Massachusetts.
> Dutch settlers built New Amsterdam (New York).
> Portuguese boats brought the first black slaves to Virginia.
> *While British Puritans were settling in Massachusetts, Dutch settlers were building New Amsterdam.*
> *Portuguese boats were bringing the first black slaves to Virginia while British Puritans were settling in Massachusetts.*
> *While Dutch settlers . . .*

1. 1630–1640
   The Puritans founded the Massachusetts Bay Colony.
   Swedes built log cabins in Delaware.
   British Catholics constructed settlements in Maryland.
2. 1640–1690
   The first Jews arrived from Portugal.
   German families came to Philadelphia.
   British Quakers founded Pennsylvania.
   French Protestants traveled to South Carolina.
3. 1690–1760
   The French explored the Great Lakes area and the Mississippi Valley.
   The Spanish built settlements in the West.
   English settlers moved to Georgia.

exercise 3 Combine the following sentences with *when* or *while*. Use correct punctuation. You may want to add, omit, or change some words when you join the sentences.

> example: Columbus reached North America.
> At least a million Indians were living there.
>
> When Columbus reached North America, at least a million Indians were living there. or
>
> At least a million Indians were living in North America when Columbus reached it.

1. Europe was changing from an agricultural to an industrial society.
   Europeans began to settle the New World.
2. The population of Europe was increasing.
   Farmland was becoming scarcer and more expensive.
3. Life became too difficult.
   Many Europeans decided to come to the New World.
4. Many people became ill or died.
   Many people were sailing to the Americas.
5. The first settlers arrived on the East Coast.
   Indians were living all along the East Coast.
6. Conflicts and fighting began.
   Settlers took Indian lands.
7. Settlers came to the New World.
   The settlers brought many diseases such as smallpox.
8. The immigrants were building a new world in the Americas.
   The Indians were fighting to save their way of life.

exercise 4 Read the sentences you wrote in Exercise 3. They tell a story. Rewrite your sentences in the form of a paragraph.

Africans being brought to North America to be slaves

B. Time Clauses with the Present Perfect and Simple Past Tenses

Since can join present and past time clauses. The main clause must be in the present perfect or present perfect continuous tense. The clause with *since* is normally in the simple past tense. *Since* (and *for*) may also begin prepositional phrases.

	examples	notes
Clause	I **have lived** here **since** I **moved** in 1983.	*Since* appears with a specific beginning time in both clauses and phrases.
Phrase	I **have lived** here **since** 1983. I **have lived** here **for** several years.	*For* appears in phrases indicating a period of time.

 Combine the following cues with *since* or *for*. Use the correct tense (present perfect or past) of the verbs.

> **example:** Germany / send / 7 million immigrants to America.
> the first German families / arrive / in 1683.
> **Germany has sent 7 million immigrants to America since the first German families arrived in 1683.**

1. over 13 million British / come / to the United States
   the Napoleonic Wars / end / in 1815
2. 1890
   over 5 million Italians / arrive / in the United States
3. 1980
   more than 15 million people / immigrate / legally to the United States
4. the last two decades
   most immigrants / come / from Southeast Asia or Mexico and Central America
5. the first immigrants / arrive / from Europe
   millions of people from every continent / move / to the United States
6. the Statue of Liberty / stand / in New York harbor
   the French / give / the statue to the U.S. in 1886
7. over 100 years
   the Statue of Liberty / be / a symbol of new opportunities
8. immigrants to the U.S. / make / major contributions to American culture
   the first / begin / arriving centuries ago

 **exercise 6**   Use the simple past, past continuous, or present perfect forms of the verbs in parentheses to complete the following eight sentences about the exploration and settlement of the Americas.

example: Columbus *discovered*_____ (discover) the Americas while

he *was looking*_____ (look) for India.

1. When Columbus _____ (see) the native people of America

for the first time, he _____ (call) them "Indians."

2. While the first immigrants _____ (settle) on the East Coast

of the United States, Champlain _____ (explore) French

Canada.

3. When settlers first _____ (arrive) in the New World, many

of them _____ (die) of illness or hunger.

4. Since the first English colonists _____ (land) in 1607, the

population of the United States _____ (grow) to over 280

million people.

5. People from every country in the world _____ (come) to the United States since the first settlers _____ (begin) their new lives here.

6. Since the beginning, different groups of immigrants _____ (have) different goals.

7. As a result, they _____ (settle) in different areas of the United States.

8. For over two hundred years, the cultures and traditions of the settlers _____ (influence) the development of each region in America.

 **exercise 7** **Review.** Fill in the blanks with the simple past, past continuous, present, or present perfect forms of the verbs in parentheses.

IMMIGRATION TO THE UNITED STATES

Since the beginning of its history, the United States has been a nation of immigrants. People _____ (come) to the U.S. because of wars,

1
unemployment, religious persecution, or natural disasters in their native countries. From 1820 to 1860, more than 5 million people_____

2
(immigrate) to the United States. Over 90% of these people

_____ (come) from England, Ireland, and Germany. After the

3
Civil War, immigration _____ (increase). Between 1860 and

4
1920, about 29 million persons _____ (arrive), mostly from

5
eastern and southern Europe. To this day, many neighborhoods in eastern cities

_____ (show) the influence of eastern Europe and Italy.

6

While the Russians, Poles, and Italians _____ (settle) in

7
the east, large numbers of Asians, especially Chinese and Japanese,

_____ (migrate) to the Pacific Coast and Hawaii. From the

8
beginning, these Asian immigrants _____ (establish / usually)

9
separate and unique neighborhoods in the cities where they

_____ (settle). Nowadays, the largest number of immigrants to

10
the U.S. _____ (come) from Mexico, Central America, and

11

Street scene in Chinatown, San Francisco

Southeast Asia. For example, many Vietnamese _____ (come) to the United States since the end of the Vietnam War. In many southwestern and eastern states, a large percentage of the population _____ (be) of Latin American origin.

Using What You've Learned

Learning About Immigrants. What do you know about the immigrants who have come to the area where you are living? Consult an almanac, an encyclopedia, or the Chamber of Commerce in your area to find out about one or more groups. Answer the questions below. Then give a report to your class.

- Which immigrant groups live in your area?
- How many have arrived since they started coming?
- Why did they come?
- How many first- and second-generation immigrants live in the area now?
- In what ways have these groups influenced the local culture?

Describing Events. Think of a recent event that has had an important impact on your country. Describe the event. Then explain how it has affected your country, your family, and you.

Contrast of Simple, Compound, and Complex Sentences

Setting the Context

previewing the passage

What do you know about colonial life in the Americas? Share your ideas and information by answering these questions about the pictures.

- When and where do you think this scene took place?
- What tools or equipment do you see in the picture?
- How did people use their time in those days?

THE MAKING OF A COUNTRY

The United States began its life as a nation in a very modest way. Its early immigrants lived in a wild land. Life was hard, and living conditions were poor. Most of the early settlers started farms even though the land along the

East Coast was not good for farming. There were resources such as coal, iron,
5 gold, and copper deep in the soil, but they remained undiscovered for much of
the country's early history.

In the beginning, the American colonies were the poorest of Britain's
colonies. The only profitable product for Britain was tobacco. As a result,
Britain paid little attention to the colonies, and the American settlers developed
10 their new land without much interference.

Although life was very difficult at first, the early settlers worked the land
and slowly made it fruitful. In many cases, after a relatively short period of
time, both rich and poor were living better than in the past. When people
worked hard, they could improve their standard of living. Eventually, many
15 men and women shared in the "American Dream"; they achieved economic
security and lived as they chose. In fact, since the first settlers came to the
American colonies, this dream has been part of the life of the immigrant.

discussing
ideas

Why did the British leave the early colonists alone? Why were the early settlers
able to improve their standard of living? What is the "American Dream"?

Contrast of Simple, Compound, and Complex Sentences

Remember that every complete sentence in English has at least one subject-
verb combination. A simple sentence has only one subject and verb. Compound
and complex sentences may have two or more subject-verb combinations.
Compound sentences use a coordinating conjunction and comma or a semicolon. Complex sentences use a subordinating conjunction. A comma is
generally used with subordinate clauses that begin sentences.

sentence type	examples
Simple	**Life** in the American colonies **was** very difficult.
Compound	**The weather** in the colonies **was** harsh, **and living conditions were** poor.
Complex	**Although life was** hard, **many colonists** soon **improved** their standard of living.

   Reread the opening passage, "The Making of a Country," on pages 240 and 241. Identify each sentence as simple, compound, or complex. Circle the connecting words in compound and complex sentences.

 exercise **2**   Indicate whether the following sentences are complete (C) or incomplete (I).

   example: __I__ Although the weather in New England was very harsh.

   1. _____ The American colonies were the poorest of Britain's colonies.

   2. _____ The weather in New England very harsh.

   3. _____ Was not good for farming.

   4. _____ Even though the land along the East Coast was not good for farming.

   5. _____ Britain paid little attention to the American colonies.

   6. _____ Because the colonies did not have many profitable products.

exercise **3**   **Error Analysis.**   Many of the following sentences are not punctuated correctly. Find and correct any errors in punctuation by adding commas and/or semicolons.

   example: When the first revolts began in the American colonies, approximately 2.2 million people had already settled there.

   1. Although the American colonies officially declared independence from Britain in 1776 fighting had actually begun several years earlier.

   2. The first protests began in Boston but colonists started demonstrating in several other cities and towns within a short time.

   3. The first protests were only demonstrations however fighting soon began.

   4. The first deaths in the American Revolution occurred in Boston when British soldiers shot at an angry crowd.

   5. After the Boston Massacre fighting spread throughout the colonies.

   6. The fighting began in Boston but it soon spread throughout the thirteen American colonies.

   7. On July 4, 1776, the Americans officially declared independence from Britain as a result the Fourth of July is celebrated every year as Independence Day.

   8. The fighting ended in 1781, and the U.S. and Britain signed the Treaty of Paris in 1783.

 exercise **4**   **Review.**   Complete the passage on the opposite page about the American Revolution with the simple past, past continuous, present perfect, or past perfect forms of the verbs in parentheses. Indicate any sentences where more than one form is appropriate.

Approximately 2.2 million people <u>had already settled</u> (settle / already) in the thirteen British colonies when the first movements toward revolution _____ (begin) in 1770. These colonists _____
1   2
(build / already) homes and communities, and they _____
3
(establish) a new way of life.

The first protests _____ (start) in Boston, Massachusetts.
4
In the beginning, these _____ (be) only demonstrations. Then,
5
on March 5, 1770, the first fight _____ (take) place when
6
British soldiers _____ (shoot) at an angry crowd and
7
_____ (kill) five people. This _____ (become)
8   9
known as the Boston Massacre.

While the British _____ (try) to keep Bostonians calm,
10
settlers in other areas _____ (start) protest movements. Soon
11
people _____ (protest) throughout the colonies. While
12
farmers _____ (fight) the first battles, the politicians
13
_____ (plan) a new government. By 1775, colonists
14
_____ (organize) a Congress, _____ (create) a
15   16
small army, and _____ (print) money. Finally, on July 4, 1776,
17
the Americans officially _____ (declare) their independence.
18
Since then, Americans _____ (celebrate) July 4 as
19
Independence Day.

 **exercise 5**   Combine the sentences here and on the next page with *because* and *although*. Add or omit words to improve your new sentences, and be sure to use commas when necessary.

example: People came in family groups to New England.
They planned to stay.
People came in family groups to New England because they planned to stay.

1. New England settlers built schools and churches.
New England settlers wanted to start communities.
2. New England was very different from England.
Many English people immigrated to New England.
3. Northern Europeans moved to the mid-Atlantic states.
The land and the climate were similar to those in their homelands.

4. Parts of Pennsylvania were very much like Germany.
   German colonists felt at home in Pennsylvania.
5. There was no real gold in Virginia.
   Tobacco, "green gold," grew well in Virginia.
6. Large landowners in the South wanted a lot of cheap labor.
   The people in the South brought men from European prisons and slaves from Africa to work.
7. Some early farmers planted cotton in the South.
   Cotton was not a very profitable crop until the invention of the cotton gin in 1793.
8. The cotton gin could clean over 50 pounds of cotton per day.
   This machine revolutionized the cotton industry.

9. The cotton gin made cotton farming very profitable.
   Southern landowners began planting this crop all over the South.
10. Landowners bought more and more slaves to cultivate cotton.
    By 1860, the slave population in the U.S. had grown to 4 million.

Replica of the cotton gin

 **exercise 6** Rewrite your sentences from Exercise 5 with transitions of reason or result *(as a result, consequently, for this [that] reason, therefore)* or of concession *(however, nevertheless, still)*. You may need to change or add words. Remember to punctuate your new sentences correctly.

example: People came in family groups to New England.
They planned to stay.
The settlers planned to stay in New England; therefore, they came in family groups.

 **exercise 7** The information on the opposite page is listed in chronological order. Combine the sentences with connecting words: *after, before, until, when, by the time (that), although, because, however, nevertheless, on the other hand.* In many cases, more than one connecting word is possible. Add or omit words to form better sentences, and change verb tenses if necessary. Remember to use appropriate punctuation.

example: Thousands of years ago, Asians traveled to the Americas. For centuries, people believed that Europeans had been the first to reach the New World.

Thousands of years ago, Asians traveled to the Americas; nevertheless, for centuries people believed that Europeans had been the first to reach the New World.

or

Although Asians had traveled to the Americas thousands of years ago, for centuries people believed that Europeans had been the first to reach the New World.

1. Adventurers from Northern Europe reached North America before 1100. Many people still think Columbus was the first European to reach the Americas.

2. The early settlers lived in the New World for a short time. The early settlers became very different from their relatives in the Old World.

3. Settlers had been living in the wilderness for some years. Settlers learned independence and self-reliance.

4. Many French people lived by fishing and hunting. Most English people started farms.

5. The American colonists valued their freedom. The American colonists rebelled against British taxes.

6. The American Revolution began in 1776. It seemed that the colonists would not win.

7. The Revolution ended. The new country did not begin to grow immediately.

8. Few settlers moved west of the Allegheny Mountains. Then railroads and canals were built.

9. Railroads and canals were built. Railroads and canals carried hundreds of thousands of immigrants to the West.

10. The area between the Alleghenies and the Rockies had tremendous natural resources. Settlers soon began to develop industries there.

Using What You've Learned

Researching Historical Events or People.   Choose an event in American or Canadian history or a famous American or Canadian that you would like to know more about. Do some research on this event or person. You may want to ask a fellow classmate, a friend, a co-worker, or a teacher for help or additional information. At another class meeting, give a brief report telling what you learned and how you found the information.

Use of Compound and Complex Sentences

Compound and complex sentences are frequently tested on standardized English proficiency exams. Review these commonly tested structures and check your understanding by completing the sample items below.

Remember that . . .

- Compound and complex sentences must use appropriate connecting words or punctuation.
- Only certain verb tenses can be used with clauses of time or condition.

Part 1. Circle the correct completion for the following.

example: Although I have studied French for years, _____.
   a. but I have difficulties speaking the language.
   b. I have difficulties in speaking the language.
   c. however, I have difficulties in speaking the language.
   d. but I have difficulties in speaking the language.

1. John has been studying Spanish _____ .
   a. since ten years
   b. for ten years ago
   c. for ten years
   d. ten years ago

2. After we _____ this project, we will take a vacation.
   a. finished
   b. have finished
   c. will finish
   d. are finished

3. If Jose Luis has time, he _____ to have a cup of coffee.
   a. will always stop by
   b. is always stop by
   c. stops always by
   d. always stops by

Part 2. Circle the letter below the word(s) containing an error.

example: If <u>native</u> and nonnative speakers <u>are combined</u>, <u>almost</u> five
      A   B   C

percent of the world population <u>is speaking</u> English.
                               (D)

1. Northern Canada is a cold, <u>treeless</u> region, but <u>however</u> many people
                                A   B

   consider it <u>extremely</u> <u>beautiful</u>.
             C   D

2. After <u>the British</u> <u>had raised</u> taxes in <u>the</u> American colonies, citizens in
        A   B   C

   Boston <u>had begun</u> to protest.
        D

3. Hopi Indians <u>have</u> been <u>raising</u> cotton to make cloth <u>for</u> centuries
            A   B   C

   <u>before</u> the arrival of Europeans in the American Southwest.
  D

CHAPTER eight

Tastes and Preferences

Clauses and Phrases of Comparison

Topic One: Positive Adjectives and Participles

Topic Two: Comparative Adjectives

Topic Three: Superlative Forms

Topic Four: Review

in this chapter

TOPIC **one**
Positive Adjectives and Participles
Setting the Context

What do you like to do in your free time? Share your opinions while answering the following questions about the pictures on the opposite page.

- What are the various people doing?
- Which of these activities are the most popular?

LEISURE TIME AND HOW PEOPLE SPEND IT

In the past, people rarely had as much leisure time as we have now. Traditionally, work took so much time that very little was left for any sort of recreation. Fortunately for us, however, life has changed. With more free time today, most of us are able to pursue other interests. We have a great many
5   choices: music, dance, drama, movies, sports, travel, painting, and so on.

What do most people do? The choices usually depend on personal tastes and preferences.

"I'm a factory worker. My work is really boring, so I fill my free time with as much excitement as possible. I'm interested in sports . . . and danger! I like
10   to skydive."

"I'm a biologist, and I like my work so much that I take it home with me. On the weekends, I spend time in my garden as often as possible. I'm developing several new varieties of roses. It's fascinating. . . ."

"I'm independently wealthy . . . I don't need to work. I have so many
15   possibilities that it's difficult to make choices. I'm fascinated with a wide variety of things: the environment, politics, the arts . . . you name it."

discussing ideas

Why do people have more leisure time today? What does *independently wealthy* mean? What are *the arts*?

A. Participles Used as Adjectives

In Chapter Five, you began to study participles *(boring, bored)*, focusing on the variety of prepositions that may follow them. This section focuses on the difference between the present and past participles when they are used as adjectives.

	examples	notes
Verb	The movie **bored** us. The language **confused** us. The plot **didn't interest** us.	See Chapter Five, page 176, for a list of verbs commonly used in this way.
Present Participle	The movie was **boring.** The language was **confusing** (to us). The plot was not **interesting.**	The present participle expresses how the subject affects someone or something.

	examples	notes
Past Participle	We felt **bored**. We were **confused** (by the language). We weren't **interested** in the plot.	The past participle expresses how the subject feels about someone or something.

exercise 1 What were these people's reactions to the movie they had just seen?

example: The older woman was _interested_ in the movie.

1. The little girl was _____ by the movie.

2. The little boy was _____ by the monsters.

3. The older gentleman was _____ .

4. The young man was _____ by the plot.

5. The young woman was _____ by the special effects.

exercise 2 Complete the sentences here and on the next page by using the present or past participle of the verb in parentheses.

example: I am _intrigued_ (intrigue) by the history of Japan.

1. Some Japanese stories are very _____ (amuse).

2. Travelers are rarely _____ (bore) when they visit Japan.

Interactions Two • Grammar

3. However, they sometimes show _____ (bore) pictures to their friends when they get home.

4. Traveling is _____ (tire) but _____ (excite).

5. Because I am _____ (fascinate) by Japan, I try to see as many Japanese movies as possible.

6. When I told her that I had seen a movie about her country, Takiko looked _____ (surprise).

7. The movie told an _____ (interest) story about life in Japan.

8. Parts of the movie were _____ (confuse), though.

B. Comparisons with (Not) As . . . As

As can be used with adjectives, nouns, and adverbs to compare two things. *As . . . as* means that two things are equal in some way. *Just* is often used to emphasize that the two things are *exactly* equal. *Not as . . . as* means that the first item is less or smaller in some way than the second. *Not quite as* is often used to show that two things are almost equal.

	examples	notes
as + *Adjective* + as	Is the music **as loud as** it was last night? Is the music **as loud as** last night? Is the music **as loud**?	A subject and verb or appropriate auxiliary verb may follow *as . . . as.* The second subject and verb are often omitted. The second *as* is also omitted if nothing follows it.
as + *Adjective* + *Noun* + as	There are **just as many people** tonight **as** there were last night. Is there **as much noise** tonight **as** there was last night?	*As many* or *as few* may come before count nouns, and *as much* or *as little* may come before non-count nouns.
as + *Adverb* + as	Tonight, the band is**n't** playing **as loudly as** it played last night. The band is**n't** playing **as loudly as** (it did) last night. Tonight, the band is**n't** playing **quite as loudly**.	Note that in conversation you may hear adjectives instead of adverbs in these expressions *(The band isn't playing as loud . . .).*

Julio Heartbreaker used to be a very popular singer, but "things have changed." Tell about Julio by completing the sentences. Choose from the following adjectives and use *as . . . as* in your sentences. Create as many sentences as you can.

creative	exciting	handsome	popular	slim	powerful
stylish	expensive	hard to get	romantic	young	enthusiastic

example: Julio isn't . . .
> **Julio isn't as slim as he used to be.**

1. His concerts aren't . . .
2. He isn't . . .
3. His music isn't . . .
4. His love songs aren't . . .
5. The tickets aren't . . .
6. His clothes aren't . . .
7. The audience isn't . . .
8. His voice isn't . . .

Everyone is nervous about Julio's concert tonight because there are many last-minute problems. Complete the speaker's sentences with *as . . . as* and an appropriate adjective or adverb.

example: Julio is talking on the phone with his agent. His agent says, "I can't come right now, but I'll come <u>as soon as I can</u>."

1. Julio is very nervous, and he wants his agent to stay with him until the performance. His agent says, "I can't stay all afternoon, but I'll stay

    _____."

2. The stage is not ready for the concert. Julio wants the stage people to work faster. They tell him, "We can't work any faster. We're working

    _____."

3. Julio is singing with a different band tonight. The band is not very experienced. They are not _____."

4. The new band is also worried. They haven't had much time to prepare for the concert. They are not _____."

5. Julio has a cold, and he hopes his voice is good enough. His agent says, "Your voice is _____."

6. It's almost concert time. Julio doesn't feel ready. He wants more help from his agent. His agent answers, "I can't help you anymore. I've helped you

    _____."

7. The concert has finally started, and the box office has closed. The ticket seller says to Julio's agent, "We can't sell any more tickets. We've sold

_____."

8. The microphones aren't working. Julio can't hear the other singers. He tells them to sing louder. They say, "We can't sing any louder. We're singing

_____."

exercise **5**   What do you know about different types of music—their similarities and differences? Pick two types of music and one adjective from the lists below. Give your ideas, using _(not) as_ + adjective + _as_. Form at least eight sentences, giving both affirmative and negative statements.

examples: **Classical music is not as loud as rock music.**
For me, jazz is just as relaxing as classical music.

TYPES OF MUSIC

classical	fusion (rock and jazz)
rock	rap
jazz	reggae
folk	country
blues	soul

ADJECTIVES

loud	enjoyable
relaxing	quiet
complicated	sophisticated
popular	violent
easy to listen to	peaceful
boring	entertaining

exercise **6**   Do you have as much free time now as you did before you came to this school? Has studying changed your lifestyle? Form complete sentences about the following, using _(not) as_ + adverb + _as_.

1. List three things that you don't do now _as often as_ you used to.
2. List several foods that you don't eat _as frequently as_ you would like to.
3. List several TV shows that you don't get to see _as often (frequently, much) as_ you would like to.

example: **Now that I am a student, I don't go to movies as often as I used to.**

C. Adjectives and Adverbs with *So . . . That*

You can use adjectives and adverbs with *so . . . that*. In these sentences, the main clause expresses a cause or reason. The clause with *that* tells the effect or result of the situation in the main clause.

	examples	notes
so + *Adjective* + that	The music was **so loud that** I couldn't hear the conversation.	This sentence means "The music was very loud. Therefore, I couldn't hear the conversation." Note that *so* (not *very*) is used to join the two sentences.
so + *Adjective* + *Noncount Noun* + that	We paid **so much money** for the tickets **that** we decided to stay.	*So much* or *so little* comes before noncount nouns.
so + *Adjective* + *Count Noun* + that	There were **so few people** at the show **that** the theater was almost empty.	*So many* or *so few* comes before count nouns.
so + *Adverb* + that	The band played **so loudly that** I couldn't hear the conversation.	Note that in conversation you may hear adjectives instead of adverbs in these expressions.

exercise  Rewrite the following sentences as two sentences with *very* and *therefore.*

example: The music was so loud that I couldn't hear anything.
The music was very loud. Therefore, I couldn't hear anything.

1. There was so much noise in the restaurant that we decided to leave.
2. The waitress spoke so quietly that we couldn't hear what she was saying.
3. The menu had so many items on it that I couldn't decide what to order.
4. I was so full from dinner that I didn't order dessert.
5. The singer gives so few concerts that it is almost impossible to get a ticket to one of his shows.
6. Tickets are so expensive now that I can't afford to see many concerts.
7. There were so many people in front of me that I couldn't see the stage.
8. The audience was so quiet that you could have heard a pin drop.

In pairs, take turns making suggestions and responding to them. Using the cues, follow the model.

example: loud / hear anything there

A: **Would you like to go to Pepper's Disco tonight?**

B: **Actually, I'd rather go to The Bistro. The Bistro is never as loud as Pepper's. Pepper's is always so loud that you can't hear anything there.**

1. crowded / get a table there
2. smoky / breathe
3. expensive / afford to buy anything

4. noisy / talk
5. hot / dance
6. formal / be comfortable

Make other comparisons of Pepper's and The Bistro, using the cues below. Following the examples as a model, use singular verbs + *much* or *little* with noncount nouns and plural verbs + *many* or *few* with count nouns.

examples: (−) parking places / park
There are so few parking places at Pepper's that we won't be able to park there.

(−) parking / park
There is so little parking at Pepper's that we won't be able to park there.

1. (+) noise / talk
2. (+) people / dance
3. (−) tables / find one

4. (+) smoke / breathe
5. (−) space / dance
6. (−) light / see well

exercise 10 Imagine that you went to the opening of a Broadway show last weekend. Tell about the events of the evening and your reactions to them by completing the following sentences. Use *so . . . that* or *(not) as . . . as*. Use *much* or *many* when necessary.

1. The tickets were . . . expensive . . .
2. The theater was . . . crowded . . .
3. The show was . . . exciting . . .
4. The hero was . . . handsome . . .
5. The music was . . . good . . .
6. After the show, there was . . . traffic . . .
7. There were . . . Rolls Royces in front of the theater . . .
8. There were . . . wealthy people . . .

Using What You've Learned

Giving Opinions.   What was the last movie you saw? What was your reaction to it? Briefly summarize the story and then talk about your reactions. Was it exciting? Boring? Were the characters and the plot interesting? Was the language confusing to you? In small groups, take turns reviewing movies.

Using Similes.   English has many idiomatic expressions using *as . . . as*. Does your language have similar ones? In small groups, discuss the meanings of the following expressions and compare them to expressions in your own language.

as blind as a bat   as quiet as a mouse
as free as a bird   as red as a beet
as hard as a rock   as strong as an ox
as light as a feather   as stubborn as a mule
as old as the hills   as white as a ghost (a sheet)

Comparing Activities.   What do you like to do with your free time? In pairs or in small groups, ask each other some of the following questions. Use these expressions as you discuss your own preferences: *as often (frequently) as I can, as seldom as possible, as much/little (many/few) as possible*.

1. Do you like to dance? What types of dancing do you enjoy? How often do you go dancing? Which club has the best bands?
2. Do you enjoy going to movies? How often do you go?
3. Do you like to visit museums? Do you prefer science museums, natural history museums, or art museums? How often do you go?

Comparative Adjectives

Setting the Context

previewing the passage

Describe the picture, telling the different types of food available along this street. Which do you think are inexpensive? Why do you think so?

EATING IN NEW YORK

New York is a city of extremes. The goods are better. The bads are worse. There's more of everything in New York, and above all there's more food. The restaurants are more numerous, and there are more unusual foods available in New York than anywhere else. Would you like to try Norwegian salmon,
5   Maine lobster, or Peruvian anchovies? You'll find them in New York.

There is a wider range of choices in New York. The restaurants are more varied and more plentiful. You can choose among nightclubs, the automat, bistros, street vendors, and ethnic restaurants. The ingredients may be fresher and more authentic in New York, but the prices are probably higher. And the
10   waiters are perhaps less friendly than almost anywhere else in the world!

Nevertheless, neither the prices nor the service will stop a true food lover. If you love food, New York is the place for you.

discussing ideas

What is the writer's opinion about food and restaurants in New York? In your opinion, what makes one restaurant better than another?

A. Comparative Adjectives

To compare two things, add *-er* to all one-syllable adjectives and to some two-syllable adjectives. Use *more* or *less* with other two-syllable and all longer adjectives. See pages 396–397 for spelling guidelines for *-er* endings and page 406 for a list of irregular forms.

	examples	notes
One-Syllable Adjectives	This restaurant is cheap, but the one across the street is **cheaper.**	Add *-er* to one-syllable adjectives to form the comparative.
Two-Syllable Adjectives	This café is dirty, but the other is **dirtier.** The waiters in this café are helpful, but the waiters in the place next door are much more **helpful.**	Add *-er* to most adjectives that end in *-y* to form the comparative. Other two-syllable adjectives take *more* or *less* in the comparative.
Multisyllable Adjectives	This restaurant is interesting, but the other one is much more **interesting.**	All longer adjectives take *more* or *less* in the comparative. *Much* may appear as an intensifier with either form.

 **exercise 1** After your teacher reads each adjective, give its comparative form.

examples: T: nice   T: beautiful
              S: **nicer**   S: **more beautiful**

1. lazy
2. colorful
3. pretty
4. crowded
5. tall

6. funny
7. interesting
8. noisy
9. good
10. bad

11. old
12. boring
13. happy
14. sad
15. enjoyable

B. Comparison of Nouns

The comparative form of adjectives may be used with nouns. *(Much) more, (many) more, less,* and *fewer* may also be used to compare nouns.

	examples	notes
All Nouns	This restaurant has **lower prices,** but that restaurant has **more interesting food.**	The appropriate comparative form of the adjective comes before the noun.

	examples	notes
Noncount Nouns *(more/less)*	This restaurant has **less atmosphere,** but it gives you much **more food.**	Use *less/more* with noncount nouns. *Much* may appear as an intensifier with noncount nouns.
Count Nouns *(more/fewer)*	That restaurant is crowded today. There are **many more customers** today. Yesterday there were **fewer people** in the restaurant.	In standard English, *fewer/more* is used with count nouns. *Many* may appear as an intensifier with count nouns. Note that you may use *more* with either count or non-count nouns.

 **exercise 2**   Make comparisons of a large supermarket and a farmer's market. Following the example as a model, use *more/less* with noncount nouns and *fewer/more* with count nouns.

example: people / supermarket
There are fewer people at the supermarket than at the farmer's market.

1. flowers / farmer's market
2. sunshine / supermarket
3. pets / supermarket
4. vendors / supermarket
5. variety / farmer's market

6. fresh air
7. vegetables
8. customers
9. fresh food
10. fruit

Complete the following interview with Mr. Alfred Charles, restaurant critic, with the comparative forms of the adjectives in parentheses.

INTERVIEWER: Mr. Charles, what general comments can you make about American restaurants?

MR. CHARLES: Obviously, American restaurants come in a variety of styles and sizes. Compared to most other kinds of restaurants, American fast food restaurants are <u>more boring</u> (boring). The food is always the same: hamburgers, fries, shakes, and soft drinks. On the other hand, American nightclubs that serve dinner are_____ (good) and _____ (interesting) because they can combine great food with great entertainment.

¹   ²

INTERVIEWER: Other countries are known for their fabulous restaurants. Compared to them, what is special about the United States?

MR. CHARLES: Above all, the United States offers a _____ (wide) variety of
³
restaurants. The choices are _____ (great) here. I think you can
⁴
find every type of food in the world in a city like New York, for example.

INTERVIEWER: What are your favorite kinds of foods, and where do you find them?

MR. CHARLES: My favorite dishes are Middle Eastern. Compared to American food, Middle Eastern food is _____ (flavorful), _____
⁵   ⁶
(spicy), and _____ (colorful). I find these restaurants
⁷
_____ (appealing) because the people are _____
⁸   ⁹
(cosmopolitan), the decor is _____ (exotic), and the
¹⁰
atmosphere is _____ (intimate).
¹¹

C. Comparisons with *Than*

Than may be used to compare two ideas in one sentence. *Than* may be followed by a subject and verb or a noun or pronoun.

	examples	notes
than + **Subject** and **Verb**	Joe's Café is **more expensive than** Sam's Grill is. Joe charges **higher prices than** Sam does.	A subject and verb may follow *than;* however, the verb is often omitted or the auxiliary is used instead.

	examples	notes
than + *Noun*	Joe's food is **better than** Sam's food. Joe's food is **better than** Sam's.	Possessives are often used without the noun(s) they modify.
than + *Pronoun*	Sam is not very friendly. Joe is **friendlier than** he (is). Joe is **friendlier than** him.	In formal English, a subject pronoun normally follows *than*. In conversational English, object pronouns are often used instead.

exercise 4   Use the pictures to help you complete the following comparisons.

examples: Sam's Grill is busier . . .
Sam's Grill is busier than Café Allegro (is).

The customers at Café Allegro look happier . . .
The customers at Café Allegro look happier than the customers at Sam's (do).

1. Café Allegro has nicer decorations . . .
2. Café Allegro is cleaner . . .
3. Café Allegro looks more expensive . . .
4. Sam's Grill is more crowded . . .
5. Café Allegro has a more romantic atmosphere . . .
6. Café Allegro looks more appealing . . .
7. The service at Café Allegro is better . . .
8. The customers at Sam's are spending less money . . .

 Make more comparisons of Sam's Grill and Café Allegro. Choose adjectives from the list to form sentences with the cues that follow.

messy	appealing	flavorful	spicy
expensive	intimate	exotic	bad
happy	busy	smelly	interesting
greasy	tasty	good	appetizing
formal	noisy	cheap	attractive

example: the waiter

The waiter at Sam's Grill is busier than the waiter at Café Allegro.

1. the tables
2. the food
3. the dishes
4. the atmosphere
5. the prices
6. the customers
7. the cook
8. the music

 In general, how do the eating habits of North Americans compare to those of people from your cultural background? Make sentences with *more, less,* and *fewer* using the following nouns and others of your own.

example: **Generally, people from Argentina eat *more meat than* Americans do. They also drink *less milk than* Americans do.**

vegetables	snacks	meals
rice	desserts	soda
wine	bread	tea
fruit	coffee	

D. Comparative Adverbs

Comparative forms of adverbs appear in comparisons of two actions. Add *-er* to one-syllable adverbs and *more* or *less* to almost all multisyllable adverbs to form the comparative. See pages 396–397 for spelling guidelines for *-er* endings and page 406 for a list of irregular forms.

	examples	notes
One-Syllable Adverbs	She lives **closer** to the museum than I do. I live **nearer** to campus.	One-syllable adverbs (*fast, hard, late, soon,* etc.) and *early* take *-er* in the comparative.
Multisyllable Adverbs	I go to the museum **more frequently** than she does.	All other adverbs take *more* or *less* in the comparative.

exercise 7   Change the following adjectives to adverbs. In some cases, the adverb and adjective are the same. Then, for each adverb, give the comparative form with *than*.

example: *close*_____   *closer than*_____

1. fast   _____ _____
2. late   _____ _____
3. frequent _____ _____
4. rapid   _____ _____
5. easy   _____ _____

6. casual   _____ _____
7. informal _____ _____
8. far   _____ _____
9. smooth _____ _____
10. hurried _____ _____

exercise 8   Complete the passage below and on the next page about cultural differences with the comparative forms of the adjectives and adverbs in parentheses.

CULTURAL DIFFERENCES OR PERSONAL PREFERENCES?

Do some of your classmates from other countries appear *friendlier*_____ (*more friendly*) (friendly) than others? Do some stand or sit _____
1
(close) to you than others? Do some look you in the eye _____
2
(frequently)? These may reflect cultural differences.

Do some people speak _____ (rapidly) than others? Do some talk
 ³
_____ (freely) about politics? Is it _____ (easy) for others to
 ⁴   ⁵
learn English? Not all of these differences are cultural. Some are personal, and

others may be political.

   Take, for example, North Americans and northern Europeans. Many North

Americans have European ancestry, but they have developed their own social

habits. People often think that Americans are _____ (informal) and
                                                              ⁶
Europeans are _____ (conservative), yet people of all types live on
                    ⁷
both sides of the Atlantic. It is true that many Americans talk, dress, and act

_____ (casually) than Europeans. However, some Americans dress
 ⁸
_____ (conservatively) and dine _____ (formally). No one
 ⁹   ¹⁰
can really say where cultural differences end and personal preferences begin.

Perhaps the two can never be separated.

exercise 9   Using the cues that follow, make statements about your food and eating
preferences. Use comparative adverbs.

   example: I eat fish more frequently than my friends do.

   1. use salt (often)
   2. eat (quickly / slowly)
   3. season food (heavily / lightly)
   4. dine (early / late) in the evening
   5. prefer to eat (simply / elegantly)
   6. dine (casually, formally)
   7. eat (heavily, lightly) in the evening
   8. try new kinds of food (frequently / infrequently)

exercise 10   Error Analysis.   Many of the following sentences have errors in the use of
comparisons. First identify all the mistakes. Then rewrite the sentences correctly.

                              from
   example: My brother is very different ∧ me. We don't even look alike. He is
              darker   heavier   more
         much <u>dark</u> and <u>heavy</u> than I am. He takes life ∧ seriously than I do.

         He reads much more and he studies <u>more</u> ̶h̶a̶r̶d̶e̶r̶ than I do.

   My best friend is more friendlier than I am. She also talks with people

much than me. I prefer to stay home and read or study. She is at home not so

often than me. She also likes sports more better and keeps activer. But we like

music the same amount. We both play the guitar good, but I play classical

guitar frequently than her. Even though I am quieter and more studious, she

enjoys more my company.

Using What You've Learned

Making Personal Comparisons.   Each individual is different from others in the same culture. In fact, even people in the same family differ greatly. Compare yourself to two people in your family: one who is quite similar to you and one who is very different from you. Use the following qualities to help you write at least ten sentences in total, five for each person.

> *Height:* tall, short
> *Weight:* heavy, light, fat, thin
> *Skin and hair coloring:* light, dark, etc.
> *Personality:* friendly, shy, talkative, quiet, serious, funny, easygoing, tense, etc.
> *Interests:* likes sports, keeps active, enjoys studying, reads, is artistic, dates, etc.

Making Cross-Cultural Comparisons.   Using the following list of adverbs, make several comparisons of customs in different cultures. You may want to work in pairs or in small groups.

example: Americans eat dinner earlier than people in Spain.

often	formally
slowly	far
widely	frequently
well	rapidly
smoothly	quickly
closely	easily
vigorously	intensely
hurriedly	

Here are some ideas of things you can compare:

> waving good-bye
> style of walking
> number of women in public places
> arriving late
> dining customs
> dating
> separation of sexes at family or social gatherings
> places for social communication
> conducting business or business meetings

TOPIC **three**
Superlative Forms

Setting the Context

*previewing
the
passage*
What do you do for excitement? Share your experiences while answering the following questions about the picture.

- Can you say which trip would be the most dangerous?
- Would you take any trips like these? Why or why not?

EXCITEMENT!

Everyone has different ideas about the most enjoyable way to spend free time. Some people prefer to stay at home and relax, while others enjoy leisure activities, spending their time at local clubs, museums, theaters, or sports arenas.

5 These activities may be personally rewarding for "normal" people, but they will not suit the most adventurous. The truly adventurous look for excitement. They take up sports and before long become "the best." They can ski the fastest, climb the highest mountains, run the farthest, dive the deepest.

When these people run out of possibilities close to home, they travel. Of
10 course, their trips are never ordinary! They will go to the most remote areas of

the world to find the greatest danger with the least amount of personal comfort! In fact, in recent years these thrill-seekers have made some of the most unusual trips on record. For instance, a young woman crossed the Australian desert alone, accompanied only by a few camels. Three British men
15 kayaked the length of the Nile River, braving crocodiles, hippos, and rushing water. And a group of adventurers from the United States piloted a balloon across the Atlantic Ocean.

discussing ideas

What are some other examples of unusual or exciting "leisure activities"? What are "thrill-seekers"? Do you know people like that? What are some of the most interesting or most difficult trips you have heard of?

Superlative Forms

Superlative forms of adjectives and adverbs occur in comparisons of three or more things. See pages 396–397 for spelling guidelines for *-est* endings and page 406 for a list of irregular forms.

	examples	notes
One-Syllable Adjectives and Adverbs	He is **the fastest** runner of all of us. He runs **the fastest** of all of us. She is **the hardest** worker that I have ever met. She works **the hardest** of anyone here.	One-syllable adjectives and adverbs take *-est* in the superlative. *The* normally comes before a superlative. These expressions often follow superlatives: *of all* (*of us, them,* etc.), *that I know, that I have met* (*tried, visited,* etc.)
Two-Syllable Adjectives Ending in -y	She is **the friendliest** person that I know. Her brother is **the least friendly,** though.	It is also possible to say *the most friendly,* but this form is less common. The opposite is the *least friendly.*
Other Adjectives and Adverbs	He is **the most reckless** skier that I know. He skis **the most dangerously** of anyone.	Longer adjectives and adverbs use *the most* or *the least* to form the superlative.
Nouns	He has **the fewest accidents** of any skier. He has **the least free time** of anyone.	Use *the most* or *the fewest* with count nouns. Use *the most* or *the least* with noncount nouns.

 **exercise 1** As your teacher reads the following adjectives, give their superlative forms.

> example: T: happy
> S: **the happiest**

1. quick
2. careful
3. pleasant
4. easy
5. dangerous

6. noisy
7. reckless
8. far
9. slow
10. fast

Now make any necessary changes to form the adverb, and then give the superlative form of the adverb.

> examples: T: happy
> S: **happily, the most happily**
>
> T: early
> S: **early, the earliest, the most early**

exercise 2 What unusual things could you see on an adventure? Animals? Plants? Buildings? Gems? Paintings? Consider some of the following. Tell about them by forming complete sentences with the cues. Use the example as a model.

> example: In Africa, you'll see the giraffe. (giraffe / tall animal)
> **The giraffe is the tallest animal in the world.**

1. In Africa, you'll see the African elephant. (African elephant / large land animal)
2. In Chicago, you'll see the Sears Tower. (Sears Tower / tall building)
3. In the Arctic and Antarctic, you'll see the blue whale. (blue whale / heavy animal)
4. In India, the Middle East, and Africa, you'll see the cheetah. (cheetah / fast land animal)
5. In London, you'll see the "Star of Africa" diamond. ("Star of Africa" / large diamond)
6. In the Americas, you'll see the three-toed sloth. (sloth / slow land animal)
7. In Japan, you'll see the Seikan Tunnel. (Seikan Tunnel / long tunnel)
8. In California, you'll see the bristlecone pine tree. (bristlecone pine tree / old living thing[*])

---

[*]Some bristlecone pines may be as much as 5,000 years old.

 **exercise 3**

In pairs, form questions and answers about world geography. Use the example as a model.

> **example:** hot place / El Aziziyah, Libya
> A: What is the hottest place in the world?
> B: **The hottest place in the world is El Aziziyah, Libya.**

1. low point of land / the shore of the Dead Sea
2. wet place / Tutunendo, Colombia
3. large freshwater lake / Lake Superior
4. high mountain / Mt. Everest
5. dry place / the Atacama Desert in Chile
6. cold place / Antarctica
7. long river / the Nile
8. deep canyon / the Colca River Canyon in Peru

 **exercise 4**

What can you do for excitement? Some people find their excitement in being the best (or worst) at something. The following is a list of some unusual world records from *The Guinness Book of World Records*. Using superlative adverbs, make questions and responses from the following cues.

> **example:** dive / far
> Mexican / 118 feet
> A: **Who dove the farthest?**
> B: **A Mexican. He dove 118 feet.**[*]

1. throw a boomerang / far
   Australian / 375 feet
2. whistle / loud
   Englishman / 122.5 decibels
3. jump / high
   American / 7 feet $7\frac{1}{4}$ inches ($23\frac{1}{4}$ inches above his head)
4. dive / deep
   Italian woman / 351 feet (without scuba equipment)
5. drive / badly
   seventy-five-year-old American
   (In twenty minutes, he got ten traffic tickets, drove on the wrong side of the street four times, and had four hit-and-run offenses.)
6. sail a boat / fast
   Frenchman / at 41.68 miles per hour
7. travel / much
   American / to all sovereign countries and all but six nonsovereign or other territories
8. reign / long
   the king of Swaziland / for 82 years

---

[*]Professional divers in Acapulco, Mexico, regularly make this dive.

Some people will try anything for excitement, even if it hurts! Form superlative adjectives or adverbs from the list (or add your own) to describe Harry's exploits. Try not to use the same form of any word more than once.

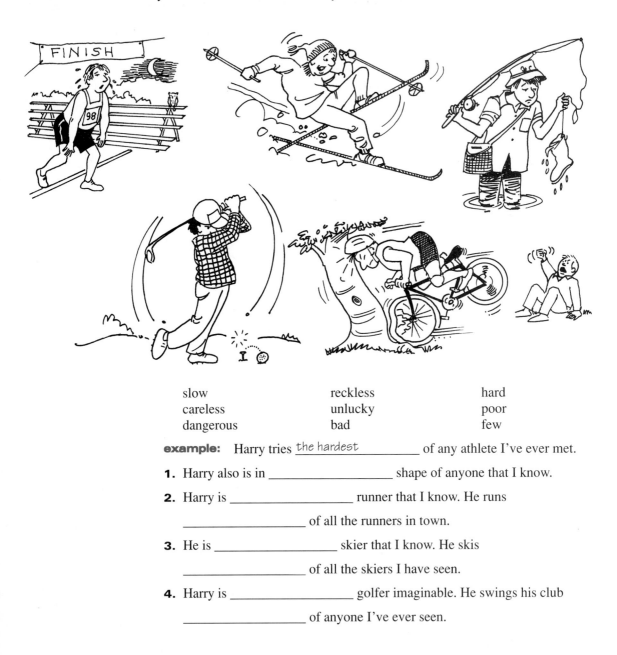

slow	reckless	hard
careless	unlucky	poor
dangerous	bad	few

example: Harry tries _the hardest_____ of any athlete I've ever met.

1. Harry also is in _____ shape of anyone that I know.

2. Harry is _____ runner that I know. He runs

_____ of all the runners in town.

3. He is _____ skier that I know. He skis

_____ of all the skiers I have seen.

4. Harry is _____ golfer imaginable. He swings his club

_____ of anyone I've ever seen.

5. Harry is the _____ bicyclist that I have ever seen. He rides his bike _____ of anyone I know.

6. Poor Harry! He's _____ fisherman I know. In fact, he catches _____ fish of anyone I've ever met!

exercise 6 Complete the following passage about driving using the superlative forms of the words in parentheses.

DRIVING

In many countries around the world, driving is one of
<u>the most dangerous</u> (dangerous) activities of all. In Central America, you

may have _____ (much) trouble with other drivers who want
₁

to race while they are passing you. _____ (easy) and
₂

_____ (good) way to deal with those drivers is to ignore them!
₃

In South Asia, the people who drive _____ (dangerously)
₄

are the ones who force you off the road because they refuse to get off the

narrow center strip. Other problems on these narrow roads are truck drivers

with _____ (large) loads imaginable. They speed down
₅

mountain roads in _____ (reckless) way, seemingly without
₆

_____ (little) care for their own safety. They must be quite
₇

skilled because a traveler seldom sees accidents there.

Around the Mediterranean, pedestrians have _____ (many)
₈

problems with cars, perhaps. A pedestrian has to be _____
₉

(careful) when the traffic is _____ (heavy) because drivers
₁₀

often use the sidewalk to pass!

exercise 7

Review. Complete the following paragraphs with the positive (simple), comparative, or superlative form of the words in parentheses. Be sure to add *the* when necessary.

1. The <u>fastest</u> (fast) way to get anywhere is certainly by plane. The Supersonic Transport (SST), for example, is so <u>fast</u> (fast) that a person can travel from New York to Paris and back in one day! However, many people don't like flying. To them, traveling by plane is _____ (comfortable) way to go anywhere. A long plane ride is _____ (bad) than staying home!

2. Flying used to be _____ (expensive) way to travel, but now most cruise ships are even _____ (expensive) than planes. Ships are not as _____ (fast) as planes, but they are much _____ (comfortable), and the food is _____ (good) because it doesn't have to be prepared ahead of time. Ships are also not as _____ (crowded) as planes, and there are _____ (many) things to do during a cruise than during a plane flight.

3. Most people agree that _____ (good) way to travel is by car because it is _____ (restricting). You can go whenever you want. It isn't as _____ (cheap) as a train, as _____ (fast) as a plane, or as _____ (luxurious) as a ship, but most people prefer car travel because it offers them _____ (much) freedom.

Using What You've Learned

activity 1

Reporting Records. What "unusual records" has your class set? First, separate into small groups and think of a topic such as sports, food, music, study habits, or clothing. Then write five questions to gather information from your classmates.

example: (food)
How many hamburgers have you eaten in one day (week)?
How long have you ever gone without eating? What is the most expensive meal you've ever had?

Rank the information that you gather according to *the most, the least, the fastest, the longest,* etc. Finally, give a report on the "unusual records" set by your class-mates.

activity **2**   **Describing Adventures.**   Where would you go to find adventure? Choose one of the places from Exercise 3 (page 269) or think of another place. Tell why you would go to the hottest, coldest, highest, etc., place on earth.

activity **3**   **Describing People.**   Who is the laziest person you know? The most energetic? Who drives the most recklessly? The most carefully? Who has the worst luck? The best luck? Tell your classmates a little about your family or friends, describing their best and worst sides! Use the following adjectives to help you.

smart	careful	athletic
energetic	funny	hardworking
boring	lucky	nice
intelligent	cheerful	nervous
tense	grouchy	dangerous
thoughtful		

TOPIC **four**
Review

Setting the Context

previewing the passage   What is body language? Share your ideas and information by answering these questions.

COMMUNICATING WITHOUT WORDS

We communicate a great deal without ever opening our mouths. Because we speak with our eyes, gestures, and expressions, our body language is an extremely important part of communication. Some researchers say that as much as sixty percent of communication is nonverbal. Nonverbal communica-
5 tion is not the same everywhere, however. Although we all use it, we may use body language in very different ways. This is because each culture has its own "unwritten rules" about appropriate gestures, eye contact, and so on. Thus, learning another language must involve the body language of that culture. Otherwise, you're learning less than half of the language.

discussing ideas   What are *unwritten rules*? Can you give some examples involving body language?

Review. Complete the following with appropriate present forms of the verbs in parentheses. In some cases, more than one tense is possible. You can also add appropriate modal auxiliaries.

1. Whenever you _visit_____ (visit) another country, you _____ (need) to learn the unwritten rules of that country. Many unwritten rules _____ (involve) time, space, eating, and driving, for example. Two of the best ways to learn the unwritten rules _____ (be) to watch people and to ask questions.

2. In some countries, when you _____ (finish) eating, you _____ (put) your silverware on your plate. In others, you _____ (place) your napkin on the table. What _____ people _____ (do) where you _____ (live) now? In some places, people _____ (talk) very little while they _____ (eat). In other places, people _____ (think) that you _____ (be) rude if you _____ (not talk). How about where you _____ (live) now?

3. What _____ you _____ (do) if you _____ (drive) a car and you _____ (arrive) at an intersection at the same time as another car? Which car _____ (go) first? It _____ (depend) on where you _____ (live) or _____ (visit). In the U.S., the car to the right _____ (go) first.

4. How _____ people _____ (form) lines? For example, how _____ people _____ (make) lines in a bank or at a bus stop? And what _____ people _____ (do) while they _____ (wait) in line? _____ they _____ (talk) to each other or not?

5. How _____ people _____ (behave) in elevators? _____ (be) everyone silent? If people _____ (talk), what _____ they _____ (talk) about?

exercise 2 **Review.** Complete the following with appropriate past forms of the verbs in parentheses.

1. When Ali _came_____ (come) to Canada from Kuwait, he _____ (study / already) a lot of English. He _____ (speak) quite well and _____ (understand) almost everything. However, he _____ (have / often) difficulties in conversation, sometimes with Canadians and often with people from other countries. He _____ (find) it especially difficult to speak with Asians. For example, while he _____ (talk) with a classmate from Asia, the person _____ (begin) to move away from him. He _____ (feel) that the person _____ (not like) him. After this _____ (happen) several times, Ali _____ (ask) another Kuwaiti about the problem. His friend _____ (laugh) and _____ (explain). In general, Kuwaitis stand close to someone in a conversation, but Asians do not. The problem _____ (not be) a dislike of Ali, but rather a difference in "personal space."

2. When Maria _____ (move) to the United States from Italy, she _____ (have) some problems with gestures. One day, she _____ (see) a friend while she _____ (walk) to class. Her friend _____ (make) a hand gesture, and Maria _____ (think) that it _____ (mean) "Come here." She _____ (run / quickly) over to her friend. Her friend _____ (laugh) and _____ (tell) Maria that _____ (be) the gesture for "Good-bye." Her friend _____ (wave) "good-bye," not signaling Maria to come. The gesture for "Come here" in Italy and "Good-bye" in the U.S. are almost the same.

Review. Have you had any particular problems in communicating? Tell about them by answering the questions below. Use the phrasal combinations in your answers.

example: Do you have specific problems when you listen to native speakers?
Whenever I listen to native speakers, I have a lot of problems with slang.

1. What problems do you have when you listen to native speakers?
2. What problems do you have when you talk to native speakers?
3. Are you confused about specific words or expressions? Which ones?
4. How do you feel when you call up someone and have to speak in English on the phone?
5. In your opinion, what is the most interesting thing about communicating among different cultures?
6. What is the most annoying thing, in your opinion?
7. In general, how do people from your culture differ from people where you live now?
8. Pick out one difference that particularly bothers you or interests you and describe it in more detail.

exercise 4

Review. These charts give some general cultural differences in body language. Use this information with the cues that follow to form sentences with comparative adverbs. Write three sentences for each one.

Distance

close together ⟵ ⟶ far apart

Middle Easterners	South Americans	Northern Europeans

Eye Contact

infrequent ⟵ ⟶ frequent

Asians	Northern Europeans	North Americans	Middle Easterners

Gestures

slowly ⟵ ⟶ rapidly

Asians	Northern Europeans	North Americans	South Americans	Southern Europeans

example: stand

Middle Easterners stand closer together than South Americans do.

1. stand
2. look into other people's eyes
3. move their hands (arms, etc.)

 **exercise 5**   **Review.**   Using the cues that follow, make five general statements about behavior in your culture. Then compare your own personal style or preferences to your generalization about your culture.

example: eaters (fast / slow)

In general, Venezuelans are fast eaters. I am a much slower eater than most people from my country.

1. eat (slowly / rapidly)
2. talk (slowly / rapidly)
3. talkers (slow / rapid)
4. stand / sit (close to / far from) other people
5. make gestures (frequently / infrequently)
6. use facial expressions (frequently / infrequently)
7. argue (more / less frequently)
8. speak (loudly / softly)
9. dress (colorfully / conservatively)
10. dressers (colorful / conservative)

exercise 6   **Review.**   First, read the following passage for meaning. Then, complete it with appropriate connecting words. Choose from these: *although, and, as a result, because, but, for example, if, in addition, than.* Finally, try to suggest any other connecting words that may be appropriate.

CULTURE, PERSONALITY, AND COMMUNICATION

Communication involves words, _____ but _____ it also involves many other things. Our nonverbal messages are also very important.

_____ we speak with our eyes, gestures, and movements, our
                    1
body language plays a major role in communication. In fact, according to some experts, we communicate more _____ sixty percent of our
                                                    2
messages through body language.

Our culture determines at least some of our body language.

_____, communication between people from different coun-
tries may be complicated _____ neither is aware of the body

language of the other. _____, a South American prefers more

eye contact _____ speaks more rapidly _____

a North American. He or she also uses gestures more frequently. In the Middle

East, people stand nearer to each other _____ North

Americans are accustomed to. _____, they often touch each

other during a conversation, _____ North Americans do not.

Differences like these can create problems in communication. Sometimes,

_____ they may not understand why, people from different

cultures feel uncomfortable during conversations. Such feelings may even

cause distrust or disapproval. _____ this happens to you, you

should pay attention to body language—both yours and the person you're

with. Words may not be the problem. The problem may be body language.

Using What You've Learned

Using Body Language.   Think of an unusual gesture or facial expression from
your culture (but don't explain it). Then, your teacher will ask for volunteers. If
you want, go to the front of the room and stand or sit, depending on what you
want to show. Demonstrate your example of body language for the class, and see
if the class can guess its meaning. Work with another volunteer, if necessary. Be
creative and try to think of ways of standing, sitting, or moving that send a particular message.

Review of Problem Areas from Chapters Five to Eight

A variety of problem areas are included in this test. Check your understanding by completing the sample items below.

Part 1.   Circle the correct completion for the following.

example: My friend is _____ learning French.
- **a.** interesting in
- **b.** interested
- **c.** interested in
- **d.** interest in

1. After the movie _____, they decided to get something to eat.
   - **a.** have finished
   - **b.** has finished
   - **c.** finishes
   - **d.** had finished

2. If John _____ the situation, he will certainly try to help.
   - **a.** understands
   - **b.** will understand
   - **c.** is going to understand
   - **d.** is understanding

3. While we were getting on the train, we _____ a robbery take place.
   - **a.** were seeing
   - **b.** saw
   - **c.** had seen
   - **d.** have seen

4. Please try to arrive as _____.
   - **a.** quick as you can.
   - **b.** quicker than you can.
   - **c.** more quickly as you can.
   - **d.** quickly as you can.

5. _____ it rains very hard, the stream overflows.
   - **a.** Whenever
   - **b.** Before
   - **c.** Although
   - **d.** As a result

Part 2: Circle the letter below in the word(s) containing an error.

example: In general, people use <u>many more</u> vocabulary in written
              A   Ⓑ
          language <u>than</u> they <u>do</u> in daily conversation.
               C   D

1. Bicycles are <u>very efficient</u> <u>that</u> they make perfect <u>use</u> of
                  A   B   C
the muscles of <u>the</u> legs.
            D

2. It is <u>often</u> said that people from <u>East Asia</u> use <u>less</u> gestures <u>than</u> people
       A   B   C   D
from the Mediterranean.

3. By 1885, hunters <u>had kill</u> <u>almost all</u> of the millions of buffalo of <u>the</u>
  A   B   C   D
Great Plains.

4. More than seven million Germans <u>has immigrated</u> <u>to</u> the United States
                                 A   B
<u>since</u> the first families <u>arrived</u> in 1683.
  C   D

5. <u>The</u> Atacama Desert in Chile is <u>the most</u> driest place on <u>earth</u>; in fact,
  A   B   C
areas exist where no measurable rain has fallen <u>decades</u>.
                                                   D

CHAPTER nine

Discoveries

The Passive Voice

Topic One: The Passive Voice with Simple Tenses
Topic Two: The Passive Voice with the Present Perfect Tense
Topic Three: The Passive Voice with the Present Continuous Tense
Topic Four: The Passive Voice with Modal Auxiliaries

The Passive Voice with Simple Tenses

Setting the Context

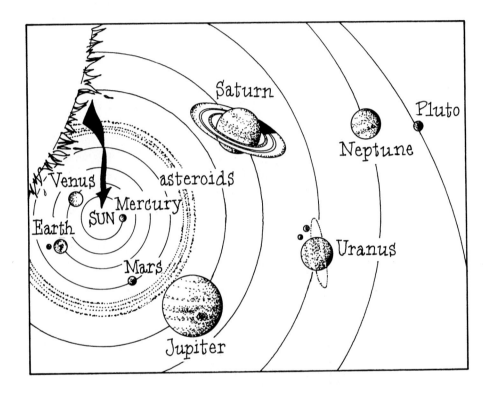

What do you know about our solar system? Share your ideas and opinions by answering these questions about the picture.

- What is the center of our solar system?
- How many planets are there in our solar system?
- Do the planets and moons move? To your knowledge, how long have we known this about our solar system?

For centuries, it was believed that the Earth was the center of the universe and that every object in the sky revolved around it. These beliefs were not changed easily. In the 1500s, Copernicus suggested that the sun was the center of the universe, but few people listened to him. Later in 1609, Galileo
5 defended Copernicus' theory. Through his use of a telescope, Galileo realized that the Earth was only one of several planets that revolved around the sun. Because he stated this publicly, Galileo was sent to prison in 1633.

Since Galileo's time, astronomers have made tremendous advances in our knowledge of the universe. Today, we know that the Earth is one of nine plan-
10 ets that orbit the sun. Our galaxy, the Milky Way, is made up of over two hundred billion stars like our sun. The universe is filled with millions of similar galaxies and countless other extraterrestrial objects.

discussing ideas

Through most of history, what was believed about the Earth and the universe? What do we know differently today? Who proved that the sun was the center of our solar system? What happened to him? Why?

A. Introduction to the Passive Voice

The passive voice occurs in both spoken and written English, and it is used very frequently in technical writing. Most verbs that take an object can be used in the passive voice. In sentences in the active voice, the primary focus is on the subject (the *agent* or doer of the action). To give primary focus to the object of the sentence, the sentence can be changed to the passive voice. Compare:

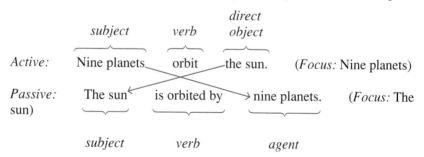

In this section, you will study the passive form of simple present and past tense verbs. Later in the chapter, you will cover other tenses and modal auxiliaries. In all cases, the verb forms have the same time frame in the

B. The Passive Voice with the Simple Present and Simple Past Tenses

To form the passive voice, use *be* + the past participle of the main verb. For the simple present tense, use *am, is,* or *are* + past participle. For the simple past tense, use *was* or *were* + past participle. The passive voice subject determines whether the verb *be* is singular or plural. The agent can be included in the passive sentence in a phrase with *by.*

	active	passive
Simple Present Tense	Nine planets **orbit** the sun. Moons **orbit** some of the planets.	The sun **is orbited** by nine planets. Some of the planets **are orbited** by moons.
Simple Past Tense	The Dutch **invented** a simple telescope. The Italians later **developed** several telescopes.	A simple telescope **was invented** by the Dutch. Several telescopes **were** later **developed** by the Italians.

Note: The following verb and preposition combinations are frequently used in the passive voice. *By* + agent is not normally used; instead, other prepositions follow these verbs.

verbs and prepositions	examples
be based on	The movie **was based on** the book.
be composed of	The moon **is not composed of** green cheese.
be involved in	She**'s involved in** a difficult situation.
be known for	He**'s known for** his great sense of humor.
be made from	Steel **is made from** iron ore.
be made up of	Our class **is made up of** people from many places.
be noted for	Miki **is noted for** her kindness and generosity.
be related to	**Are** you **related to** Karen Muse?
be used for	Machines **are used for** measuring distances in space.
be used to	Machines **are used to** measure distances in space.

Other participle and preposition combinations include verbs of emotion such as *bore (be bored with), interest (be interested in),* and so on. See Chapters Five and Eight for more information on these.

exercise 1 Which of the following sentences are in the active voice (A), and which are in the passive voice (P)? Label each. Then label the subject (S), verb (V), object (O), and/or agent (A) in each sentence. Finally, tell the primary focus of the sentence.

> example: ___A___ Galileo invented one of the first telescopes in 1609.
>   *Focus:* Galileo
>
>   ___P___ One of the first telescopes was invented by Galileo in 1609.
>   *Focus:* One of the first telescopes

1. _____ The first telescopic maps of the moon were drawn by Thomas Harriot in 1609. _____

2. _____ Johannes Kepler invented the first astronomical telescope in 1611. _____

3. _____ The former Soviet Union began the "Space Age" when it launched the first space satellite. _____

4. _____ The first space satellite, Sputnik, was launched by the former Soviet Union in 1957. _____

5. _____ In 1969, Apollo 11 reached the moon, and two Americans touched the moon's surface for the first time. _____

6. _____ In 1990, a giant telescope was launched into space by the United States. _____

7. _____ This telescope orbits the earth. _____

8. _____ The telescope is used by scientists to "see" far into the universe. _____

exercise 2 Form passive sentences from the following cues. Use the simple present tense.

> example: the sun / orbit / by nine planets
> **The sun is orbited by nine planets.**

1. some planets / orbit / by moons
2. Jupiter / orbit / 16 moons
3. the universe / fill / with many galaxies
4. astronauts / send / into space to learn more about the universe
5. high-powered telescopes / use / to study other galaxies
6. new discoveries about the universe / make / every year

exercise 3   Underline the direct object in each of the following sentences. Then use the direct object as the subject and change the sentences from the active voice to the passive voice. Pay attention to verb tenses.

> **example:**   Scientists around the world study <u>the moon</u>.
> **The moon is studied by scientists around the world.**

1. The moon reflects sunlight.
2. The reflection of sunlight produces moonlight.
3. Large craters cover the moon's surface.
4. Volcanos made some of the craters.
5. Meteors probably caused other craters.
6. Most small telescopes reveal the details of the moon's surface.

exercise 4   Complete the following passage about the moon with either present or past passive forms of the verbs in parentheses.

THE DISTANCE TO THE MOON

     The distance to the moon <u>was calculated</u> (calculate) long ago when

measurements _____ (make) by ancient astronomers.
₁

Observations _____ (take) from two different places on the
₂

ground. The moon and these two locations on the Earth formed a triangle. This

imaginary triangle _____ (use) by ancient astronomers to
₃

calculate the real distance to the moon.

     Although this method was fairly accurate, it _____ (not
₄

use) anymore. Today, laser beams _____ (use) instead. In the
₅

1970s, mirrors _____ (place) on the surface of the moon. Now,
₆

laser beams from the Earth _____ (reflect) by the mirrors, and
₇

the moon's position _____ (measure) to the nearest few
₈

centimeters. Its average distance from Earth is 384,000 kilometers (equal to

traveling around the Earth ten times).

C. Uses of *By* + Agent

> *By* + noun (or pronoun) can be used in a passive voice sentence to tell who or what performed the action of a verb. Use *by* + agent with new or important information.

	examples	notes
Active	Galileo first **used** the telescope in astronomy.	The subject *Galileo* is important to the sentence. It cannot be omitted from the passive sentence.
Passive	The telescope **was** first **used** in astronomy **by Galileo.**	

Many passive sentences do not include *by* + agent. Do *not* use *by* + agent with information that is obvious or unimportant.

	examples	notes
Active	People **make** telescopes with a series of lenses.	The subject *people* is obvious. It is not important to the sentence. It can be omitted from the passive sentence.
Passive	Telescopes **are made** ~~by people~~ with a series of lenses.	

exercise 5  In the following sentences about the solar system, decide whether you can leave out *by* + agent without changing the meaning of the sentence.

example: The sun is orbited by nine planets.
The phrase with **by** must be used in this sentence.

1. Until recently, little was known by scientists about the closest planet to the sun, Mercury.
2. Mercury is rarely seen by people because it is often obscured by the sun.
3. The planet Venus is covered by a heavy atmosphere.
4. Radar is used by scientists to get information about the surface of Venus.
5. Seventy-one percent of the earth's surface is covered by water.
6. For a long time, it was believed by people that Mars was inhabited by little green men.
7. *The War of the Worlds,* a story about a Martian invasion, was written by H. G. Wells in 1898.
8. No life was found on Mars by the Mariner space missions.

Saturn · December 1, 1994
Hubble Space Telescope · Wide Field Planetary Camera 2

Change the following sentences from the active to the passive voice. Decide whether the agent is necessary. If it is, include it in a phrase with *by*.

example: Nine planets orbit the sun.

The sun is orbited by nine planets. (**By nine planets** *is necessary to the meaning of the sentence.*)

1. Sixteen moons orbit Jupiter.
2. Galileo discovered the four largest moons.
3. Christian Huygens first saw Saturn's rings in 1655.
4. William Herschel identified Uranus on March 13, 1781.
5. Astronomers found many irregularities in the orbit of Uranus.
6. Astronomers calculated the size of Neptune before anyone saw it.
7. Clyde Tombaugh discovered Pluto in February, 1930.
8. Astronomers use powerful telescopes to observe Pluto.

D. *It* with the Passive Voice

It is sometimes used with the passive voice to avoid naming the agent or source of the information. This construction is often used with verbs such as *believe, feel, hope, report, say,* and *think*. A clause with *that* follows the verb.

active	passive
People believed that the Earth was the center of the universe.	**It was believed that** the Earth was the center of the universe.
Some people thought that everything revolved around the Earth.	**It was thought that** everything revolved around the Earth.

 **exercise 7** The following statements were once believed to be true. Now they have been disproven. Change the quotations to the past. Begin each statement with, "It was believed (said, thought, etc.). . . ."

> **examples:** "The earth is flat."
> **It was believed that the earth was flat.**

1. "The moon is made of green cheese."
2. "Little green men live on Mars."
3. "The stars are holes in the sky."
4. "The Earth is the center of the universe."
5. "A comet in space causes bad luck on Earth."
6. "Meteors are stars falling from the sky."

 **exercise 8** Complete the following passage on the exploration of the moon with active or passive past tense forms of the verbs in parentheses.

EXPLORING SPACE

During the 1960s, the first spaceships _were sent_ (send) to the moon. These American spaceships _____ (call) Rangers. Each spaceship _____ (carry) six television cameras. Each ship _____ (design) to send back pictures to Earth just before it _____ (crash) on the moon. The first six missions _____ (end) in failure. Finally, a Ranger _____ (reach) its goal in 1963. People on Earth _____ (watch) the first "live" TV pictures from the moon. Between July of 1964 and March of 1965, 17,000 pictures of the lunar surface _____ (send) back to Earth.

From 1966 to 1968, ten spaceships _____ (launch) to land on the moon or to orbit it. Then on July 20, 1969, humans _____ (touch) the moon for the first time. On that historic day, Neil Armstrong and Edwin Aldrin _____ (walk) on the lunar surface. Between December of 1968 and December of 1972, twenty-four people _____ (send) to the moon. Twelve actually _____ (walk) on the moon's surface.

Using What You've Learned

activity 1

Describing Equipment and Processes.   Every type of work has equipment that is helpful or necessary in order to do the job. For example, a thermometer and a blood-pressure gauge are important equipment to a doctor or nurse. A balance sheet is important to an accountant. A tennis racket is absolutely necessary for a tennis player. In pairs or in small groups, think of equipment that is important in a hobby or field that you are interested in. Use the following questions to help you describe the equipment.

1. When and where was it developed?
2. What is it made of?
3. How is it made?
4. How is it used?

Give a brief (two-to-four minute) presentation, individually or as a group. Then save your notes to use in the activity at the end of Topic Two.

activity 2

Explaining Beliefs and Superstitions.   Most cultures have traditional beliefs or customs regarding the moon, the planets, the stars, the weather, and so forth. Some are superstitions, but others may be true. What beliefs or superstitions are common in your culture? In groups or as a class, share them. Try to list four or five beliefs each.

examples: **In my culture, it's believed that the full moon makes people crazy.**
For a long time, it was believed that eclipses were signs from God.

activity 3

Learning More About Your Classmates.   In pairs or small groups, practice using the passive voice by asking and answering the following questions. Be sure to write down the most interesting answers. Then, come together as a class and compare notes.

- What is your hometown best known for?
- What personality types is your family composed of? (For example, serious people, funny ones, ones who take many risks, and so on)
- In your family, what are you especially noted for? (For example, for being a hard worker, for talking a lot, and so on)
- Are you related to anyone famous (or infamous)?
- Are you involved in any special political, social, or environmental groups?
- Are you involved in any special research or projects right now?

The Passive Voice with the Present Perfect Tense

Setting the Context

What do you know about our galaxy? Share your ideas and opinions by answering these questions about the picture.

- What is the name of our galaxy?
- Is our galaxy unique? How do we know this?

NEW DISCOVERIES

   Much has been learned about our universe since the time of Copernicus and Galileo, but most of the discoveries have been made during this century. During the last several decades, powerful telescopes, satellites, and spaceships have been developed. Through these advances in technology, many of the
5 mysteries of the universe have been solved.
   Until sixty years ago, it was believed that our galaxy, the Milky Way, was unique. It was believed that our galaxy *was* the universe. In recent years, through improved technology, these ideas and many others have been disproven. It has been estimated that trillions of galaxies like our own fill the
10 universe. The universe itself is calculated to be between fifteen and eighteen billion years old.

Who has made these recent discoveries? What new space technology has been developed? What is now known about the age and size of the universe?

The Passive Voice with the Present Perfect Tense

To form the passive voice of the present perfect tense, use *has* or *have + been* + past participle. The passive voice subject determines whether the verb is singular or plural.

	active	passive
Present Perfect Tense	The Soviet Union **has launched** many spaceships. Scientists **have improved** technology.	Spaceships **have been launched** by the Soviet Union. Technology **has been improved.**

 **exercise 1** Underline all verbs in the present perfect tense, passive voice, in the passage "New Discoveries" on the previous page. In each case, try to tell who or what the agent of the action was.

 **exercise 2** Change the following sentences from the active voice to the passive voice. Omit the agent to avoid repetition.

example: Astronomers have learned much about the universe.
Much has been learned about the universe.

1. Astronomers have discovered new stars.
2. Astronomers have designed powerful new telescopes.
3. Astronomers have launched spaceships.
4. Astronomers have sent astronauts into space.
5. Astronomers have photographed the solar system.
6. Astronomers have mapped many parts of the sky.
7. Astronomers have measured the distance from the sun to each of the planets.
8. Astronomers have calculated distances throughout the universe.

 **exercise 3** Colonel Mariko Kanno of Aerospace Control Central is reading a checklist to an astronaut in a spaceship that is about to be launched. In pairs, take turns asking and answering questions based on the following cues. For your answers, use "abbreviated" speech. That is, use the past participle as an affirmative answer.

example: speed / calculate
A: **Has the speed been calculated?**
B: **Calculated!**

This is Control Central to Moonbeam. This is our final checklist.

1. computers / program
2. rockets / test
3. windows / close
4. oil / check
5. radar / set
6. food / load
7. doors / lock
8. engines / start

 **exercise 4**   Colonel Kanno is giving a talk about Operation Moonbean. Complete it with either the active or passive form of the present perfect tense of the verbs in parentheses.

"Good morning. I am here today to announce our newest space program, Operation Moonbeam. We _have completed_ (complete) plans for a space colony on the moon. At this point, all the necessary technology _____ (develop). A spaceship _____ (build) to carry the astronauts and their equipment.

"In addition, a dome _____ (construct) to cover a small part of the moon's surface. Machines _____ (design) to 'produce' weather. With the help of these machines, we _____ (produce) wind and rain.

"We _____ (begin / also) to select astronauts for this mission. To date, twenty members of the team _____ (choose) by our staff. So far, one physicist, five biologists, four chemists, and ten astronomers _____ (select). We _____ (include) both single people and married couples. But there will be no children on this first mission.

"Are there any questions?"

exercise 5

In small groups, choose one person to "be" Colonel Kanno. Ask "her" questions about the upcoming Operation Moonbeam. Form questions from the cues following, using the passive voice in the present perfect tense. Then add some questions of your own. "Colonel Kanno" will have to use his or her imagination for some of the information for the answers.

example: How many spaceships / build?
A: **How many spaceships have been built?**
B: **Ten spaceships have been built.**

1. pilots of the spaceships / train?
2. what kinds of safety measures / take?
3. special clothing / design?
4. special food / develop?
5. the weather dome / test?
6. colony managers / choose carefully?
7. what kind of entertainment / plan for the colonists?
8. the space station / check for safety?

exercise 6

The following passage gives you information on star formation. First, read the passage for meaning, checking any vocabulary that may be difficult for you. Then complete it with simple past, simple present, or present perfect tense, active or passive, of the verbs in parentheses. In some cases, more than one tense is appropriate. Try to give all possibilities.

STAR FORMATION

Gas and dust _exist_____ (exist) throughout space, and new stars

_are formed___ (form) from this gas and dust. First, gas and dust

_____ (form) a sphere or ball, and the "ball" _____ (begin) to

rotate. When the pressure and temperature _____ (rise) inside the

"ball," it _____ (begin) to produce radiant energy—light. At this

point, the "ball" _____ (become) a star.

Young and middle-aged stars _____ (fuel) by the burning of
hydrogen. Radiant energy _____ (produce) when hydrogen
_____ (burn). During this nuclear reaction, mass _____
(change) into energy.

After the hydrogen _____ (use up), the star _____ (begin)
a different nuclear reaction. Heavier elements _____ (burn) until all
sources of fuel _____ (exhaust). At that point, smaller stars
_____ (burn out) and _____ (collapse). Medium-sized stars,
on the other hand, _____ (explode) in a fiery death. Giant stars
_____ (collapse). They _____ (become) "black holes."

When the universe _____ (form), only hydrogen and helium
_____ (exist). Everything else in our universe _____
(compose) of heavier elements that _____ (create) by star explosions.
These star explosions, which _____ (burn) brighter than a billion
stars, _____ (call) supernovas. Our planet and all of its continents,
seas, and living things _____ (form) from the gas and dust that
_____ (leave) in space by the explosion of nearby dying stars.

Using What You've Learned

Describing Equipment and Processes.   Use the information and notes that you
prepared for Activity 1 in Topic One on page 290 to plan a follow-up presentation.
Again, you may do this individually or in small groups. Give more detailed information, including the following:

1. Give a brief summary of your first presentation.
   a. When and where was the equipment developed?
   b. Who developed it?

2. Now give information on the changes that have taken place?
   a. How has this equipment been improved?
   b. Why have these improvements been made?
   c. How have they changed the way the equipment is used?

Finally, use all of this information to write a short composition on your topic.

The Passive Voice with the Present Continuous Tense

Setting the Context

*previewing
the
passage*

Do you enjoy science-fiction movies or books? Share your ideas and opinions by answering these questions about the picture.

- What kind of story is the man going to write?
- Have you read stories like these?

SPACE-AGE TECHNOLOGY

Only a few years ago, science-fiction writers were writing amazing stories about spaceships, ray guns, robots, and satellites. Even more amazing: today these things are no longer part of science fiction. They exist, and they are being used!

5   Today, spaceships are being launched regularly. The space shuttle is being perfected. Satellites are being sent into orbit to beam radio, television, and telephone signals worldwide. Space stations are being designed. And lasers, powerful rays of directed light, are being used in all areas of high technology.

    Yesterday's science fiction has become today's reality. Perhaps today's
10 science fiction will be tomorrow's reality. It is not impossible!

What type of space exploration is taking place today? Did some science-fiction writers predict this activity?

The Passive Voice with the Present Continuous Tense

To form the passive voice of the present continuous tense, use *am, is,* or *are* + *being* + past participle. The passive voice subject determines whether the verb *be* is singular or plural.

	active	passive
Present Continuous Tense	The Soviet Union **is sending** ships into outer space. Researchers **are launching** a new rocket today.	Ships **are being sent** into outer space. A new rocket **is being launched** today.

exercise 1

First underline all the examples of *by* + agent in the following sentences. Then change them from the passive to active voice. If a sentence does not have an agent, use *scientists* as the active subject.

> **example:** New discoveries are being made almost daily. (no agent)
> *Scientists are making new discoveries almost daily.*

1. Joint research projects are being developed by several countries.
2. Jets are being designed to fly above the atmosphere.
3. Communication satellites are being used by many countries.
4. Space shuttles are being tested.
5. Computer technology is being improved.
6. Space colonies are being planned by many countries.
7. Spaceships are being launched.
8. Robots are being programmed to run spaceships.

exercise 2

Form passive statements from the following cues.

> **example:** food / load
> **The food is being loaded.**

1. control panel / check
2. computers / program
3. radar / set
4. radio / test
5. doors / close
6. climate control / adjust
7. engines / start
8. ship / launch

Complete the following conversation with either the active or passive voice, in the present continuous tense.

Ladies and gentlemen. Operation Moonbeam is being prepared for take-off. At this moment...

OM: Operation Moonbeam to Control Central. We <u>are beginning</u> (begin) our descent to the moon! Can you hear us?

CC: Operation Moonbeam, this is Control Central. We hear you loud and clear! In fact, your voices _____ (hear) by people around the world. People
everywhere _____ (watch) you make history!

1

2

OM: I'm sure everyone wants to know what we _____ (do) right now. At the
moment, the ship _____ (prepare) for landing. The spacesuits and
oxygen equipment _____ (test) one last time, and the shuttle
_____ (check)—just in case. We _____ (plan) to spend an hour
on the ground before we actually get off the ship.

3

4

5

6

7

CC: Could you describe the scene for us, please? I am sure that everyone
_____ (look) forward to a full description.

8

OM: Better yet, you will have pictures in a moment. Right now pictures
_____ (transmit) directly to you. These pictures_____ (take) by
special cameras on the spaceship. The cameras_____ (take) over fifty
pictures a minute.

9

10

11

CC: Operation Moonbeam, we will let you return to your landing preparations, and we will give the TV audience a chance to see these fascinating pictures. Over and out. . . .

exercise 4   **Review.**   The following passage gives you information on Sputnik, the first satellite in space. First, read the passage for meaning, checking any vocabulary that may be difficult for you. Then complete it with active or passive forms of the verbs in parentheses. Choose from the simple present, simple past, present perfect, or present continuous tenses.

THE RACE TO SPACE

On October 4, 1957, a 187-pound sphere (83.6 kilograms) <u>was sent</u> (send) into orbit. It <u>carried</u> (carry) a radio transmitter and enough batteries for two weeks. It _____ (launch) into orbit by the former Soviet Union. This satellite _____ (know) as "Sputnik."

    Sputnik _____ (not be) very sophisticated, but it _____ (show) the technology of the Soviets. Sputnik _____ (not carry) any scientific equipment, and it _____ (not take) any measurements in space. Nevertheless, a satellite _____ (be) in orbit for the first time,

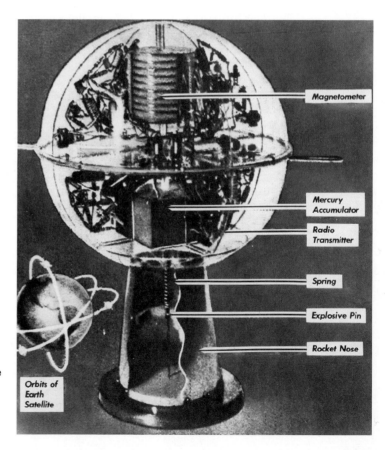

Sputnik: Cutaway diagram of the
Soviet satellite

Magnetometer

Mercury
Accumulator

Radio
Transmitter

Spring

Explosive Pin

Rocket Nose

Orbits of
Earth
Satellite

and Sputnik _____ (begin) a scientific and technological competition
that _____ (continue) to this day.
    People around the world _____ (surprise) by the launching of
Sputnik. Five months later, the Americans _____ (finalize) plans for a
space program.

    Since 1957, all of those plans and more _____ (finalize). Hard,
soft, and manned landings _____ (make) on the moon. Robots
_____ (send) to Mars and other planets. Measurements
_____ (take) and experiments _____ (make) in space.
Satellites _____ (launch) for worldwide communication. Today, these
satellites _____ (use) to send radio, television, and telephone signals
around the world. Weather forecasting and map-making _____
(improve) through use of satellites and high-flying rockets. New discoveries
_____ (make) about distant stars and galaxies. Lasers _____
(develop) for use in many fields.

    It _____ (be) difficult to imagine that all of this _____
(begin) little more than thirty years ago and that it _____ (start) with
one small satellite: Sputnik.

Using What You've Learned

Talking About Hobbies or Interests.   Write answers to the following questions
about new developments in an area that interests you. After writing, share your
information with your classmates.

examples: What equipment is being used now?
            My hobby is photography. Both manual and automatic cam-
            eras are being used. Many kinds of lenses are available . . .

            I'm interested in computer science. Three types of computers
            are being used now: mainframe computers, minicomputers, and
            microcomputers.

1. What equipment is being used now in your hobby?
2. What types of things are currently being designed?
3. Are any of these being developed now?
4. What types of things are being tested?
5. What is currently being improved?
6. What is being planned for the future?

Giving "Eyewitness" Reports. In small groups, give an "eyewitness" account of a breakthrough in science or technology. Some of the group members may role-play the event while others are giving the "eyewitness" news story on it. Be sure to include an "anchor person" at your news station, as well as "special correspondents" who are at the scene. You may choose from the following ideas or create your own situations.

1. A flying saucer has just landed outside of your classroom and several extraterrestrials are getting off. Inspect the saucer, describe it, and interview some of the crew members. Find out where they are from, how long they have been traveling, how their spaceship is operated, etc.

2. A famous astronomer has just discovered that the moon is, in fact, made of green cheese. Interview the astronomer and his or her assistants to learn how this discovery was made, what is being done to verify it, and what impact this discovery will have on the future.

3. The first space colony has just been established on the moon. You are being sent to interview the residents of Operation Moonbeam. Ask about their new world and how they like it.

TOPIC **four**

The Passive Voice with Modal Auxiliaries

Setting the Context

previewing the passage

What would life be like on a space colony? Share your ideas and opinions about the picture.

- Describe the drawing on the previous page.
- What purposes could space colonies possibly serve?

SPACE COLONIES

The technology already exists to send people into space and to bring them back to Earth safely. Now scientists have started thinking about the next step: building colonies in space. But where will space colonists go? Can a place be found or created that will support human life?

5   Perhaps space stations could be launched, or artificial environments might be created on the moon or on another planet. This could be done by building domes and importing air and water. An urban Earth environment could be imitated, complete with parks, libraries, even swimming pools!

    As countries continue to develop their space programs, a space colony may 10 even be launched during our lifetime. Perhaps technology will be improved so much that ordinary people will have a chance to live in space. Ordinary activities like language classes may someday be conducted in space!

discussing ideas

Are space stations and artificial environments possible now? Would you like to be one of the first people to live in a space colony?

The Passive Voice with Modal Auxiliaries

To form the passive voice of modal auxiliaries, use modal + *be* + past participle. Note that modal auxiliaries have the same functions in the passive voice as they do in the active. See Chapter Three if you need to review functions of modals.

	active	passive
Modal Auxiliaries	We **could launch** space stations. We **should start** space colonies. Scientists **will perfect** the necessary technology soon.	Space stations **could be launched.** Space colonies **should be started.** The necessary technology **will be perfected** soon.

 At a conference, scientists are talking about the technology that is needed for people to live in space. Use the modals and verbs in parentheses to form sentences in the passive voice.

> **example:** Attractive space stations _may be developed_____ (may develop).

1. In order for people to live in space stations, they

_____ (must make) safe.

2. An atmosphere _____ (must create).

3. Station managers _____ (train).

4. Comfortable housing _____ (should design).

5. Parks and other recreation areas _____ (might built).

6. For humans to settle on Mars, the environment

_____ (must modify).

7. First, energy _____ (must produce).

8. Then, the Martian ice caps _____ (can melt).

9. In this way, a regular supply of water _____ (could develop).

10. In addition, oxygen _____ (produce).

Following are other ideas expressed by scientists at the conference. In each sentence, first underline the direct object. Then change the sentence from the active voice to the passive voice. Omit the agent.

> **example:** Someday, something may destroy <u>life on earth</u>.
> *Someday, life on earth may be destroyed.*

1. Then humans must find other places to live.
2. We will need very advanced technology.
3. Scientists can plan test colonies now.
4. We should start training programs for space colonists now.
5. We can use computers to study life in space.
6. Governments should spend more money on space research.

The year is 2020. You are planning to spend your summer vacation on a space colony. The cues are a checklist of things that must or should be done before you leave for your trip. Write each item as a complete sentence, using the passive voice.

> **example:** warm clothes / pack
> *My warm clothes must be packed.*

1. travel schedule / confirm one week before departure
2. passport / renew
3. camera / repair
4. bills / pay before I leave
5. friends / tell where to write to me
6. space suit / clean

You've been at the space colony for two weeks now. Life is simple and rather boring. Read the list of complaints below. Then use the cues and any appropriate modal to make suggestions for improving life at the colony.

> **example:** Mail from home comes only once a week.
> (mail / deliver twice a week)
> **Mail should be delivered twice a week.**

1. The food here is tasteless. (hamburgers / import from Earth)
2. There aren't any gardens. (flowers / plant)
3. There isn't any good music. (rock and roll / broadcast from Earth)
4. These dorm walls are colorless. (posters of Earth / hang)
5. It's too hot to go outdoors. (the indoor environment / improve)
6. We don't have any sports events here. (a stadium / build)

What are your opinions about the "race into space"? Answer the following questions in your own words, using the passive voice.

1. Should space colonies be developed?
2. Should money be spent on this kind of research?
3. In your opinion, what kinds of research should be done?
4. Should people be sent into space for long periods of time?
5. Should tests for the ability to survive in space be performed on humans?
6. Should animals be used for these tests?

exercise 6   **Review.**   The following passage gives you information about the future of our solar system. First, read the passage for meaning, checking any vocabulary that might be difficult for you. Then complete it by using active or passive modal auxiliaries with the verbs in parentheses.

THE FUTURE OF OUR SUN

Life on earth _may continue_ (may continue) for a very long time, or it _might be destroyed_ (might destroy) by our sun. Sometime, in thousands of millions of years, the sun _____ (will burn) all of its hydrogen. Then, the sun _____ (will expand) into a red giant star. Mercury _____ (will swallow) up by the sun. Venus _____ (may consume) by the expanding sun, and the Earth _____ (might destroy).

If this happens, it _____ (will mean) the end of all life in the solar system. Any life on planets near the sun _____ (will destroy). And life on some other planets _____ (will freeze) by the extreme cold. Eventually the sun _____ (will shrink) to a white dwarf star. After the sun shrinks to a white dwarf star, it _____ (will look) like a beautiful, bright diamond in the sky.

Using What You've Learned

Researching a Topic.   Is there more that you would like to know about the solar system? Other galaxies? Choose a topic and research it. Then report back to the class what you found out. Here are some possible topics:

- black holes
- a mythological story about a constellation
- light
- stars: their birth and death

focus on testing

Use of the Passive Voice

Verbs in the passive voice are frequently tested on standardized English proficiency exams. Review these commonly tested structures and check your understanding by completing the sample items on the next page.

Remember that . . .

- The passive voice is formed with the correct tense of *be* + past participle.
- *Be* is singular or plural, depending on the subject.

Part 1. Circle the correct completion for the following.

example: French _____ in many parts of the world.
a. is spoken
b. is speaking
c. spoken
d. is being speaking

1. Water _____ hydrogen and oxygen.
a. is composed by
b. is composed of
c. compose of
d. composes by

2. Is that woman _____ the famous movie star?
a. relate to
b. related
c. relating
d. related to

3. Specialized drills _____ deep wells.
a. is used for digging
b. is used to digging
c. are used to dig
d. are used for dig

Part 2. Circle the letter below the word(s) containing an error.

example: In terms of native languages, Spanish is use by around 330
           A   Ⓑ   C

million people worldwide.
                 D

1. Until the Martian space probes, it was believe that life forms might exist
       A   B   C   D

on Mars.

2. When Sputnik is launched by the Soviets in 1957, the "race to space"
       A   B   C

began in earnest.
      D

3. Galileo put in prison because of his public statements regarding
                     A   B   C

the rotation of the Earth around the sun.
       D

CHAPTER **ten**

Medicine, Myths, and Magic

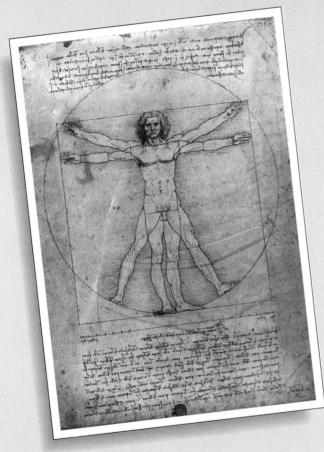

Adjective Clauses

Topic One: Adjective Clauses with *That*
Topic Two: Adjective Clauses with *Who, Which,* and *Whose*
Topic Three: Adjective Clauses with *That, Which,* and *Who(m)*
Topic Four: Adjective Clauses with *When* and *Where*

Adjective Clauses with That

Setting the Context

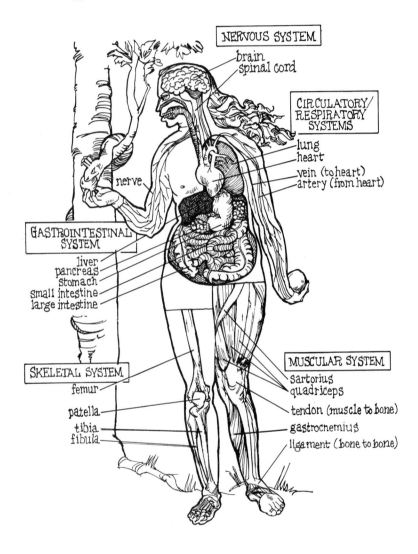

NERVOUS SYSTEM
brain
spinal cord

CIRCULATORY/
RESPIRATORY
SYSTEMS
lung
heart
vein (to heart)
artery (from heart)

nerve

GASTROINTESTINAL
SYSTEM
liver
pancreas
stomach
small intestine
large intestine

MUSCULAR SYSTEM
sartorius
quadriceps
tendon (muscle to bone)
gastrocnemius
ligament (bone to bone)

SKELETAL SYSTEM
femur
patella
tibia
fibula

previewing the passage

What do you know about the way your body works? Share your ideas and opinions by answering the following questions about the picture.

- What are the major systems of the body?
- How does your blood move through your body?
- What are nerves? Do they extend throughout your body?

THE MAJOR SYSTEMS OF THE BODY

During the last one hundred years, medical researchers have discovered a great deal about the way the human body works. We now know about the various systems of the body that keep us alive. The systems that are most important include the circulatory, respiratory, nervous, musculoskeletal, and
5 gastrointestinal systems. Each of these systems controls major body functions. The system that controls the flow of blood through the body is the circulatory system. It includes the heart, the arteries, the capillaries, and the veins. The nervous system connects the brain to the rest of the body through the spinal cord and the nerves. The system that supports the body and allows it to move
10 is the musculoskeletal system. The system that controls breathing is the respiratory system. It includes the nose, mouth, throat, trachea, bronchi, and lungs. Finally, the gastrointestinal system, the part of the body that controls digestion and elimination, consists of the esophagus, the stomach, and the small and large intestines. Two of its most important organs are the liver and
15 the pancreas.

discussing ideas

Which system connects the brain to the rest of the body? What system includes the liver and the pancreas? What does each of the following systems do: circulatory, respiratory, nervous, musculoskeletal, gastrointestinal?

A. Introduction to Adjective Clauses

An adjective clause is a clause that modifies or describes a noun or pronoun. An adjective clause usually comes immediately after the word(s) that it describes. It usually begins with a relative pronoun: *that, which, who, whom, whose, when,* and *where.*

B. Clauses with *That:* Replacement of Subjects

To form an adjective clause, *that* may replace the subject of a simple sentence. It may be used to refer to ideas, things, and people. Note that *who(m)* is usually used for people, however.

	examples
Two Simple Sentences	The body is like a **complex machine. This machine** automatically repairs itself.
One Complex Sentence with that	The body is like a complex machine **that automatically repairs itself.**

 **exercise 1**   Underline the adjective clauses (*that* clauses) in the opening passage, "The Major Systems of the Body." Circle the words that the clauses modify.

 **exercise 2**   Combine the following sentences. The second sentence should become a clause beginning with *that*. Omit words and change *a* or *an* to *the* when necessary.

example: Blood is a liquid. This liquid circulates through the body.
           Blood is the liquid that circulates through the body.

1. The heart is an organ. This organ pumps blood through the body.
2. Blood is a liquid. This liquid carries food and oxygen through the body.
3. Blood is carried in vessels. The vessels are called arteries and veins.
4. The lungs are filled with air. This air contains oxygen.
5. The body is supported by a bone and muscle structure. This structure is responsible for body posture and movement.
6. The body is covered with skin. The skin protects the body from bacteria.
7. The brain is the control center for the nerves. The nerves carry messages to and from the body.
8. Digestion of food is an essential process. This process takes place in the intestine.

 **exercise 3**   Combine the following sentences to form one sentence with a clause with *that*. Omit words when necessary.

example: In Ancient Egypt, there were many doctors. These doctors cured patients with the help of magic and spirits.
           In Ancient Egypt, there were many doctors that cured patients with the help of magic and spirits.

1. Egyptians believed sickness came from spirits. These spirits were angry and evil.
2. The Egyptian doctor would put a magic spell on the angry spirit. This spirit had caused the person's illness.
3. The magic spell always included words. The words had to be repeated in a certain way.
4. Egyptian doctors also used medicine. This medicine came from the organs of wild animals.

...rugs

...is kind of

...schools were

...Greek philosopher, w... ...e important books.
...books discuss medical problems that we still face today.

exercise 4 Adjective clauses with *that* are often used to define words. Use the following cues to define various parts of the body. Be sure to use appropriate singular or plural verbs in the adjective clauses and to add articles or pronouns when necessary.

example: heart / organ / pump blood / through / body
The heart is the organ that pumps blood through your body.

1. spine / set of bones / support / body
2. arteries / major blood vessels / carry / blood away from / heart
3. spinal cord / set of nerves / lead to / brain
4. nerves / fibers / communicate messages to and from / brain
5. knees / joints / allow you to bend / legs
6. tendons / tissues / connect muscles to / bones
7. Quadriceps / muscle / extend the leg
8. Femur / bone / reach from the hip to the knee

exercise 5 In pairs, use the diagram at the beginning of the chapter to help you make definitions of the following terms. Complete each sentence in Column A with one of the items in Column B.

example: **Your brain is the organ that controls the body through nerves.**

A

√ 1. Your brain is the organ
2. Your heart is the organ
3. Your lungs are the organ
4. Your intestine is the organ
5. Your bones and muscles are the structures
6. Your arteries are the blood vessels
7. The veins are the blood vessels
8. The elbow is the joint
9. The pancreas is the organ
10. The stomach is the organ

B

a. that carry blood back to the heart.
b. that brings oxygen to your blood.
√ c. that controls the body through nerves.
d. that connects the upper arm and forearm.
e. that digests your food.
f. that carry blood from your heart to your organs.
g. that receives food you eat.
h. that support the body and provide movement.
i. that pumps blood through the body.
j. that makes insulin.

well

hand

3. nose   **6.** teeth

Adjective Clauses with Who, Which, and Whose

Setting the Context

How has medicine changed during the last century? Share your information by answering these questions about the picture on the opposite page.

- What is shown in the picture?
- Are any of these treatments useful?

EARLY MEDICINE

Medicine and pharmacology are two sciences that have changed a great deal in recent times. Long ago, medicine was a guessing game. Medical care was given by doctors, pharmacists, and even barbers! All of them experimented freely on their patients, who often died as a result.

5 Early pharmacists depended on plant remedies that had been developed over the centuries. One popular remedy during the Middle Ages was poppy juice, which contains opium (a narcotic). Other remedies were animal fat and even crocodile blood, which was considered a "cure" for poor eyesight.

Other common practices were dangerous and sometimes fatal. For 10 instance, bleeding patients to let out "bad blood" often resulted in the death of the patient. A common practice that was equally dangerous involved drilling a hole in the patient's skull. Perhaps this was done to treat head wounds or to relieve pressure inside the head.

People whose diseases were "incurable" often looked for help from the 15 spirit world, astrology, and magic. Astrology, which was valued as a method of diagnosis, was even taught in many medical schools.

Medicine has become a reliable science only in recent times. Even now, however, it still involves a certain amount of experimentation.

discussing ideas

Why was early medicine a guessing game? What different types of people gave medical care? What were some common early medicines and treatments? Do you know of any other early remedies or treatments?

A. Clauses with *Who* and *Which:* Replacement of Subjects

To form adjective clauses from simple sentences, *who* may replace subjects that refer to people. *Which* may replace subjects that refer to things or ideas.

examples	
Two Simple Sentences	The **physician** was Dr. Andrews. **He** treated the patient.
One Complex Sentence with who	The physician **who treated the patient** was Dr. Andrews.
Two Simple Sentences	**Aspirin** is a common treatment for headaches. **Aspirin** is a pain reliever.
One Complex Sentence with which	Aspirin, **which is a pain reliever,** is a common treatment for headaches.

 **exercise 1** Use the cues to form sentences with adjective clauses with *who*. Add *a* or *an* when necessary and use appropriate singular or plural verbs in your adjective clauses.

examples: orthopedist / treat bone, joint, or muscle problems
An orthopedist is a doctor who treats bone, joint, or muscle problems.

orthopedists / treat bone, joint, or muscle problems
Orthopedists are doctors who treat bone, joint, or muscle problems.

1. radiologist / read / X-rays
2. surgeons / perform / operations
3. pediatrician / take care of / children
4. ophthalmologist / treat / diseases or injuries of the eye
5. internists / specialize in / diagnosis and treatment of diseases in adults
6. gynecologist / specialize in / functions and diseases of women
7. neurologist / take care of / patients with nerve or brain disease
8. psychiatrists / treat / mental problems

 **exercise 2** Use the following cues to form sentences with adjective clauses with *which* (or *that*). Be sure to add articles when necessary.

example: rubber hammer / tool / be used for testing reflexes
A rubber hammer is a tool that is used for testing reflexes.

1. stethoscope / instrument / be used for listening to a person's heart
2. scalpel / instrument / be used for cutting during surgery

3. opium / narcotic / produce a feeling of great happiness
4. anesthetic / drug / put people to sleep before surgery
5. aspirin / drug / relieve pain
6. thermometer / instrument / measure temperature

 **exercise 3** Combine the following sentences about early medical practices with *who* or *which*. Make the second sentence of the two into an adjective clause when you combine them. Change words when necessary.

> **example:** Some prehistoric *people* performed brain operations. These *people* lived in Europe in about 10,000 B.C.
>
> Some prehistoric people who lived in Europe in about 10,000 B.C. performed brain operations.

1. These brain surgeons used simple *knives*. The *knives* were made of stone.
2. Many *skulls* have been found in Europe. The *skulls* had small holes cut into them.
3. The *surgeons* probably removed pieces of bone. *They* operated on the head.
4. In early times, however, *some people* went to magicians rather than doctors. These *people* had physical problems.
5. *People* would ask for help from a magician. *They* thought spirits or magic caused illness.
6. During the Middle Ages, some doctors used different *cures*. These *cures* did not treat the body at all.
7. For example, a *swordsman* was not treated with medicine. The *swordsman* had been hurt in a fight. (The sword was treated instead!)
8. Another *remedy* was to wear a card with the word "abracadabra" on it. This *remedy* became very popular in the Middle Ages.

 # B. Clauses with *Whose:* Replacement of Possessives

Whose may also be used to form adjective clauses. It does not act as the subject of a clause. Instead, it replaces a possessive noun or adjective that modifies the subject of the clause.

examples	
Two Simple Sentences	The woman thanked **the doctor. His** treatment had cured her.
One Complex Sentence with whose	The woman thanked **the doctor whose** treatment had cured her.

Combine the following sentences with *whose*. Make the second sentence into the adjective clause.

> **example:** The villagers gave a gift to *the pharmacist. His* secret medicine had cured their mysterious disease.
>
> The villagers gave a gift to the pharmacist whose secret medicine had cured their mysterious disease.

1. A *person* sometimes gets well unexpectedly. *His* or *her* will to live is very strong.
2. Another *person* might die unexpectedly. *His* or *her* belief in witchcraft is strong.
3. Some *doctors* can be successful. *Their* treatments are not always scientific.
4. Some *people* refuse to see a doctor. *Their* condition is serious.
5. *People* may be afraid of doctors. *Their* faith in modern medicine is not very strong.

C. Restrictive Versus Nonrestrictive Clauses

In some cases, commas come before and after adjective clauses. Commas are used with adjective clauses that give additional information. These clauses often modify proper nouns (Dr. Nie, Athens, the Tower of London) or names of unique people, places, or things (the sun, vitamin C, the equator). *Who, which, whom,* and *whose* (but not *that*) may be used in these clauses. They are called nonrestrictive clauses.

In contrast, commas are not used with adjective clauses that specifically identify the word(s) they modify. *That* may be used in this type of clause only; *who, which, whom,* and *whose* may also be used. These clauses are called restrictive clauses.

	examples	notes
Nonrestrictive Clauses	Dr. Fox, **who has been a friend of ours for years,** is both a pediatrician and an internist. Dr. Carlson, **who works with Dr. Fox,** specializes in radiology.	Nonrestrictive clauses give additional or extra information about the noun(s) they modify. They do not explain *which* people, places, or things the speaker or writer is referring to—this information is probably known. Commas are used before and after these clauses.

	examples	notes
Restrictive *Clauses*	Doctors **who treat children** are called pediatricians. Doctors **who read X-rays** are called radiologists.	Restrictive clauses explain *which* people, places, or things the speaker or writer is referring to. No commas are used.

In the passage "Early Medicine" on page 313, reread the sentences with adjective clauses. Try to explain why commas are or are not used with each clause.

In the following pairs of sentences, underline the adjective clause. Then indicate whether the clause gives essential or additional information. Next, add commas where necessary.

example: Typhoid and cholera, <u>which have been common problems for</u> <u>thousands of years,</u> have now disappeared from some areas. (Additional information—commas are used.)

1. The bubonic plague which is a contagious disease is carried by rats.

2. This plague which was also called the "black death" killed half the population of Europe in the fourteenth century.

3. Physicians who treated plague victims never found a cure for the disease.

4. During the plague, many people who touched the sick or the dead died after a short time.

5. People who lived in major seaports were more likely to become plague victims.

6. Thousands of people died in Marseilles which was a major seaport.

Combine the sentences here and on the next page with *who, which,* or *whose.* Change the second sentence into an adjective clause. Be sure to use commas where necessary.

example: Mumps and chicken pox are not treated with antibiotics. They are diseases caused by viruses.
Mumps and chicken pox, which are diseases caused by viruses, are not treated with antibiotics.

1. Certain illnesses cannot be treated with antibiotics. These illnesses are caused by viruses.

2. The ordinary cold is a viral infection. The cold is our most common sickness.

3. A careful diet can be a good treatment for people. Their internal organs do not function properly.
4. People can be treated effectively with drugs. These people suffer from tuberculosis.
5. People must take hormone pills every day. Their thyroid glands have been removed.
6. Many people take vitamin C every day. These people are trying to avoid colds.
7. Antibiotics are chemicals. These chemicals are produced from microorganisms.
8. Antibiotics can kill or control some bacteria. Some bacteria cause diseases.
9. Sir Alexander Fleming received the Nobel Prize in 1945. He discovered penicillin.
10. Penicillin is perhaps the most valued medicine today. Penicillin stops the growth of many bacteria.

Using What You've Learned

activity

Giving Definitions. In small groups, test your skills at a vocabulary game. The object of this game is for one person to describe people, places, objects, ideas, and so forth. The other people in the group must guess who or what they are. In this version of the game, the clues must include adjective clauses with *that, who, which,* or *whose.*

examples: A: **I'm thinking of an instrument which is used to listen to a person's heart.**
B: **A stethoscope.**
A: **I'm thinking of a physician whose specialty is treating children.**
B: **A pediatrician.**

TOPIC three

Adjective Clauses with That, Which, and Who(m)

Setting the Context

previewing the passage

What are "medical myths"? How do such myths originate? Share your ideas and opinions by answering these questions about the picture.

- What is shown in each part of the drawing?
- Does your culture have similar myths?

MEDICAL MYTHS

In the past, people believed a number of medical myths that we laugh at today. During the Middle Ages, for example, many people believed the bubonic plague was caused by arrows that Christ had shot. In eighteenth-century England, even people whom others considered sophisticated had faith
5 in strange remedies. They believed they could cure an earache by sleeping with a roasted onion in the aching ear. The same people thought a growth on the eyelid could be cured by rubbing it with the tail of a male cat.

Since then, we have learned many things: bubonic plague is caused by bacteria, roasted onions cannot cure earaches, and cats do not cure growths.
10 Nevertheless, there are medical myths that people still believe today. There are many misconceptions about the common cold, for example. People believe they will catch a cold if they sit in a draft or become chilled. Yet, we know a cold is due to a virus which is passed on through personal contact with people who have the germ. There is no myth about this!

discussing ideas

What are some ancient medical myths? What are some modern medical myths? Do you know of any others?

A. Clauses with *That* and *Which*: Replacement of Objects

That and *which* may replace objects of verbs to form adjective clauses. *Which* refers to things or ideas. *That* may refer to things, ideas, or people, although *who(m)* is generally preferred for people. *That* may be used only in restrictive clauses (clauses without commas) and is preferred in these clauses. Both *that* and *which* can also be omitted from restrictive clauses.

Two Simple Sentences	Many people believe in **predictions.** Astrologers make **them.**
One Complex Sentence with that or which	Many people believe in predictions **that (which) astrologers make.**
One Complex Sentence with No Relative Pronoun	Many people believe in predictions **astrologers make.**

B. Clauses with *Who(m):* Replacement of Objects

Who(m) may replace objects of verbs to form adjective clauses. *Who(m)* refers to people. In this type of clause, *whom* is correct and preferred in formal English. However, *who* is very frequently used, especially in conversation. Both *who* and *whom* can also be omitted from restrictive clauses.

examples

Two Simple Sentences	The woman believed **the astrologer.** She had consulted **the astrologer.**
One Complex Sentence with who(m)	The woman believed the astrologer **who(m) she had consulted.**
One Complex Sentence with No Pronoun	The woman believed the astrologer **she had consulted.**

 **exercise 1**   Underline the adjective clauses in the passage "Medical Myths" on page 319. Indicate whether the clause is restrictive or nonrestrictive. Also note whether the subject or the object of the original clause has been replaced.

Add adjective clauses (in parentheses) to these sentences. Use commas where necessary. In sentences with restrictive clauses (without commas), write both possibilities: using the relative pronoun and omitting it. Remember that you cannot omit the relative pronoun from a nonrestrictive clause.

example: Every society has myths. (which people believe in)
Every society has myths which people believe in.
Every society has myths people believe in.

1. Many societies have a spiritual healer or magician. (whom everyone asks for medical advice)
2. Medical practices differ from culture to culture. (that superstitious people believe in)
3. Copper bracelets are also worn as jewelry. (which many people wear to cure arthritis)
4. Amulets are necklaces. (which some people wear to prevent disease)
5. One belief is that chicken soup will cure any illness. (that many Europeans and Americans have)
6. In the past, the color red was never used in sick rooms. (which some cultures considered unlucky)

Combine the following sentences by using *that, who(m),* or *which.* Use commas where necessary. For each sentence, write all possible combinations. Then, tell which sentence is preferred in formal English. Remember that you cannot omit the relative pronoun from a nonrestrictive clause.

example: Many cultures still have healers or magicians. Sick people consult the healers or magicians.
Many cultures still have healers or magicians whom sick people consult. (Preferred in formal English.)
Many cultures still have healers or magicians who sick people consult.
Many cultures still have healers or magicians that sick people consult.
Many cultures still have healers or magicians sick people consult.

1. There are many medical myths. Even educated people believe them.
2. A common saying is "An apple a day keeps the doctor away." Mothers repeat this saying to their children.
3. Most of us think of doctors as special people. We can trust doctors with our most personal problems.
4. In many places, there are no doctors. Sick people can consult doctors.
5. In my town, there was one old woman. Everyone asked her about their health problems.
6. This woman always made herbal tea. She gave the tea to the sick.

Use the following cues to form questions with adjective clauses beginning with *who(m)*, *which*, or *that*. Work in pairs and take turns asking and answering the questions. Many answers are possible.

> **example:** medicine / you take most often
> A: **What is the medicine that you take most often?**
> B: **Aspirin.**

1. doctor / you usually visit when you're sick
2. foods / you eat when you have the flu
3. fruit / you eat most often
4. meat / you like the best
5. mineral / you should take when you feel tired
6. person / people in your family consult when they need medical advice
7. food / you eat to live a long life
8. food / people eat to have healthy hair and nails

Following the example as a model, use the cues to write definitions. Add connecting words, articles, prepositions, and any other necessary expressions.

> **example:** flu / illness / many people get / in the winter
> The flu is an illness that many people get in the winter.

1. sugar / food / people eat for quick energy
2. onion / food / some people eat to live longer
3. black / color / Western societies associate with death
4. mushrooms / plants / many people believe have mysterious powers
5. storks / birds / many children believe deliver babies
6. thirteen / number / many people believe is unlucky

Using What You've Learned

Comparing Traditional Beliefs. Are there foods that people from your culture believe have special effects? For example, are there foods that make people live longer, have more children, see better, and so forth? Discuss these questions in small groups. Find out if there are foods that are recommended for a certain purpose in more than one culture. Does science support the idea that these foods are effective for these particular purposes?

activity 2

Describing Myths and Superstitions.   This activity concerns several "medical myths" and folk remedies that people have believed in. Look at the list of medical problems. Do you know any medical myths about their causes or cures? Where did you hear about them? In small groups, share your stories and information.

colds   skin rashes
flu   allergies
rheumatism   headaches
hiccups   depression

TOPIC **four**
Adjective Clauses with When and Where

Setting the Context

previewing the passage

What do you know about medical care in North America? Share your ideas and experiences by answering these questions about the picture.

- What is shown in each picture?
- Why is hospital care so expensive today?

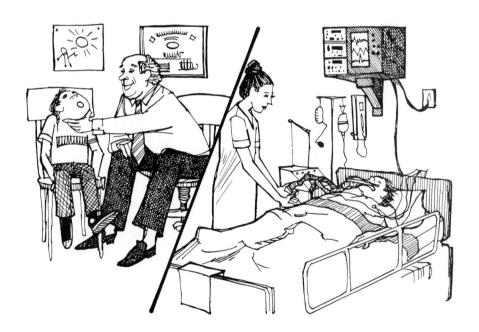

Medical care has changed greatly since the days when the family doctor treated all family members for every type of medical problem. Today's physician is usually a specialist who treats only problems within his or her specialty.

5 Today's specialists often work together in a large group in order to share costs. The group will buy expensive equipment for its own offices rather than use hospital facilities. The physician's office usually has a laboratory where a variety of medical tests can be done. So, unlike the family doctor, who often visited patients at home, today's doctors normally see patients in their offices,
10 where they can use specialized equipment.

Likewise, many changes are taking place in hospitals, where the cost of medical equipment and care is skyrocketing. Because of the high costs, patients now spend a limited number of days in the hospital, depending on their illness. Even new mothers, who used to have a five-to-ten-day hospital
15 stay after the birth of their babies, are now being sent home in twenty-four hours.

Medical technology certainly has led to great advances in the diagnosis and cure of many illnesses. However, some people want to bring back the "good old days" when the family physician was also a family friend.

discussing ideas

What was medical care like in the past? How is it different now? Why? Are changes also taking place in your country? Why or why not?

Adjective Clauses with *When* and *Where*

When and *where* can introduce adjective clauses if they come after nouns. *When* usually modifies a noun that has the meaning of time or a time period. *Where* usually modifies a noun that has the meaning of a physical place or an abstract area or field.

examples

Two Simple Sentences	The 1950s were a **time**. At that **time,** doctors still made house-calls.
One Complex Sentence with when	The 1950s were a time **when doctors still made house-calls.**

Two Simple Sentences	We can expect continued progress in **the medical field.**
	New discoveries are made every day in **the medical field.**
One Complex Sentence with where	We can expect continued progress in the medical field, **where new discoveries are made every day.**

 **exercise 1**

Combine the following sentences with *when* or *where*. Add commas where necessary.

> example: Treatment for cancer will be more effective in the future. In the future, scientists will know more about the body's immune system.
>
> *Treatment for cancer will be more effective in the future, when scientists will know more about the body's immune system.*

1. It's interesting to visit a hospital laboratory. In the laboratory, there is a lot of sophisticated equipment.
2. Teaching hospitals often have the most modern facilities. In these hospitals, new doctors are educated and trained.
3. We are now in an age. Medicine is very specialized.
4. The doctor's office is now a complicated place. In the doctor's office, many tests and even surgery can be performed.
5. Medicine will become a very competitive field in the future. In the future, there will be too many doctors in the United States.
6. University hospitals around the U.S. are places. A great deal of research on cancer is taking place there today.
7. The whole world is hoping for the time. A cure for cancer will be discovered then.
8. We would all like to see the day. That day, good medical care will be available to everyone.

exercise 2

Complete the following sentences by adding adjective clauses with *when* or *where*.

> example: An intensive care unit is a place . . . *where critically ill or injured patients are cared for.*

1. A hospital is a place . . .
2. The emergency room is the place . . .
3. A laboratory is a place . . .
4. The twentieth century is a time . . .
5. The Middle Ages was a time . . .
6. A pharmacy is a place . . .
7. A nursing home is a place . . .
8. Your visit to the doctor is the time . . .

An operating room in a modern Western hospital

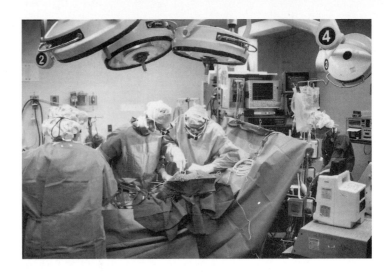

Review. Complete the following passage about traditional medicine with the correct relative pronoun.

TRIBAL MEDICINE

In most areas of the world, people _who_ are sick are taken to a doctor or a hospital for treatment. But there are still many places

_____ patients are taken instead to a local medicine man, or healer,

1

_____ is a combination of doctor, priest, and psychologist.

2

In Western thinking, disease is something _____ people regard as

3
natural. In tribal cultures, however, people consider illness an unnatural condition; it is a sign of deep anger, hatred, fear, or conflict. To discover the reason for an illness, a healer might use astrology or ask the patient about his dreams. Once the cause of illness is known, the patient may go to a healing shrine or

temple, _____ he cleans himself. After that, he returns to the

4

healer, _____ performs different ceremonies to chase the evil spirits

5
out of the patient's body. The patient, _____ family also participates

6
in the healing ceremony, may be put into a trance, _____ is a state of

7
deep, unconscious concentration. While the patient is in the trance, the healer performs different ceremonies to chase the evil spirits out of the patient's body.

Finally, the healer suggests changes _____ the person must make so

8
that the disease does not return.

Why does tribal medicine work? There are several explanations. Perhaps it works because the people _____ participate in these ceremonies believe in its power. Or it may work because the patient sees that all the people _____ he cares about are involved in making him well. Another reason may be that the healing ceremonies produce chemical changes in the body _____ then help to cure the disease. Finally, many of the plants_____ are used in these ceremonies are known to have healing powers.

People _____ live in westernized societies may be able to learn a lesson from tribal medicine. In these times, _____ most people no longer have a strong sense of faith or community, perhaps we need to examine more closely some of the social and spiritual aspects of healing.

Using What You've Learned

Playing the Dictionary Game.　You will need a dictionary for this game. First, divide into groups of four. Take turns selecting a word from the dictionary. Choose a word no one in the group knows the meaning of. The person who chooses the word writes the correct meaning on a piece of paper. The other people write false definitions that they think "sound" real. Then the person who chose the word reads all the definitions aloud (without laughing!). Each person in the group votes for the definition he or she believes is correct. The object is to get your classmates to choose your definition rather than the correct one. You score one point for every person who voted for your definition.

focus on testing

Use of Adjective Clauses

Adjective clauses are frequently tested on standardized English proficiency exams. Review these commonly tested structures and check your understanding by completing the sample items on the next page.

Remember that . . .

* In object clauses, *whom* (not *who*) is grammatically correct.
* The original object is omitted in object clauses.
* The relative pronoun may not be omitted from a nonrestrictive clause.
* The verb in an adjective clause is singular or plural, depending on the word it modifies.

Part 1.   Circle the correct completion for the following.

> example: I have a friend _____ neighbors are from France.
> **a.** that
> **b.** whom
> **(c.)** whose
> **d.** who

1. The doctor _____ was a specialist in orthopedics.
   a. that saw
   b. whom I saw
   c. who I saw
   d. which I saw

2. Aspirin is a pain reliever _____ been used for centuries.
   a. which it has
   b. that it has
   c. that has
   d. that have

3. In traditional medicine, a healer is someone _____ may use a combination of rituals and remedies to treat a sick person.
   a. whose
   b. who
   c. that
   d. whom

Part 2.   Circle the letter below the word(s) containing an error.

> example: There are many languages used around the world today
>   A   B
> which they do not have a form of writing.
>   ©   D

1. The system that it controls the flow of blood through the body is the
       A   B   C   D
circulatory system.

2. Over the centuries, three alcoholic liquids that has been used
                                A   B   C
as medicine are beer, brandy, and gin.
   D

3. Aristotle, his writings about medicine were used by physicians and
                  A   B   C
barbers for hundreds of years, believed the brain to be a cooling
                                                    D
system for the heart.

CHAPTER eleven

The Media

Gerunds, Infinitives, and Related Structures

Topic One: Gerunds

Topic Two: Infinitives

Topic Three: Infinitives Versus Gerunds

Topic Four: Causative and Structurally Related Verbs; Verbs of Perception

in this chapter

Setting the Context

*previewing
the
passage*

How has communication changed in the last one hundred years? Share your opinions and information while answering the following questions about the picture.

- When did each of these scenes take place?
- What are the people in each scene doing?

REPORTING THE NEWS

Today newspapers, magazines, radio, and television share the responsibility of reporting the news to the public. However, communicating through printed and electronic media is a relatively new development. For centuries, the news traveled in a wide variety of ways. In Rome, in the fifth century B.C., for
5 instance, Roman barbers were the major source of news. They reported on recent happenings as they were cutting people's hair. Later, Romans learned the news by reading handwritten reports that were posted on the walls of public buildings. In England and North America in the eighteenth century, the news was delivered by a town crier. His job was shouting out the latest news as
10 he walked the city streets.

In less populated areas, news was often spread by "word of mouth" or other methods. In West Africa, for example, the news traveled from one village to another via the "talking drum." In North America, the American Plains

Indians communicated over long distances by sending smoke signals back
15 and forth over hills and plains.

Methods of reporting important events changed when people began print-
ing daily newspapers. For a long time, newspapers were the chief medium for
learning about the day's events. The transistor radio, however, revolutionized
communication. Nowadays, listening to the latest news on the radio is an event
20 that takes place in even the most remote corners of the world.

discussing ideas

Can you think of some other traditional ways of reporting news? How do you
usually communicate with other people (letters, telephone, telegrams, etc.)? Why
do you prefer these methods?

A. Introduction to Gerunds and Infinitives

Gerunds and infinitives are verb forms that may be used in place of a noun or
pronoun. This section presents common uses of gerunds; the following section
presents common uses of infinitives. Compare:

	examples	notes
Noun Gerund	I like **books.** I like **reading.**	A gerund is the simple form of a verb + *ing*. See Appendix pages 396–397 for spelling rules for -*ing* endings.
Noun Infinitive	I like **magazines.** I like **to read.**	An infinitive is *to* + the simple form of a verb.

B. Uses of Gerunds

	examples	notes
Subject	**Reporting** the news is the job of television, radio, magazines, and newspapers.	Gerunds may replace nouns or pronouns as subjects, objects, or complements.
Object of a Preposition	Most newspapers are interested in **reporting** the news accurately.	Where a verb form is used after a preposition, it must be the gerund form.

	examples	notes
Object of a Verb	Reggie enjoys **working** for the evening paper.	In conversational English, nouns or object pronouns are sometimes used with gerunds instead of possessives.
Complement	His job is **researching** stories.	
Negative Gerund	Many people complain about **not getting** accurate news.	*Not* is used before the gerund to form the negative.
Possessive with a Gerund	**Reggie's (His) reporting** is normally very accurate.	*Formal:* I don't like *John's (his)* saying that. *Conversational:* I don't like *John (him)* saying that.

 **exercise** Reread the passage at the beginning of this section. Circle all the gerunds and determine their grammatical function in the sentence (subject, object, object of a preposition, or complement).

C. Gerunds After Prepositions

These are some common phrases with prepositions that are often followed by gerunds. Note that an infinitive *cannot* be used after them. See Chapter One, Chapter Five, and Chapter Eight for a review of prepositions and phrasal combinations with prepositions.

common phrases with prepositions		examples
angry about	believe in	Lois was **angry about losing** her job as a reporter.
bored with (by)	care about	
certain of	consist of	She's **bored with living** in a small town.
concerned about	depend on	She is **excited about moving** to New York City.
excited about	dream about	All of the reporters **care about writing** good articles.
happy about	insist on	
interested in	succeed in	A reporter's job **consists of gathering** information **and writing** articles.
nervous about	take care of	
responsible for	talk about	Our editor **insists on checking** every detail.
satisfied with	think about	He **worries about making** mistakes.
thrilled about (by)	work (hard) at	
	worry about	

common phrases with prepositions	examples
be accustomed to* be used to* look forward to*	I'm **accustomed to reading** a lot. I'm not **used to reading** in English. I always **look forward to getting** news from home.

*Do not confuse the preposition *to* with the *to* in infinitives. Compare: I am used to getting up early. I used to get up early.

**exercise 2**   Complete the sentences with the gerund forms of the verbs in parentheses.

example: I finally succeeded in _getting_____ (get) a job.

1. I'm looking forward to _____ (begin) my new job as a newspaper reporter.

2. I'm excited about _____ (work) for a major newspaper.

3. I'm nervous about _____ (make) mistakes.

4. A reporter must work at _____ (gather) information, _____ (check) all the facts, and _____ (write) a good article.

5. Reporters for major newspapers are used to _____ (work) long hours.

6. They are also accustomed to _____ (get) large salaries!

7. The editor's job consists of _____ (make) corrections, _____ (choose) which stories to print, and _____ (decide) what to put on each page.

8. Editors are also responsible for _____ (write) editorials.   **333**

exercise 3 Complete the following sentences by adding gerunds. Choose from these verbs. In some cases, several choices are possible.

advertise	edit	manage
attract	gather	report
check	get	sell
deliver		

example: The managing editor is responsible for *checking* all news stories.

1. His job consists of . . . all stories.
2. The advertising manager earns money for the paper by . . . ads.
3. Businesses attract new customers by . . . in the newspaper.
4. A reporter begins his work by . . . facts.
5. The business department is interested in . . . the budget.
6. The circulation department works at . . . new readers.
7. The paperboy is responsible for . . . the paper each day.
8. A sports writer takes care of . . . football games.
9. Newspaper readers are concerned about . . . accurate news.

exercise 4 Complete the following passage with the missing prepositions and the gerund forms of the word(s) in parentheses. In some cases, you will not need to repeat a preposition that was already used.

...Our top story today: still no word on the kidnapping...

KEEPING UP WITH THE NEWS

Many people get bored <u>with (by)</u> <u>hearing</u> (hear) or <u>reading</u> (read) long, detailed news reports. They believe that the media should entertain. These people care only _____ _____
(listen) to music or _____ (watch) entertainment programs.

There are other people who really do care _____ _____

4
5
(be) informed; however, they don't have enough time to follow the news in
detail. They have to be satisfied _____ _____ (watch) the

6
7
latest news on short TV programs or _____ (hear) ten-second items

8
on the radio. They might not be thrilled _____ _____ (get)

9
10
such limited information, but they have little choice.

Of course, some people insist _____ _____ (get) detailed

11
12
news from various sources. They are not only used _____

13
_____ (read) a morning newspaper, but they are also accustomed

14
_____ _____ (receive) one or more news magazines in the

15
16
mail. They worry_____ _____ (get) accurate news and

17
18
believe _____ _____ (be) well-informed. They feel each

19
20
individual is responsible _____ _____ (know) what is

21
22
happening in the world.

D. Common Verbs Often Followed by Gerunds

If a verb form follows these verbs, it must be the gerund form.

verbs	examples
avoid	Some people **avoid writing** because it's difficult.
be worth	Good books **are worth reading.**
can't help	I **can't help worrying** about him.
consider	He **is considering applying** for a newspaper job.
enjoy	He **enjoys writing.**
finish	He's finally **finished writing** his first story.
imagine	Can you **imagine working** on a book?
involve	It would **involve doing** a lot of research.
miss	I would **miss having** free time.
spend time (hours, days, etc.)	I would rather **spend time doing** other things.

E. Common Verbs Often Followed by Gerunds or Infinitives (1)

Like gerunds, infinitives may be used as objects of verbs. Either a gerund object or an infinitive may follow these verbs with little or no difference in meaning.

verbs	examples
begin	I've **begun understanding (to understand)** most news stories.
can't stand	I **can't stand reading (to read)** late at night.
continue	I've **continued reading (to read)** several papers.
dislike	He **dislikes reading (to read)** the paper.
hate	I **hate being (to be)** uninformed.
like	All of us **like spending (to spend)** hours with the Sunday paper.
love	My brother **loves reading (to read)** the comics first.
prefer	My sister **prefers reading (to read)** the editorial page.
start	I've **started reading (to read)** several different papers.

 **exercise 5** Complete the passage by adding gerunds; form them from the following list of verbs. In some cases, you'll need to use the same gerund more than once. Finally, mark any instances where either the gerund or the infinitive can be used.

advertise	have	mix	read
buy	look	notice	

WHERE'S THE NEWS?

When you pick up a newspaper, you can't help _noticing_____ the amount

of _____. In fact, the typical newspaper today is 40 percent news and

1

60 percent ads. At least half of the news is text, but the rest is usually pictures.

If you can't stand _____ at advertisements, read just the front page

2

and the editorial pages! Normally, these are the only pages without ads.

Editors arrange the newspaper visually by _____ pictures and

3

headlines with advertisements. In this way, the newspaper does not look dull.

Apparently, few people like _____ newspapers without pictures or art

4

work. In general, people prefer _____ a lot of art work with the text

5

because they enjoy _____ at the pictures. According to marketing
                           6
researchers, most people avoid _____ newspapers with "too much
                                              7
print." In fact, the majority of people who buy newspapers spend only a short
time _____ the articles.
        8

Using What You've Learned

Interviewing a Classmate.   Using the following cues, interview one of your classmates about his or her newspaper-reading habits. Feel free to ask questions besides the ones you form from the cues.

> examples: avoid / read / newspapers in English
> **Do you avoid reading newspapers in English?**

1. enjoy / read / newspaper / in the morning
2. how much time / spend / read / paper
3. when you are on vacation / miss / read / local paper
4. like / read / the comics
5. prefer / buy / morning paper / or / afternoon paper
6. begin / read / English newspaper / regularly
7. ever / consider / become / journalist

Solving Problems.   Imagine that you work for a local newspaper. The paper is in serious financial trouble and may go bankrupt. Some of the problems include: few human-interest stories, boring comics, little advertising, poor circulation, no home delivery, and little material of interest to young people. In small groups, try to find possible ways to save the newspaper and your jobs. Complete the following sentences with gerund phrases and add sentences of your own. Finally, choose one member of your group to report to the class on your recommendations.

> In my opinion, people don't like . . .
> People are (not) interested in . . .
> Our readers are bored with . . .
> People enjoy . . .
> We should consider . . .
> Everyone will have to work hard at . . .
> If we don't find a solution, we'll all have to get used to . . .
> I don't look forward to . . .

TOPIC **two**
Infinitives

Setting the Context

previewing the passage
Do you know much about moviemaking? Share your information while answering the following questions about the picture.

- What is happening in the picture?
- What are the responsibilities of the various people shown?

MAKING MOVIES

For centuries, people such as Leonardo da Vinci dreamed about "photographing" objects in motion. Finally, in the twentieth century, inventors succeeded in developing a movie camera.

Leland Stanford was one of the first people to experiment with movement
5 and pictures. Because he wanted to study the motion of a running horse, Stanford asked a friend to take a series of photographs of one. He hoped to find out if the horse ever managed to have all four feet off the ground at the same time. To prove new theories is often difficult, and Stanford's project wasn't easy to do. His photographer needed to use twenty-four cameras set
10 close to each other to take pictures one after the other. After developing the pictures, he was able to report that a running horse did not, in fact, touch the ground at all times.

Later, the inventor Thomas Edison asked Stanford to show him the pictures and to introduce him to the photographer. During this meeting, Edison began to develop his ideas for the first motion-picture camera. It wasn't difficult to interest others in Edison's work. Soon, many kinds of cameras were invented, and within twenty years, filmmaking was a major industry.

discussing ideas Who were some important people in the development of the movie camera? What were some important steps in the history of filmmaking?

A. Uses of Infinitives

	examples	**notes**
Subject	**To make** a good movie is not easy.	Infinitives may replace nouns as objects of verbs and as subjects.
*With **it***	It is difficult **to make** a good movie.	Infinitives often follow the anticipatory *it* as the subject of a sentence.
Object of a Verb	I've always wanted **to learn** more about films.	
Infinitive of Purpose	I am taking classes **(in order) to learn** more about filmmaking. To begin, I've enrolled in three classes.	Infinitives can be used to show the purpose of an action. In these cases, *in order* is sometimes used before the infinitive.
Negative Infinitive	One of the most important things is **not to shake** the camera.	*Not* is used before the infinitive to form the negative.
For + Noun or Pronoun	It's difficult **for me to hold** the camera steady.	*For* + a noun or object pronoun is often used with an infinitive.

Note: An infinitive is never used as the object of a preposition. Compare:
correct: Practice is necessary to learn a new skill.
incorrect: Practice is necessary for to learn a new skill.

Reread the opening passage. Underline all the infinitives and discuss their grammatical functions.

Use infinitives to complete the following passage about the first motion picture. Choose from these simple forms:

attract	go	see
be	keep	study
create	learn	watch

LIGHTS, CAMERA, ACTION!

It is interesting <u>to study</u> the history of today's motion-picture indus-

try. In order _____ about its beginnings, we have _____ to
$\quad\quad\quad\quad\quad\quad$1$\quad\quad\quad\quad\quad\quad\quad\quad\quad\quad$2

New Jersey in the year 1891. There, at Thomas Edison's workshop, the first

movie audience got the opportunity _____ a film of a man bowing to
$\quad\quad\quad\quad\quad\quad\quad\quad\quad\quad\quad\quad$3

the audience. The viewers were thrilled _____ able _____ the
$\quad\quad\quad\quad\quad\quad\quad\quad\quad\quad$4$\quad\quad\quad\quad\quad\quad\quad\quad$5

first movie actor smiling, waving, and taking off his hat. Although this first

movie was thrilling, it did not contain enough _____ the audience
$\quad\quad\quad\quad\quad\quad\quad\quad\quad\quad\quad\quad\quad\quad$6

interested for very long. _____ audiences, moviemakers soon needed
$\quad\quad\quad\quad\quad\quad\quad\quad\quad\quad\quad$7

_____ film that actually told a story.
$\quad\quad$8

Complete the following seven sentences about early movies. Use all the verbs listed below.

be	make	take charge
control	produce	view
go	see	watch

example: In the early days, moviegoers were able <u>to view</u> only short

$\quad\quad\quad\quad\quad\quad\quad$comedies or "newsreels."

1. People liked _____ to the movies because they showed another

world.

2. It was thrilling (and frightening) _____ a train thundering toward

you on the screen.

3. It was exciting for the audience _____ a "good guy" defeat a "bad

guy."

4. In the early days, the actors, actresses, artists, and writers all expected

_____ able _____ the content of the films they were

making.

5. Later, because of rising costs and competition from radio, bankers began

_____ of films.

6. Bankers and businesspeople wanted _____ money-making films.

7. They learned _____ the same types of film again and again

because these types were always money-makers.

exercise **4**   Without changing the meaning, rewrite the paragraph by replacing each gerund with an infinitive. Use the *anticipatory it* whenever possible.

example: Creating new films took a few years.
    It took a few years to create new films.

EARLY FILMMAKING

 After Edison's first movie, creating new films took a few years. The Lumière brothers showed the next motion pictures in 1896. Producing good-quality images was impossible at that time, so the pictures were "jumpy." Also, making films of any length was very difficult, so the Lumière brothers' three
5 "movies" were only 30 to 90 seconds long. Yet watching them was probably a thrilling experience for those early audiences. In the twentieth century, present-ing an interesting story became important. Soon, entertaining audiences was the purpose of movies.

B. Common Verbs Often Followed by Infinitives

If a verb form is used after the verbs below, it must be in the infinitive form.

Verb + Infinitive

These verbs are followed directly by an infinitive.

verbs	examples
agree	My friend **agreed to take** a film class with me.
be (able)	I was **able to find** several good film classes.
decide	I **decided to take** several classes.
fail	My friend **failed to enroll** in time.
forget	He **forgot to enroll** before the first of the month.
have	All students **had to enroll** before the first of the month.
hope	My friend **hopes to take** a class next semester.
know how	I don't **know how to use** a movie camera.
learn (how)	Last night we **learned (how) to load** the film.
manage	Several people **managed to ruin** their films.
offer	The teacher **offered to help.**
plan	I **plan to be** very careful with my camera.
seem	You **seem to be** happy with your new hobby.
wait	I can't **wait to buy** a new camera.

Verb + (Noun or Pronoun) + Infinitive

These verbs may be followed directly by an infinitive, or they may use a (pro)noun object before the infinitive. *Note: For* is not used in this pattern.

verbs	examples
ask	I **asked to enroll** in the class. I **asked my friend to enroll** in the class.
expect	I **expect to learn** a great deal about early films. My teacher **expects me to learn** a great deal.
need	I **need to buy** some film. I **need you to buy** some film for me.

verbs	examples
promise	We **promised to do** all of the work.
	We **promised our teacher to do** all of the work.
want	I **want to help.**
	I **want you to help.**
would like	I **would like to help.**
	I **would like you to help.**

Verb + Noun or Pronoun + Infinitive

When these verbs are in the active voice, they are not directly followed by an infinitive. A (pro)noun object *must* come before the infinitive. When they are in the passive voice, they may be directly followed by an infinitive. Note: *For* is not used in this pattern.

verbs	examples
advise	I **advise you to take** some classes.
convince	A friend **convinced me to enroll** in three classes.
encourage	A friend **encouraged me to buy** a new camera.
force	My budget **forced me to buy** a used camera.
invite	I **invited my friend to attend** a film class with me.
remind	The teacher **reminded us to bring** our cameras.
teach	The teacher **taught us to focus** carefully.
tell	The teacher **told us to adjust** the lights.

 Decide if the following verbs can be used in pattern A, B, or C.

A. He . . . to go to the movies.
B. He . . . John to go to the movies.
C. Either is possible.

example: hope
      Hope **is possible only in A.**

1. tell

2. expect

3. advise

4. ask

5. agree

6. plan

7. forget

8. want

9. invite

10. promise

11. encourage

12. offer

exercise 6   In pairs, ask and answer questions using the following cues. Add a noun or pronoun object when necessary.

> **example:** advise / not to see *Snake Pit*
> A: **Have you advised John not to see *Snake Pit*?**
> B: **Yes, I advised him not to see *Snake Pit*.**

1. tell / see *Star Wars*
2. remind / not use the free tickets until next week
3. encourage / watch French films
4. invite / come with us Saturday
5. convince / not go out Wednesday
6. promise / not cry during the movie
7. ask / go to see *Dracula*
8. offer / pay for the tickets

exercise 7   Complete the following passage by putting the words in parentheses in the correct form and order. In each case, change the appropriate verb to an infinitive.

THE PLOT THICKENS . . .

The first films that <u>managed to tell</u> (tell / manage) a story were George

Méliès' *A Trip to the Moon* and Edwin S. Porter's *The Life of an American*

Fireman and *The Great Train Robbery*. Moviemakers _____

(audiences / expect / enjoy) these early motion pictures, although they lasted
1

only ten minutes and were actually quite boring. Soon, however, audiences

_____ (producers / ask / make) more interesting films. People
2

_____ (want / see) short comedies or newsreels when they
3

_____ (plan / go) to a movie. Before long, audiences _____
4   5

(begin / demand) even more. They _____ (show / producers / expect)
6

them a fantasy world in their films. Viewers _____ (create / encourage /
7

moviemakers) illusions on the screen.

 C. Infinitives with *Too* and *(Not) Enough*

Adjectives or noun phrases + infinitives are often used in expressions with *too* and *(not) enough*. *For* + (pro)noun is often added for clarity.

	examples	notes
too	The movie was **too long** (for us) **to sit** through.	*Too* often implies a negative result: *The movie was very long, so we didn't sit through it.*
enough	The film was **good enough** (for me) **to watch** five times.	*Enough* often implies a positive result: *The film was good, so I watched it five times.*
not enough	There were**n't enough people** in the audience **to show** the movie.	*Not enough* often implies a negative result: *There weren't many people, so they didn't show the movie.*

exercise **8**   Complete the passage here and on the next page with the infinitive form of the verbs in parentheses and *too* or *enough*.

THE BIRTH OF HOLLYWOOD

In the early twentieth century, the motion-picture industry moved to California for one simple reason: The weather in the East was _too_ unpredictable _to make_ (make) movies outdoors. In the West, however,

there was _____ sun year-round _____ (light) the scenes. In
those days, technology was not advanced _____ _____
(provide) adequate lighting for indoor scenes. Thus, even indoor scenes were
filmed outside in the sun. Unfortunately, the illusion did not work. Outdoor
light was _____ strong _____ (seem) like indoor light.
Finally, indoor film lighting was invented.

    Nevertheless, indoor lighting did not solve all problems. A few important
ones remained. For instance, it was _____ hot _____ (use)
certain objects under the lights, so substitutions had to be made (for example,
mashed potatoes for ice cream). The lights also made some actors
_____ uncomfortable _____ (work) effectively.

exercise 9   Change the following sentences to use *too* or *(not) enough* with infinitives and *for*
+ (pro)noun where necessary.

    example: The weather in the East was unpredictable, so filmmakers couldn't
                     work outdoors regularly.
                     **The weather in the East was too unpredictable for filmmakers
                     to work outdoors regularly.**

1. In the East, there wasn't very much sunlight in the winter, so producers
   couldn't film outdoors.
2. In California, there was sun year-round; therefore, producers could make
   films without worrying about weather.
3. Soon the technology of indoor lighting became more advanced, so
   filmmakers could begin shooting films inside.
4. The first indoor film lights were so hot that actors couldn't work for long
   periods of time.
5. Many actors felt so uncomfortable that they couldn't perform well.
6. Some early movies were very good, so people still enjoy them today.
7. Today film technology is very advanced; therefore, we can shoot pictures
   anywhere, anytime.
8. A few movies are extremely popular, so they bring in millions of dollars in
   profits.
9. Other movies aren't successful; therefore, they cannot even cover the costs
   of making them.
10. Some movies would be very expensive, so they are never made.

D. Infinitives of Purpose

    Infinitives can be used to tell why an action is performed. These infinitives
may appear at various points within a sentence.

examples	meanings
(In order) To create the illusion of blood, filmmakers used chocolate syrup in black and white films.	These infinitive phrases often begin with *in order to*. However, *in order* is not necessary to give this meaning.
Chocolate syrup was used in black and white films **to create** the illusion of blood.	Infinitives of purposes are often used at the beginning of a sentence or after the verb (and direct object).

 **exercise 10** Match the events in Column A with their purposes in Column B. Then make the items in Column B into infinitive phrases. Finally, make new sentences by combining the items in Column A with the phrases in Column B.

examples: **In black and white films, producers used chocolate syrup to produce the illusion of blood.** *or*
To produce the illusion of blood in black and white films, producers used chocolate syrup.

A

1. In black and white films, producers used chocolate syrup.
2. Red food dye was used.
3. In old westerns, actors would hit a place on their shirts.
4. Nowadays, packets of "blood" have small wires in them.
5. The computer is programmed.

B

a. It created an illusion of blood in color films.
b. The wires connect the packets to a computer.
c. It explodes the packet at exactly the right time.
d. It produced the illusion of blood.
e. They broke a hidden packet of "blood."

Using What You've Learned

 **activity** **Describing Trends.** In pairs or small groups, share information about movies in North America and in your country. What kinds of movies are being produced today? What kinds of movies make a lot of money for the producers? What kinds of movies do people like to watch? As you discuss current trends in filmmaking and audience preferences, try to use as many of the following expressions as possible.

Today, movies seem . . .
People in my culture (don't) enjoy . . .
They like . . .
They can't stand . . .
It's boring . . .
They're used to . . .

Audiences usually prefer . . .
Most people would like . . .
It's (more) exciting . . .
Films today are too . . .
It's (not) worth . . .

TOPIC three
Infinitives Versus Gerunds

Setting the Context

previewing
the
passage

What do you know about radios and communication? Share your information while answering the following questions about the picture.

- What sort of equipment is shown in the picture?
- What is it used for?

RADIO

Like the film business, radio communication seemed to grow overnight. Within a few years, radio developed from an experimental idea into a useful piece of equipment and a huge industry. Today radio technology plays a very important role in many aspects of our lives.

5   Radio technology is used in a wide variety of ways. The most common is, of course, commercial broadcasting. Radio also has many specialized uses. For example, teletypewriter signals are sent by transmitting radio waves. Another form of radio is radar. Objects of all kinds may be located with radar, which is frequently used for both civilian and military purposes. Armies use shortwave

10　radio to coordinate their activities. Likewise, many political groups have tried to organize their resistance by operating a network of radio communications. Because of the effectiveness of such communication, some governments have stopped allowing private use of radio.

　　A more common (and less controversial) use of radio is to send and receive
15　emergency information. Professionals such as doctors often carry "walkie-talkies" or beepers. If a hospital needs to contact a doctor, radio waves can be used to signal him or her. In this way, the doctor can be certain of getting emergency calls at any time or place.

　　Nowadays, few people can remember not having radios, and it's difficult to
20　imagine getting along without the benefits of radio technology. Certainly if radio did not exist, we would all miss being entertained and informed by the music, news, and other programs that have come over the radio waves.

discussing ideas

What are the major uses of radio? Which do you think are most important? Can you think of other uses of radio?

exercise 1

Reread the opening passage. Circle all the gerunds and underline all the infinitives. Pay special attention to the verbs that are used with both the infinitives and the gerunds.

exercise 2

Using the verbs in parentheses, complete the sentences here and on the next page with either infinitives or gerunds. In some cases, either may be possible.

1. In 1920, station KDKA started _transmitting (to transmit)_ (transmit) in Pittsburgh, Pennsylvania.

2. By the end of 1922, over 500 radio stations had begun

_____ (broadcast) around the United States.

3. The first stations were created by radio equipment companies in order

_____ (develop) a market for their products.

4. These companies were concerned about _____ (sell) more radio equipment to stations, and they also wanted

_____ (tell) the public about their products.

5. Soon many types of companies were interested in

_____ (advertise) their products, so radio stations

decided _____ (sell) "air time."

6. Early commercials were very long. In some cases, an announcer would

spend ten minutes _____ (encourage) people

_____ (buy) cosmetics or _____

(rent) an apartment.

7. Radio became popular very quickly. People throughout the United States

dreamed about _____ (have) a radio, and by 1930

12,000,000 Americans had managed _____ (buy) a set.

8. People everywhere enjoyed _____ (listen) to the early

radio programs.

9. Americans were thrilled about _____ (be) able

_____ (hear) performers like Al Jolson or Amos and

Andy in their own homes.

10. People also loved _____ (follow) radio melodramas

and looked forward to _____ (hear) their favorite "soap

opera" every night.

exercise **3** Complete the following passage with infinitive or gerund forms of the verbs in
parentheses. In some cases, both may be possible.

NONCOMMERCIAL RADIO

Although many radio listeners dislike _hearing (to hear)_____ (hear)

commercials, few noncommercial stations exist in the United States. It is

difficult for these stations _____ (survive) because, finan-
                                                     1
cially, they have _____ (depend) on _____
                              2   3
(receive) donations from their listeners. Sometimes listener-sponsored stations

succeed in _____ (raise) large amounts of money, but often
                          4
they fail _____ (get) enough funds _____
                       5   6
(cover) their budgets. Managers of these stations constantly worry about

_____ (have) enough money _____ (pay)
              7   8
their employees and their bills. In fact, financial problems have forced many

listener-sponsored stations _____ (begin)
                                                   9
_____ (sell) air time for _____ (advertise).
              10   11

As a result, the only major commercial-free station in the United States is National Public Radio, which receives funds from the U.S. government, in addition to donations from its listeners.

 When did you last listen to the radio? Did you listen to the news or weather? Did you hear a commercial? Tell about the radio broadcast by completing the following sentences. Include either an infinitive or a gerund phrase in each sentence.

1. The weatherperson advised people . . .
2. It (the weather) should continue . . .
3. The newscaster said that the government plans . . .
4. The government will avoid . . .
5. The president (governor, mayor, etc.) hopes . . .
6. He or she expects . . .
7. The sportscaster was excited (nervous, angry) about . . .
8. The sportscaster reminded people . . .
9. The commercial tried to convince me . . .
10. It encouraged me . . .

Common Verbs Often Followed by Infinitives or Gerunds (2)

In Topic One you saw that some verbs can take either an infinitive or a gerund object with little or no change in meaning. The following verbs may take either an infinitive or a gerund object, but the meaning of the verb changes, depending on which is used.

	examples	notes
Infinitives with remember	Did you **remember to buy** the tickets?	*Remember* tells the first (or earlier) action, and the infinitive tells the second (or later) action.
Gerunds with remember	I **remember telling** you about that.	The gerund tells the first (or earlier) action, and *remember* tells the second (or later) action.
Infinitives with try	I **tried to buy** several tickets.	When *try* is followed by an infinitive, it means "attempt."
Gerunds with try	I **tried calling** the theater, **going** to the box office, **and asking** all my friends for extra tickets.	When *try* is followed by a gerund, it means "experiment with different possibilities or alternatives."

	examples	notes
Infinitives with quit **and** stop	He **stopped to have** coffee. He **stopped** at Mary's house **(in order) to have** coffee.	When an infinitive follows *stop* or *quit* it means that the subject stopped whatever he or she was doing for the reason or purpose given by the infinitive. *In order* can usually be added: *in order to have coffee.*
Gerunds with quit **and** stop	He **stopped (quit) having** coffee because it made him very nervous. He drinks juice, instead.	When a gerund follows these verbs, it tells "who" or "what" was stopped—often a habit or custom that had existed for a long time.

exercise 5 Complete the following passage with infinitive or gerund forms of the verbs in parentheses.

LIFE BEFORE TV

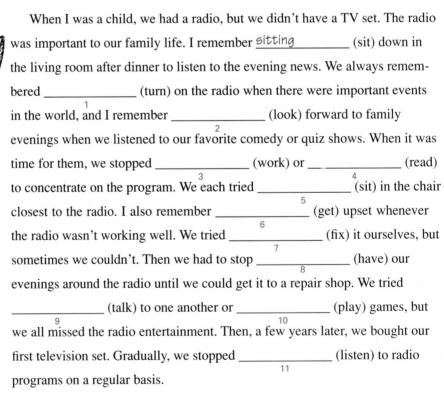

When I was a child, we had a radio, but we didn't have a TV set. The radio was important to our family life. I remember _sitting_____ (sit) down in the living room after dinner to listen to the evening news. We always remem- bered _____ (turn) on the radio when there were important events in the world, and I remember _____ (look) forward to family evenings when we listened to our favorite comedy or quiz shows. When it was time for them, we stopped _____ (work) or __ _____ (read) to concentrate on the program. We each tried _____ (sit) in the chair closest to the radio. I also remember _____ (get) upset whenever the radio wasn't working well. We tried _____ (fix) it ourselves, but sometimes we couldn't. Then we had to stop _____ (have) our evenings around the radio until we could get it to a repair shop. We tried _____ (talk) to one another or _____ (play) games, but we all missed the radio entertainment. Then, a few years later, we bought our first television set. Gradually, we stopped _____ (listen) to radio programs on a regular basis.

exercise 6 Rephrase the following people's opinions by completing the sentences. Use infinitive or gerund phrases in your new sentences.

My favorite radio program is CITY HOME COMPANION. Everyone should listen--It's great! I can't wait to hear it next week! I wish there were more programs like CITY HOME COMPANION.

I don't like sports on radio. TV's much better. Tonight there's a great baseball game on the tube.

We always listen to the TOP FORTY so we know the most popular songs. Our mom always complains about the volume. She says the radio is so loud that she can't think. We like loud music--it doesn't bother us.

1. This woman enjoys . . .
2. She's looking forward to . . .
3. She encourages everyone . . .
4. She would like . . .
5. This man avoids . . .
6. He prefers . . .
7. He plans . . .
8. These girls are interested in . . .
9. They spend a lot of time . . .
10. For the girls, it's fun . . .
11. According to their mother, the radio is too loud . . .
12. According to the girls, they're used to . . .

Using What You've Learned

activity **1**

Persuading. Individually, in pairs, or in small groups, create your own commercial or political advertisement. In either case, you will try to convince your audience to do something. Use as many expressions with infinitives and gerunds as possible in your ad. Finally, perform your ads for the class.

> example: Homemakers everywhere! Do you want to avoid ironing hundreds of shirts each year? Can you imagine not having to iron another shirt again? Then buy . . .

activity **2**

Conducting a Talk Show. Many radio stations have talk shows that give advice or information on a wide variety of topics. Conduct a talk show in your class, taking turns being the host of the show, the guest speaker(s), and radio listeners. The guest speakers may want to be counselors, political figures, or "experts" on dating, sports, etc. If possible, make arrangements with your local phone company to use a Telezonia Telephone Kit for your "radio" listeners to call in on. (Just ask the telephone company about this.)

> example: **"Hello, Linda Lovelorn? I would like to get your advice on how to meet women and have more dates . . ."**
> **"Well, if you want to have a date every night, I advise you to learn how to dance. Women everywhere love to dance, but most men are too embarrassed to learn well. A man who knows how to dance well . . . ."**

TOPIC **four**

Causative and Structurally Related Verbs; Verbs of Perception

Setting the Context

previewing the passage

How do televisions work? Share your information while answering the following questions about the picture on the opposite page.

- Describe the process of sending a television picture.
- Describe the process of receiving a television picture.

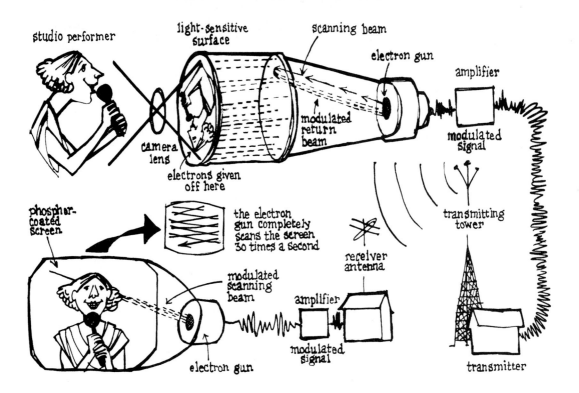

Labels in figure:
studio performer · light-sensitive surface · scanning beam · electron gun · amplifier · modulated return beam · modulated signal · camera lens · electrons given off here · phosphor-coated screen · the electron gun completely scans the screen 30 times a second · transmitting tower · receiver antenna · modulated scanning beam · amplifier · modulated signal · electron gun · transmitter

TELEVISION

     Television broadcasting began in the United States and England in 1926. Radio stations let the scientists who were experimenting with television use their radio transmitting equipment for these early broadcasts, which lasted only a few minutes and did not include sound. Early broadcasters had difficulty
5 getting investors to support their experiments because few people believed at the time that television had any future.

     Obviously, TV did have a future, and today life without television is almost unimaginable. Television provides us with entertainment and lets us know what is happening around the world. For example, we can watch an orchestra
10 performing in Rome or see athletes swimming in Moscow. Television also educates; it has helped people to learn everything from languages to cooking, and it has gotten all of us to experience new things, ideas, places, and people without even leaving our living rooms.

     But television may also affect us negatively. For example, it has been
15 suggested that violent TV programs might make some people go out and commit similar violent acts. Many parents also worry that watching a lot of television may make their children become passive. As a result of these concerns, some governments have tried to have TV viewing limited. Various countries, for instance, do not let television stations broadcast during daylight hours.
20 Naturally, some people are angry about having their freedom of choice limited in this way.

What are some positive and negative effects of TV? In your opinion, should governments regulate how much TV people can watch?

A. Causative and Structurally Related Verbs

The verbs *get, have, help, let,* and *make* are often called "causatives." They are followed by a direct object and then an infinitive, a simple form (the infinitive without *to*), or a past participle.

	active sentences	passive sentences	notes
get have	I **got** him **to wash** the car. I **had** him **wash** the car.	I **got** the car **washed.** I **had** the car **washed.**	*Get* and *have* are similar in meaning: "arrange for." Note that *get* is followed by an infinitive in the active form.
help	I **helped** him **wash** the car. *or* I **helped** him **to wash** the car.		*Help* means "aid" or "assist." Note that *help* can be followed by the simple form or the infinitive of a second verb.
let make	I **let** him **wash** the car. I **made** him **wash** the car.		*Let* means "allow." *Make* is similar in meaning to "force."

exercise  Appliances and other machines often break down. Using the cues, suggest solutions for the following common problems. Use modal auxiliaries (*ought to, should, could,* etc.) and the causative verb *have* in your suggestions.

example: The picture on my television set is very poor.
television / repair
picture tube / replace
You should have your television repaired.
You could have the picture tube replaced.

1. My television set isn't working well.
TV / fix
antenna / install

2. The sound on my stereo is very poor.
stereo / repair
speakers / replace
wiring / check

3. The lights go out when I use more than one major electric appliance at the same time.
house / rewire
new fuse box / put in

4. My car isn't running well.
engine / tune
oil / check
spark plugs / replace

 **exercise 2**

In pairs, form questions and answers using *get*. Follow the example.

example: car / wash
A: **Do you normally wash your car yourself?**
B: **No, normally, I get my car washed.**

1. typewriter / clean
2. hair / cut
3. suits / dry-clean

4. piano / tune
5. watch / repair
6. computer / fix

exercise 3

Which of the following things did your parents let you do when you were fifteen years old? Compare your answers with those of your classmates.

example: drive the car
When I was fifteen years old, my parents wouldn't let me drive the car.

1. watch television until midnight during the week
2. go out alone in the evening
3. stay home from school if I felt like it
4. choose my own clothes
5. drink wine with dinner
6. work while I was in school

exercise 4

Two local television executives are discussing a change in sports programming. Complete their conversation here and on the next page by using *get, let, make,* or *have*. In some cases, more than one verb may be appropriate.

JACK: People have stopped watching our Saturday afternoon sports show. How can

we _____*get*_____ more viewers to watch on Saturdays? Perhaps we

should offer different sports programs. I think everyone is tired of football

and baseball.

ANDERS: I think we should _____ our viewers decide which sports we tele-
vise. Why don't we _____ our viewing audience write us letters?
₁
₂

JACK: We've already received a lot of letters requesting more soccer games on TV.
Do you think we can _____ the national TV networks to broad-
cast more soccer matches? How can we _____ them understand
that people want more soccer on TV? The national networks think that soccer
has only a few fans. How can we _____ them change their
minds?

ANDERS: That will be difficult. Well, here's an idea. Let's _____ our viewing audience to write letters to the national networks, too!

B. Verbs of Perception

The verbs *feel, hear, listen to, look at, see, smell,* and *watch* can be followed
by a second verb. Depending on the meaning, the second verb can be a present
participle or the simple form. A noun or object pronoun is used after the main
verb.

	examples	notes
Simple Form	I saw **them film** the commercial. I heard **them discuss** the price.	In most cases, there is little difference in meaning between the simple form and present participle. The simple form can imply that the action was completed, however.
Present Participle	I saw **them filming** the commercial. I heard **them discussing** the price.	The present participle may refer to an action in progress. This sentence means "I saw them *while* they were filming the commercial."

 **exercise 5**   Complete the passage on the opposite page with the present participle or simple
form of the verbs in parentheses. Be prepared to discuss any difference in mean-
ing when both forms are possible.

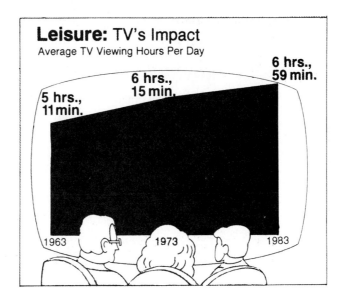

Leisure: TV's Impact
Average TV Viewing Hours Per Day

5 hrs., 11 min.

6 hrs., 15 min.

6 hrs., 59 min.

1963   1973   1983

THE IMPACT OF TV

Most of us have been watching entertainers _perform (performing)_ (perform) on TV for most of our lives. We have listened to musicians

_____ (sing) or _____ (play) instruments,
 1 2

have seen dancers _____ (move) to music, and have heard
 3

actors and actresses _____ (say) their lines. We have probably
 4

learned a lot from television programming.

Our children are also learning a lot from television, but what exactly are they learning? Many people are afraid that children are learning to be violent. Children today spend hours watching actors _____ (be) hurt
 5

or killed. They see and hear people _____ (fight),
 6

_____ (hit) each other, _____ (shoot) guns,
 7 8

and _____ (use) other weapons.
 9

Because of the types of programs on TV today, some parents believe that we should not let our children _____ (watch) whatever they
 10

want on TV. Instead, we should help them _____ (choose)
 11

valuable shows and make them _____ (think) and
 12

_____ (talk) about what they have seen.
 13

exercise 6

Imagine that you could visit the filming of your favorite television show. Describe your visit by completing the following, telling everything you saw, heard, etc.

> **example:**   I saw the stagehands . . .
> **I saw the stagehands setting up the scenery.**

1. I saw cameramen and women . . .
2. I heard the director . . .
3. I watched the actors and actresses . . .
4. I listened to the stars . . .
5. I heard the studio audience . . .
6. I watched my favorite actor (actress) . . .
7. I looked at the crowd of fans . . .
8. I felt my heart . . .

exercise 7

Review.   Complete the passage below and on the opposite page about television transmission with either gerund or infinitive forms of the verbs in parentheses.

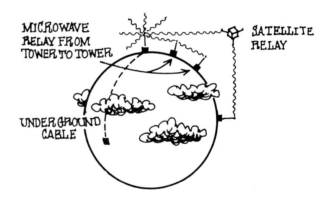

TELEVISION TRANSMISSION

TV TRANSMISSION

Scientists know how _____ (transmit) TV pictures from
the moon to Earth. But within the Earth's atmosphere, we have learned

_____ (send) a TV picture only a short distance. Most stations
are able _____ (transmit) just a little beyond the horizon—as
seen from the transmitter.

Very high frequency TV waves travel in straight lines. They continue

_____ (travel) right out into space, or they strike the Earth and
are absorbed. Thus, stations need _____ (build) high antennas
in order _____ (transmit) over long distances.

For _____ (transmit) over very long distances, TV stations
use either cables or microwave relay stations, depending on the landscape.

Stations prefer _____ (use) microwave relay when there are
mountains or large bodies of water to be crossed. In cities or across level areas,

it is easier _____ (use) cables.

exercise  8 **Review.**   Fill in the blanks here and on the next page with the correct forms of
the verbs in parentheses. In some cases there may be two correct answers.

UNPLUGGING THE TV

This is the story of a family that did a very unusual thing: They decided
_____ (stop) _____ (let) television
_____ (control) their lives. In fact, they agreed
_____ (not watch) television at all for a while. How did they
make this decision?

It was dinnertime on a typical day. Jane Wilkins was starting
_____ (prepare) dinner for her family. She could hear the
evening news _____ (blare) in the next room. Suddenly, there
was a loud BOOM! Then silence. The television set had fallen on the floor and
broken.

The Wilkins family had been accustomed to _____
(watch) television four or five hours every day. It was normal for them
_____ (eat) or _____ (do) homework in front
of the TV. But now the TV was broken. Jane Wilkins had a thought: What
would their family life be like if they didn't have the TV
_____ (fix)?

She remembered that, when her children were little, they all used to
_____ (take) walks and play together. She had enjoyed
_____ (read) to her children. It also seemed that she and her
husband had spent a lot more time _____ (talk).

Jane thought it would be worth _____ (try) to go a week
without _____ (watch) TV. When she suggested this to her
husband and children, they agreed _____ (do) it. During the

week, the family did things together. Jane was thrilled about

_____ (have) time to be with her husband and children again.
      17
At the end of the week, the family had another meeting, where they decided

_____ (try) another week without TV. One of the children
      18
said, "I thought I would miss _____ (watch) TV every day.
                                      19
But I don't. _____ (not watch) television lets me
                    20
_____ (have) more free time for other things. I really like
      21
that."

Using What You've Learned

activity 1

Expressing Opinions.   What do you think about the types of programs shown on North American TV? On TV in your area or country? What would you change? What would you offer more or less of? In small groups share your opinions by completing the following sentences. Be sure to add original sentences, too.

> I (don't) like . . .
> I (don't) enjoy . . .
> Personally, when I turn on the TV, I (don't) want to watch actors and actresses . . .
> I prefer (not) . . .
> It's (not) good . . .
> I would have networks . . .
> In my opinion, the government should(n't) let . . .
> It should(n't) make TV networks . . .
> It's important . . .

Then, as a group, write a letter to the local station telling them what you like (that they already do) and what other programs you would like to see in the future.

Discussing Rights.   In your opinion, which of the following things do governments have the right to make people do? Compare your opinions with those of your classmates.

> examples: limit the number of children people have
> **In my opinion, governments do not have the right to make people limit the number of children they have.**

1. serve in the military
2. pay taxes
3. wear a helmet when riding a motorcycle
4. wear seat belts in the car
5. quit smoking in public places
6. move (if the government wants the land)

Use of Gerunds, Infinitives, and Other Verb Forms

Adjective clauses are frequently tested on standardized English proficiency exams. Review these commonly tested structures, and check your understanding by completing the sample items below.

Remember that . . .

- Certain verbs can be followed by gerunds, others by infinitives, and some verbs by either.
- Gerunds (not infinitives) are used after prepositions.
- Certain verbs may be followed by the simple form or the present or past participle of another verb.

Part 1. Circle the correct completion for the following.

   example: I have a friend who hopes _____ live in France.
   a. be able to
   b. to be able
   c. be able
   d. to be able to

1. Mary was quite _____ her work.
   a. boring with
   b. bored with
   c. boring
   d. bored

2. Companies use commercials _____ their products.
   a. to convince people buy
   b. convince people buy
   c. to convince people to buy
   d. convince people to buy

3. In the U.S., many children spend _____ TV than they do in any other activity.
   a. time more watching
   b. more watching time
   c. more time to watch
   d. more time watching

Part 2. Circle the letter below the word(s) containing an error.

example: <u>To raise</u> a child multilingually, one of <u>the best</u> methods is
       A   B

to <u>have</u> different people <u>to speak</u> different languages to
C   Ⓓ

the child from the time of birth.

1. In <u>the</u> early 1900s, the <u>motion-picture</u> industry moved from the East
    A   B

Coast to California <u>in order</u> be able <u>to film</u> outdoors year-round.
                     C   D

2. The first television broadcasts in the United States and England <u>were</u>
                                                           A

not able <u>transmit</u> sound, and the broadcasts <u>lasted</u> <u>only a few</u>
         B   C   D

minutes.

3. A reporter's job <u>consists</u> of <u>gathering</u> information and <u>to write</u> <u>news</u>
               A   B   C   D

stories.

CHAPTER **twelve**

Prejudice, Tolerance, and Justice

Hope, Wish, **and Conditional Sentences**

Topic One: *Hope* and *Wish:* Present and Future
Topic Two: Conditional Sentences: Present or Unspecified Time
Topic Three: Past Wishes and Conditions
Topic Four: Review

in this chapter

TOPIC **one**

Hope and Wish: *Present and Future*

Setting the Context

Amnesty International members demonstrating in Boston, Massachusetts

previewing the passage What are human rights? Do you know about any international organizations that work for human rights? Share your information while answering the following questions about the picture.

- What is this group of people doing?
- What does amnesty mean?

PEACE ORGANIZATIONS

Most of us wish that we could end war, poverty, and hunger; we wish there were no censorship and no political prisoners, and we wish we had more power to change conditions in the world. But how many of us actually spend any of our time working to make such changes happen?

5   There are several outstanding organizations that work to solve these problems. One important one is UNESCO. The purpose of this United Nations organization is to promote peace. Its constitution says: "Since wars begin in the minds of men, it is in the minds of men that the defenses of peace must be constructed." UNESCO hopes that education will help build a peaceful world

10 based on human rights.

Amnesty International is also working to protect human rights. It began in 1961, and it has groups in about 110 countries. Each of these groups adopts at least two political prisoners in other countries. By pressuring governments, writing letters, and demonstrating, they hope they can free these prisoners.

15   Most "peace demonstrations" need help from many individuals in the
countries where they operate. So if you wish that we could solve the world's
problems, get involved!

**discussing
ideas**

How does UNESCO work for peace? What kind of work does Amnesty International do?

Hope and *Wish:* Present and Future

Hope and *wish* express different points of view about the present and future.
Hope refers to real possibilities. *Wish* is used to express impossibility or
improbability—that the speaker or writer wants reality to be other than it is.
Compare:

hopes versus wishes	implied meanings
I **hope** that they **will (can)** help us.	It is possible that they will (can) help us.
I **wish** that they **would (could)** help us.	They probably will not (cannot) help us.

Hopes: Present and future hopes are expressed by using present or future
verbs or modal auxiliaries such as *can* in the dependent clause.

Wishes: Present and future wishes are expressed by using *would, could,* or
a special verb form—the subjunctive—in the dependent clause. In most cases,
this form is the same as the simple past tense. In formal English, *were* is used
for all forms of the verb *be*. However, in informal English, *was* is sometimes
used with *I, he, she*, and *it*, although it is not considered correct. Use of *that* is
optional in these sentences.

	examples	implied meanings
Wishes About the Present	I **wish** (that) they **were** here.	They aren't here.
	I **wish** (that) they **were coming.**	They are not coming.
	I **wish** (that) they **came** here more often.	They don't come here very often.
	I **wish** they **could come.**	They cannot come.
Wishes About the Future	I wish they **were going to come.**	They are probably not going to come.
	I wish they **would (could) come** next week.	They probably won't (can't) come next week.

exercise 1

Complete the following by using either the present or past forms of the verbs in parentheses.

example: I wish there <u>weren't</u> (not be) so many problems in the world.

1. The teacher hopes that the students _____ (understand) her explanation.

2. The students wish that they _____ (understand) English grammar better.

3. Everybody wishes there _____ (be) peace in the world.

4. I hope there _____ (be) enough time to discuss this problem.

5. The representatives at the peace conference wish they _____ (not disagree) about so many things.

6. They hope they _____ (reach) some kind of an agreement.

exercise 2

Complete these sentences with *can, could, will, would,* or *be going to* + the simple form of the verb in parentheses.

example: My friend and I wish we <u>could work</u> (work) together, but we can't.

1. I hope we _____ (be able to) work together some day.

2. After meeting at the conference, the two delegates hope they _____ (meet) again soon.

3. Government leaders hope the peace talks _____ (end) the fighting.

4. I wish I _____ (meet) you this evening, but I have to go to a meeting.

5. I wish they _____ (call) us.

6. I hope they _____ (come) with us to the meeting.

exercise 3

Complete the sentences with the correct forms of the verbs in parentheses. Add modal auxiliaries when necessary. (In which sentences are both *could* and *would* correct?)

example: There are many conflicts among nations, but we wish there

<u>weren't</u> (not be).

1. We wish we _____ (know) a way to end wars forever.

2. We wish we _____ (establish) a permanent peace.

3. We wish governments _____ (agree) to stop the arms race.

4. Many people wish governments _____ (ban) nuclear weapons.

5. We wish there _____ (be) more organizations working for peace.

6. We wish we _____ (be able to) protect human rights for everyone.

7. We wish more individuals _____ (work for) peace.

8. We wish that somehow we _____ (guarantee) the survival of the human race.

exercise 4 **Error Analysis.** Correct the following sentences.

      were

1. I wish I ~~would be~~ in Mexico now.

2. I wish I can talk to Maia now.

3. I hope I would see you tomorrow.

4. I wish I will be in college next semester.

5. I wish I went to New York next year.

6. I hope I could feel better now.

7. I wish I am able to help you with the project.

8. I hope I wouldn't have homework this weekend.

exercise 5 The Peace Corps is an organization that sends volunteers to developing countries to help people improve their living conditions. In the following passage, a Peace Corps volunteer in Lesotho, Africa describes her experiences. Complete the passage below and on the next page with the correct forms of the verbs in parentheses. Add modal auxiliaries when necessary.

PEACE CORPS VOLUNTEERS

    "I came here two years ago because I wanted to teach people about modern health care. I will be leaving in about two months; I wish I _could stay_ (stay) longer, but it's time for me to go home.

    "My work here has been very interesting. I am learning so much. I always wish that there _____ (be) more hours in the day so that I could do
                            1
more. Maybe it's silly, but I worry about what will happen to the villagers after I leave. I hope that my students _____ (remember) the things I've
                                         2
tried to teach them. I hope that in the future there _____ (be) less
                                                3
disease and that the children _____ (be) healthier. And of course,
                                4
I hope that they _____ (not forget) me. I've become so close to the
                   5

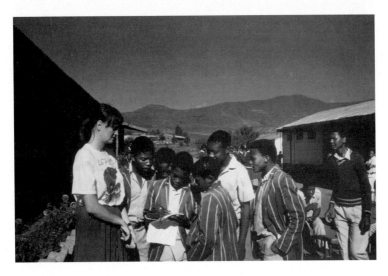

Peace Corps volunteer in Lesotho

people here, I wish I _____ (take) them home with me! But of course that's impossible, so I hope I _____ (visit) them in the future. I wish
₆
more people _____ (join) the Peace Corps. It's so rewarding, and
₇
there's so much work to be done.
₈

 **exercise 6**   Several students are talking about the problems in their countries. Complete the sentences with statements expressing their *hopes* or *wishes*.

example: "My city is very big, so people drive their cars everywhere. We have terrible traffic jams. We need better public transportation."

a. This student wishes people wouldn't drive their

cars everywhere.

b. She hopes that the government will develop a

better public transportation system.

1. "We don't have enough schools or teachers in my country. Few people can get a good education. This is one of our biggest problems, something we want to change."

a. This student wishes _____

_____

b. He hopes _____

_____

2. "We have a serious problem with medical care in my country. There aren't enough doctors, and hospital care is very expensive. I want to study medicine so that I can help my people."

a. This student wishes _____

_____

b. She hopes _____

_____

3. "My country is fighting a war right now. I don't know what is happening to my family. I want this war to end soon."

a. This student wishes _____

_____

b. He hopes _____

_____

4. "We didn't have enough rain last year, so this year we are having a food shortage. Many people are hungry. Maybe next year we will have more rain."

a. This student wishes _____

_____

b. He hopes _____

_____

Using What You've Learned

Expressing Hopes and Wishes.   Does your city or country have a problem that particularly concerns you? Have you done any work to help solve the problem? What would you like to do? What do you hope will happen? Discuss this problem with your classmates. Briefly state the problem. Tell what you wish that you, personally, could do. Then say what you hope will happen.

example: **Inflation is my country's biggest problem. Prices keep going up and people are uncertain about the future. I wish that people would try to stop buying so many foreign products. I hope that we can solve this problem soon.**

TOPIC **two**
Conditional Sentences: Present or Unspecified Time

Setting the Context

previewing the passage

What are *civil rights*? Where do they come from? Share your knowledge while discussing the answers to the questions about the picture.

- What are the protestors hoping to achieve?
- What is freedom of speech?

CIVIL RIGHTS

Civil rights are the freedoms and rights that a person may have as a member of a community, nation, or state. For Americans, these rights are described in a part of our Constitution that is called the *Bill of Rights*. A few of these rights are explained below.

5   *Freedom of speech:* The Constitution guarantees freedom of speech. If Americans did not have this freedom, someone who spoke against the government could go to jail.

    Freedom of religion: The Constitution also guarantees freedom of religion. If Americans did not have this right, it would be possible to discriminate
10 against people because of their religious beliefs.

Due process: This means that a person accused of a crime must receive fair treatment. For example, the police must have a reason for arresting someone. In addition, an accused person has the right to be represented by a lawyer. Due process is a very important part of the American legal system. If the United
15 States didn't have due process, accused people wouldn't have any legal protection at all.

discussing ideas

What important rights are guaranteed by the Constitution? What do you think *freedom of speech* means? What is *due process*?

Conditional Sentences: Present or Unspecified Time

Imaginary conditions express ideas that the speaker thinks of as unlikely, untrue, or contrary to fact. They may be wishes and dreams, or they may express advice to others. The following conditional sentences refer to the moment of speaking or to habitual activities, depending on the context. In these sentences, a modal auxiliary (usually *would, could,* or *might*) is used in the main clause. The subjunctive form is used in the *if* clause. In most cases, the subjunctive form is the same as the simple past. For the verb *be,* however, *were* is used for all persons in formal English.

examples	implied meanings
If we **had** more police, there **might be** less crime.	We don't have enough police. Because of this, there is a lot of crime.
If the government **spent** less money, it **could lower** taxes.	The government spends a lot of money; therefore, it cannot lower taxes.
I **would lower** taxes if I **were** president.	I'm not president, so I can't lower taxes.

exercise 1

What could we do if we raised taxes? Or do you believe taxes should be lowered? Complete the sentences here and on the next page with *would, could,* or *might* + the simple forms of the verbs in parentheses.

example: If I were president, I <u>would raise</u> (raise) taxes.

1. If the government did not have enough money, it _____ (not protect) people's rights.

2. If we raised taxes, we _____ (improve) schools.

3. If we had no taxes, rich people _____ (get) richer.

4. If there were no sales tax, some poor people _____ (not pay) any taxes.

5. If tax laws were simpler, more people _____ (calculate) their own taxes.

6. If the sales tax increased, business activity _____ (decrease).

exercise Laws protect citizens in many ways. What would happen if we didn't have this protection? Complete the following statements with the correct form of the words in parentheses. Be sure to pay attention to the order of the clauses; add *would, could,* or *might* to the main clauses.

> **example:** If there <u>were</u> (be) no police, crime <u>would be</u> (be) worse.

1. If we _____ (not have) freedom of speech, people _____ (not criticize) the government.

2. If we _____ (not have) laws, people _____ (behave) in any way they liked.

3. An accused person _____ (have to) defend himself or herself in court if there _____ (be) no lawyers.

4. If we _____ (not have) trial by jury, all cases _____ (be) tried by judges.

5. If all cases _____ (be) tried by judges only, then judges_____ (have) too much power.

6. Trial by jury _____ (be) impossible if citizens _____ (not be) willing to support the jury system.

exercise **3** First, think about the ideal society and the ideal place to live. Then, in pairs, take turns asking and answering the questions on the opposite page. Give reasons for your answers. Finally, add a few of your own questions.

> **examples:** If you could live anywhere, where would you live?
> **If I could live anywhere, I'd live on the top of a very high mountain where I could watch everything surrounding me. And only people who really cared about me would climb up to see me . . .**

1. Where would you live if you could live anywhere in the world?
2. If you had all the money in the world, what would you build or create there?
3. If you could choose the people who would live there, who would you choose?
4. If you had to create laws, what types of laws would you want?
5. If you could live at any time in history, what time might you choose?

exercise Complete the following sentences with your own ideas. Pay attention to verb forms.

> example: If I had more time, . . .
>
> If I had more time, **I'd read more books.**

1.   If I won $1 million in the lottery, . . .
2. I might get married if . . .
3. The world would be a better place if . . .
4. If I didn't eat for a week, . . .
5. If I were president, . . .
6. We wouldn't need to learn English if . . .
7. If I were an American citizen, . . .
8. If people had wings, . . .
9. You could borrow my car if . . .
10. I might go to China next year if . . .

Using What You've Learned

 **Planning a New Society.**   If you had the opportunity, how would you organize a legal system? What laws would you put into effect? Consider the following four issues; several positions have been listed for each. Choose one of these or state your own position on the topic. Make at least two statements about your position. Use *if* clauses that explain your choice.

> example: control of handguns
> **a.** It would be legal for anyone to have a handgun.
> **b.** I would ban all handguns.
> **c.** Only the military and police would have handguns.
> **In my system, only the military and police would have handguns. If only the military and police had handguns, there would be fewer violent crimes, murders, and assassinations. If criminals could not obtain handguns, our society might be safer.**

1. education
   a. Students would be able to attend the school of their choice.
   b. Only primary education would be free.
   c. Everyone would pay for education. There would be no scholarships.

2. religion
   a. All religions would be allowed.
   b. Only one religion would be allowed.
   c. All religions would be prohibited.

3. voting
   a. Every person, including children, would be allowed to vote.
   b. Everyone over age eighteen would be allowed to vote.
   c. There would not be any elections.

4. censorship
   a. I would allow complete freedom of the press.
   b. I would form a government agency to monitor the press.
   c. The government would control (and censor) all newspapers, magazines, television, and movies.

TOPIC**three**
Past Wishes and Conditions

Setting the Context

previewing the passage
What are the largest minority groups in the United States? What special problems do they have? Share your knowledge while discussing the following questions.

- What is happening in the photo on the opposite page?
- How do you think the students feel?

THE BAKKE CASE

In the past, members of minority groups without a good educational background were not admitted into good universities. To help minority students, some universities now have "affirmative action" programs. These programs give special consideration to minority applicants. This help may include schol-
5 arships or special admission requirements. Many Americans support these programs, but there is also a growing number of people who oppose them.

The famous Bakke case questioned the use of affirmative action programs in universities. In both 1973 and 1974, a California medical school refused to admit Allan Bakke, who was a white engineer in his mid-thirties. The school
10 said that Bakke's grades and test scores should have been higher. With a better academic record, the school might have accepted him. However, Bakke discovered that his grades and scores were higher than those of some minority students who had been accepted as part of a special affirmative action program. So Bakke sued the university. He said that the university would
15 have accepted him if he hadn't been a white male.

In the end, the Supreme Court decided that Bakke was right. It said that the medical school should have accepted him and that the affirmative action program was unfair. Of course, many people disagreed with the court. They believed that the court should have supported the special affirmative action
20 program for minorities.

discussing ideas

What is *affirmative action*? Why didn't the medical school admit Bakke? Why did Bakke sue the university?

A. Perfect Modal Auxiliaries

Perfect modal auxiliaries describe past activities or situations that are not real or that did *not* occur. Often, they express our wishes about these past events. Perfect modals follow this pattern: modal + *(not) have* + past participle.

	examples	notes
would have	He **would have gone** to medical school, but his grades were too low.	*Would have* refers to past intentions that were not fulfilled.
should have	He **should have applied** earlier, but he didn't.	*Should have* refers to actions that were advisable, but that did *not* take place.

	examples	notes
could have	He **could have gone** to any school he wanted.	*Could have* refers to past possibilities or choices. In many cases, the speaker or writer is uncertain if the action occurred.
might have	He **might have gone** to Harvard; I'm not sure.	*Might have* refers to past possibilities. In many cases, the speaker or writer is uncertain if the action occurred.

 You applied for a job, but you didn't get it even though you were very well qualified. You think the interviewer may have discriminated against you because of your age. What would you have done differently? Make statements using the following cues.

example: wear a new suit for the job interview
I would have worn a new suit for the job interview.

1. be enthusiastic about working for that company
2. ask a lot of good questions about the company
3. describe my work experience in detail
4. discuss my good health and high level of energy
5. explain why I was a good candidate for the job
6. try to relax more

 You were fired from a job you had had for many years, so you stopped working and left quietly. Now you are beginning to question your decision, and you ask your friends what they would or would not have done. In pairs, ask and answer questions using the following cues.

example: sue the company
A: **Would you have sued the company?**
B: **Yes, I would have.**

1. write a letter to the company president
2. talk to someone in the personnel department
3. ask for another job in the same company
4. tell your co-workers about the problem and ask for their advice
5. discuss the case with a lawyer
6. ask for a meeting with a company representative

 In the following situations, a friend of yours tells you what he or she did or didn't do. You think your friend made a mistake; respond with *should (not) have*. In pairs, take turns making the statements below and responding to them.

example: A: I didn't get the job I wanted, so I just gave up. Now I'm receiving unemployment insurance.

         B: **You shouldn't have given up. You should have looked for a job with a different company.**

1. I didn't vote in the last election.
2. I drove home from a party after drinking nine bottles of beer.
3. I saw somebody shoplifting in a department store, but I didn't tell anybody about it.
4. I was fired from my last job. I don't think it was fair, but I didn't complain about it.
5. When my boss criticized me, I got angry and shouted at him.
6. I quit my job because I didn't get a raise.

exercise 4

Read the following three situations. For each one, think of other things the person in the situation *could have* done. Use the words in parentheses and your own ideas.

example: When Allan Bakke wasn't accepted by the medical school, he sued the school. What else could he have done?

         A: **He could have applied to another medical school.**

         B: **He could have continued working as an engineer.**

1. The nurses at Community Hospital were complaining about their working conditions. They felt that their salaries were too low. However, nobody did anything to change the situation. What could they have done?

    a. (go on strike)

    b. (quit)

    c. _____

2. A foreign student wasn't accepted at a famous university because her TOEFL score was only 450. As a result, she went back to her country.

    a. (take the TOEFL again)

    b. (apply to a different university)

    c. _____

3. George M. works for a large corporation. Recently it was discovered that a large sum of money had been stolen from the company, and George was blamed for it. George knew that one of his co-workers actually stole the money, but he had no proof. George was fired. What could he have done?

    a. (tell his boss the truth)

    b. (go to the police)

    c. _____

exercise 5   Following are three short "mysteries." Decide what things *might have* or *could have* happened in each case. Use the words in parentheses and your own ideas.

1. Charles H. was hired by the XYZ Corporation. He was supposed to start work on Monday, but he never showed up. The secretary called him at home, but he never answered the phone. By Wednesday, he still had not appeared.
   a. (have accident)
   b. (get another job)

   c. _____

2. Mr. Purl feeds his cat every evening at exactly six o'clock, as soon as he comes home from work. On this particular evening, Mr. Purl's cat has not come home for dinner even though it is already seven o'clock. Mr. Purl is very worried. What happened to his cat?
   a. (find better food at the neighbors' house)

   b. _____

   c. _____

3. Mr. and Mrs. Yan have spent the evening at the opera, and they are now walking back to their car. To their great surprise, their car is not where they left it. What happened to it?

   a. _____

   b. _____

   c. _____

exercise 6   John Q. applied to law school and was rejected seven years ago. Now he is talking about it with Bill, his next-door neighbor. Complete the conversation below and on the next page with *would, could, should,* or *might + have + past participle*. In some cases, more than one answer may be correct.

JOHN: When I didn't get into law school, I was shocked. All my dreams were ruined. I

   didn't know what to do, so I went to work in a bank.

BILL: What do you think you _could (might, should) have done_ (do) differently?

JOHN: Looking back, I think there were several possibilities. First, I _____
   1
   (work) for a year to get some legal experience and then applied again. I also

   _____ (take) the entrance exam again; I _____ (get) a
   2   3
   higher score the second time. Finally, I _____ (apply) to more
   4
   schools instead of just the university. I'm sure I _____ (be) accepted
   5
   somewhere. Anyway, I _____ (not give up) so easily.
   6
BILL: Why didn't you try harder?

JOHN: Well, I was already married at the time, and we didn't have much money. I felt

that I couldn't afford to waste another year. But now I'm sure that we

_____ (find) a way of supporting ourselves if I'd been accepted.
7

BILL: Did you ever think of trying again?

JOHN: As a matter of fact, yes. I'm taking the entrance exam again next week.

BILL: Good luck!

B. Past Wishes

Wishes about the past express feelings or thoughts that did not happen, that are contrary to reality. To show the unreality of the wish, a subjunctive form, which is the same as the past perfect tense, is normally used in the dependent clause.

examples	notes
The workers went on strike. I wish (that) there **hadn't been** a strike. The negotiators didn't agree. We wish (that) they **had (agreed).**	In most cases, *had* + past participle is used with past wishes. The past participle can be omitted if the meaning is clear. *That* can also be omitted.
The negotiators couldn't agree. We wish (that) they **could have (agreed).**	In some cases, perfect modals (*could* [*would*, etc.] *have* + past participle) are used to express past wishes.

exercise  The following sentences express regrets. Complete each sentence with your own ideas. Be sure to use *had* + past participle.

example: I spent only three years in college. I wish I . . .
I wish I had finished school.

1. I started working full-time at sixteen. I wish . . .
2. I got married when I was twenty. I wish . . .
3. I left home for good when I was eighteen. I wish . . .
4. I never did any volunteer work. I wish . . .
5. I was never very good at learning languages. I wish . . .
6. I have always wanted to be a doctor. I wish . . .

exercise 8 In the following passages, several people are speaking about missed opportunities. Complete each with the correct form of the verbs in parentheses. In some cases, you may want to add modal auxiliaries.

1. "Last week I had two big exams on the same day. So what did I do the night before? I went to a movie with my friends. Of course, I didn't do very well on my tests. I wish that I _hadn't gone_ (not go) to the movies. I wish I _____ (study) instead. I wish that I _____ (get) better grades on the tests."

2. "I voted for Jack Hopkins for mayor of this town and, as you know, he won. But I'm pretty unhappy with what he's done since he was elected. Taxes are higher, there's more crime, and the schools are more crowded than ever. To tell you the truth, I wish I _____ (vote/never) for him. I wish I _____ (work) for the other candidate. Better yet, I wish that I _____ (be) a candidate myself!"

3. "I really wish that I _____ (go) to college, but my parents didn't have the money to send me to school. I wish there _____ (be) scholarships in my day. I wish that I _____ (got) a job to pay for my own education."

Conditional Sentences: Past Time

The conditional can be used to describe ideas about past situations or events that did *not* take place. The past perfect tense is used in the *if* clause. A modal auxiliary (usually *would, could,* or *might + have +* past participle) is used in the main clause.

examples	implied meanings
If Schweitzer **had not gone** to Africa, he **wouldn't have received** the Nobel Prize.	Schweitzer did go to Africa and received the Nobel Prize for his work there.
Martin Luther King, Jr. **could have worked** for more reforms if he **had lived** longer.	King was assassinated, so he was not able to work for more reforms.

exercise 9 Read the information about other Nobel Peace Prize winners. Then complete the sentences using the past perfect and *would, could,* or *might + have.*

example: Dag Hammarskjöld, a Swede, was Secretary General of the United Nations from 1953 to 1961. He helped to solve conflicts in the Middle East and in Africa. He died in a plane crash and was awarded the Nobel Prize after his death.

If Hammarskjöld ___had lived___ (live), he _would have received_ (receive) the prize in person.

1. The International Red Cross has won the Nobel Peace Prize three times for its efforts to reduce human suffering. For example, following earthquakes in Nicaragua in 1972 and in Guatemala in 1976, it sent emergency food and medicine to these countries. Fewer people _____ (be helped) if the Red Cross _____ (not coordinate) these rescue operations.

2. Andrei Sakharov, born in 1921, was a Russian physicist best known for his efforts to support human rights and world peace. He criticized the Soviet government for refusing to give its citizens basic human rights; as a result, his government arrested him. If Sakharov _____ (remain) silent, he _____ (not go) to prison.

3. Linus Pauling, the famous American chemist, was one of the first people to speak out against the dangers of atomic power. Because of his great influence, 9,000 scientists signed a petition to stop atom bomb tests in the late 1950s. Pauling received the peace prize in 1962. If Pauling _____ (not be) a famous scientist, people _____ (not start) to pay attention to the dangers of nuclear power.

Linus Pauling

Complete the following sentences with your own ideas. Pay attention to your verb forms and modal auxiliaries.

example: If I had gotten up earlier this morning, . . .
I might not have been late.

1. If I had been born in the United States, . . .
2. He could have gotten a better grade on the test if . . .
3. I couldn't have come to this country if . . .
4. If my family had had more money, . . .
5. We wouldn't have run out of gas if . . .
6. Yesterday I would have stayed home if . . .
7. If I had learned English when I was a child, . . .

Using What You've Learned

Expressing Regrets and Giving Advice. Have you made any mistakes—large or small—since you've been in this country? Think of a specific event or action and tell the members of your group what happened and what you might, could, or should have done differently. The members of your group will comment on what you should, could, or might have done, and what they would have done instead.

example: A: **When I came to this city, I took the first apartment I found. I didn't know that it was in the most expensive part of town. I think I should have looked at some more apartments. Unfortunately, I also signed a year's lease.**

B: **You shouldn't have done that. Now you have to pay a high rent for a whole year. I would have asked somebody for advice before I signed anything. You could have saved yourself a lot of money that way.**

TOPIC **four**
Review

Setting the Context

previewing the passage   Do you know anyone who has won the Nobel Peace Prize? What special thing did this person do? Share your ideas and information while answering the following questions about the pictures on the opposite page.

- Who are the people in the pictures?
- What did they do?

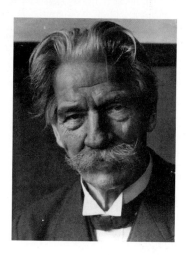

Albert Schweitzer

Mother Teresa

Dr. Martin Luther King, Jr.

THE NOBEL PEACE PRIZE

What kind of person wins the Nobel Peace Prize? Almost always, these are individuals who have worked all their lives to fight injustice, poverty, and discrimination. Here are three famous examples.

Albert Schweitzer (1875–1965) was a German physician, philosopher,
5 musician, clergyman, missionary, and writer. In 1913, he established the first hospital in the rural areas of West Africa. After many years of humanitarian work, he received the Nobel Peace Prize in 1952. Schweitzer used this award money to help Africans who had leprosy. If Schweitzer had not gone to Africa, thousands of Africans that Schweitzer treated might have died.

10 Martin Luther King, Jr., (1929–1968) received the 1964 Nobel Peace Prize for his efforts to create social, political, and economic equality for American black people. He encouraged people to oppose discrimination by using nonviolent methods. As a result of the efforts of Dr. King and other civil rights workers, Congress passed the Civil Rights Act of 1964 and the Voting
15 Rights Act of 1965. These laws might not have passed if King had not spent years fighting for them. Sadly, King was assassinated in 1968.

Mother Teresa is the Yugoslavian-born nun who started the Missionaries of Charity, a group of Catholic nuns and brothers who serve the poorest people in the world. She received the Nobel Peace Prize in 1979, after starting homes in
20 India for victims of leprosy, homeless children, and retarded people. Would anyone else have helped these people if Mother Teresa had not? It is doubtful. Unfortunately, there are very few Mother Teresas in the world.

Other winners of the Nobel Peace Prize include Willy Brandt, Henry Kissinger, George Marshall, Lester Pearson, René Cassin, and Woodrow
25 Wilson. How would history have been different if these people had never been born?

Why did Schweitzer, King, and Mother Teresa win the Nobel Peace Prize? What do you know about the other people mentioned in the passage?

exercise 1

Review. Complete the following with appropriate active or passive forms of the verbs in parentheses. Choose from a variety of tenses.

UNICEF

UNICEF, the United Nations Children's Fund, was founded in 1946. It _____ (form) to give temporary help to children of countries
 1
devastated by World War II. UNICEF _____ (provide) food, clothing,
 2
and medicine to children after that war. However, UNICEF_____
 3
(become) so popular by the early fifties that the General Assembly _____ (decide) to make it a permanent part of the U.N.
 4
UNICEF is not part of the U.N. budget. Contributions from countries and individuals _____ (support) UNICEF. Money _____ (raise /
 5   6
also) around the world through the selling of cards and calendars, but most of the money _____ (donate) by governments.
 7
Since it _____ (found) in 1946, UNICEF _____ (succeed)
 8   9
in getting food and medical care to children in every part of the world. In addition, family planning and human rights _____ (support) by
 10
UNICEF. For the last twenty years, racial problems _____ (be) a main
 11
concern.

In 1965, UNICEF _____ (award) the Nobel Prize for its work.
 12

exercise 2

Review. Combine the following ten sentences with *that, who, which,* and *whose.* Use commas where necessary.

1. Nobel Prizes are prestigious awards. They are given each year.
2. Alfred Nobel was a Swedish inventor. He lived from 1833 to 1896.
3. Alfred Nobel was a scientist. He invented dynamite.
4. Dynamite is an explosive. People often use dynamite for destructive purposes.
5. Nobel left $9 million dollars in a fund. Nobel created this fund to benefit humanity.
6. Nobel created a fund. Its money is distributed as awards each year.
7. The prizes are for talented people. Their major contribution was made in physics, chemistry, medicine, economics, literature, or peace.
8. A sixth yearly award was begun in 1969. This award is in Economic Science.

9. The Nobel awards are obviously both financially and professionally important to the recipients. The awards averaged 1.2 million dollars each in 1992.

10. The Nobel Prize is perhaps the most important award. A person or institution can earn this award.

 **exercise 3**

Review. Fill in the blanks with the correct forms of the verbs in parentheses. Refer to the Appendix pages 403–405 for a list of verbs followed by gerunds or infinitives.

THE NOBEL PRIZE

A Swedish inventor, Alfred Nobel, decided _____ (give) five
                                                              1
generous cash prizes every year for outstanding achievement in physics,

chemistry, physiology-medicine, literature, and peace. Recently, the Swedish

government has also become involved in _____ (fund) a prize.
                                                    2
It funds the Nobel Memorial Prize for Economic Science.

In most fields, prizes are awarded for inventions or discoveries. In litera-

ture, however, the Nobel Committee considers _____ (award) a prize
                                                              3
only to someone whose work has passed the test of time. Often the Committee

recommends _____ (offer) the prize to more than one person. In 1994,
                     4
Yitzhak Rabin and Yasir Arafat shared the Nobel Peace Prize.

The winners must plan on _____ (travel) to Stockholm, Sweden,
                                       5
to receive the prize. They need _____ (be) prepared _____
                                        6   7
(attend) a formal dinner. Recipients rarely miss _____ (go) to the
                                                            8
dinner because it is always a magnificent occasion.

exercise 4

Review. Mohandas Gandhi is honored by the people of India as the father of their nation. He helped free India from British control through nonviolent resistance. Gandhi took many risks in his life and often had to suffer the consequences. Read the information on pages 388 and 389 about the life of Gandhi. After each section, write at least one sentence, using the example as a model.

example: In 1893, Gandhi went to South Africa to do some legal work. There, people would not respect him because he was not white.

The people in South Africa might have respected Gandhi if he
had been white.

Gandhi might not have had problems with the South Africans
if he had been white.

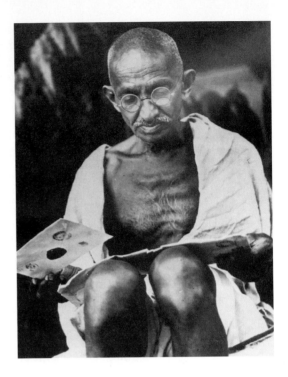

Mohandas Gandhi in London negotiating for India; he wore traditional Indian clothing even to meet King George at Buckingham Palace.

1. Gandhi spoke out against British rule, and he went to prison many times.

_____

_____

_____

2. Gandhi did not stay in Africa. Instead, he returned to India in 1935. Soon, he became leader of the Indian nationalist movement.

_____

_____

_____

3. Gandhi believed that it was honorable to go to jail for a good cause. He spent seven years in prison for political activity against the British.

_____

_____

_____

4. Gandhi wanted people of all races and religions to live together peacefully. He frequently spoke in favor of this. He was assassinated by a man who disagreed with him.

_____

_____

_____

_____

Using What You've Learned

 _activity_

Describing Turning Points.   Events, experiences, and decisions that change your life in a major way are called "turning points." What turning points have you experienced? Was your decision to study English or to come to this school a turning point? Are you at a turning point now? First, think of a major turning point in your life. How would your life have been different if you hadn't had that experience or if you had made a different decision? How would your life be different now? Are you happy with the outcome? Or do you wish you had done things differently? What are your hopes for the future in this regard? Then share your turning point and the results of it with your classmates—in pairs, in small groups, or in a letter to your class.

example:

Dear Class:

Now that we are nearing the end of our session, I want to say good-bye and to tell you how much I've appreciated all of you. Learning to speak another language has changed my life, and you are all part of that change. If I hadn't learned English, I couldn't have come here. And if I had not studied in this class, I would never have met all of you.

Meeting all of you has been a wonderful experience for me, and I only wish I could have gotten to know everyone much better. I wish I had been able to speak more English in order to talk with you more. I wish that the time hadn't gone so fast. Above all, I hope that you will all come to visit me at my home.

Love,
Patricia
(from Argentina)

Review of Problem Areas from Chapters Nine to Twelve

A variety of problem areas are included in this test. Check your understanding by completing the sample items below.

Part 1. Circle the correct completion for the following.

example: If they had enough time, they _____ more often.
a. will write
b. had written
c. would write
d. write

1. If John were rich, he _____ all of his money on sports and cars.
   a. would have spent
   b. spends
   c. will spend
   d. might spend

2. She _____ getting up early in the morning.
   a. is used
   b. is used to
   c. used to
   d. use to

3. The book _____ was expensive.
   a. that we bought it
   b. which we bought it
   c. we bought it
   d. we bought

4. If you _____ in Boston at that time, you would have met him.
   a. lived
   b. had lived
   c. have lived
   d. were living

5. The project _____ on time.
   a. was not completed
   b. was not completing by them
   c. not completed
   d. not complete by them

Part 2. Circle the letter below the word(s) containing the error.

example: If everyone <u>would had voted</u>, we <u>might have chosen</u> a <u>better</u>
                          Ⓐ   B   C
candidate <u>for the office</u>.
                    D

1. <u>Seventy-one</u> percent of <u>the earth's surface</u> <u>is cover</u> <u>by water</u>.
        A   B   C   D

2. Mother Teresa is a <u>Yugoslavian-born</u> nun <u>which</u> started <u>a group of</u>
                                  A   B   C
   missionaries <u>to help</u> the poorest people in the world.
                          D

3. The owners <u>would get</u> a larger profit if <u>the employees</u> <u>would work</u> more
                          A   B   C
   <u>efficiently</u>.
         D

4. UNICEF <u>was founded</u> in 1946 <u>in order</u> <u>giving</u> help to children <u>who</u>
                      A   B   C   D
   survived World War II.

5. In <u>both traditional and modern</u> medicine today, many doctors continue
                      A
   <u>using</u> plant remedies <u>that</u> <u>has been developed</u> over centuries.
       B   C   D

Appendix

Common Irregular Verbs

simple	past	past participle
be	was/were	been
become	became	become
begin	began	begun
bite	bit	bitten
blow	blew	blown
break	broke	broken
bring	brought	brought
build	built	built
buy	bought	bought
catch	caught	caught
choose	chose	chosen
come	came	come
cost	cost	cost
cut	cut	cut
do	did	done
draw	drew	drawn
drink	drank	drunk
drive	drove	driven
eat	ate	eaten
fall	fell	fallen
feel	felt	felt
fight	fought	fought
find	found	found
fly	flew	flown
forget	forgot	forgotten
freeze	froze	frozen
get	got	got/gotten
give	gave	given
go	went	gone
grow	grew	grown
have	had	had
hear	heard	heard
hide	hid	hidden
hit	hit	hit
hold	held	held
hurt	hurt	hurt
keep	kept	kept
know	knew	known
lay	laid	laid

simple	past	past participle
leave	left	left
lend	lent	lent
let	let	let
lie	lay	lain
light	lit	lit
	lighted	lighted
lose	lost	lost
make	made	made
mean	meant	meant
meet	met	met
pay	paid	paid
prove	proved	proven/proved
put	put	put
quit	quit	quit
read	read	read
ride	rode	ridden
ring	rang	rung
run	ran	run
say	said	said
sell	sold	sold
send	sent	sent
set	set	set
see	saw	seen
show	showed	shown/showed
shut	shut	shut
sing	sang	sung
sit	sat	sat
sleep	slept	slept
speak	spoke	spoken
spend	spent	spent
stand	stood	stood
steal	stole	stolen
swim	swam	swum
take	took	taken
tear	tore	torn
tell	told	told
think	thought	thought
throw	threw	thrown
understand	understood	understood
wear	wore	worn
write	wrote	written

Spelling Rules for *-s, -ed, -er, -est,* and *-ing* Endings

This chart summarizes the basic spelling rules for endings with verbs, nouns, and adjectives. Chapter 2 gives more information on nouns, including irregular plural forms. Chapter 8 gives information on adjectives and adverbs, including irregular forms.

rule	verb	-s	-ed	-er	-est	-ing
For most words, simply add s, ed, er, est, or ing without making any other changes	clean cool	cleans cools	cleaned cooled	cleaner cooler	cleanest coolest	cleaning cooling

Spelling changes occur with the following:

rule	verb	-s	-ed	-er	-est	-ing
For words ending in a consonant + *y*, change the *y* to *i* before adding *s, ed, er,* or *est.*	carry happy lonely study worry	carries studies worries	carried studied worried	carrier happier lonelier worrier	 happiest loneliest	
For most words ending in *e*, drop the *e* before adding *ed, -er, -est,* or *-ing.* *Exceptions:*	dance late nice save write agree canoe		danced saved	dancer later nicer saver writer	 latest nicest	dancing saving writing agreeing canoeing
For most words ending in one vowel and one consonant, double the final consonant before adding *-ed, -er, -est,* or *-ing.* *Common exceptions*[*]:	begin hot mad plan run win bus happen open travel	 buses	 planned bused happened opened traveled	beginner hotter madder planner runner winner opener traveler	 hottest maddest	beginning planning running winning busing happening opening traveling
words ending in *u, x,* or *y*	fix play sew		fixed played sewed	fixer player sewer		fixing playing sewing

[*]In words ending in one vowel and one consonant, do *not* double the final consonant if the last syllable is not stressed.

Appendix

rule	verb	-s	-ed	-er	-est	-ing
For most words ending in *f* or *lf,* change the *f* to *v* and add *-es.*	half	halves	halved			
	load	loaves				
	shelf	shelves	shelved			
Exceptions:	belief	beliefs				
	chief	chiefs				
	proof	proofs				
	roof	roofs				
	safe	safes				
For words ending in *ch, sh, x, s, z,* and sometimes *o,* add *-es.*	church	churches				
	wash	washes				
	class	classes				
	fix	fixes				
	quiz	quizzes				
	tomato	tomatoes				
Exceptions:	dynamo	dynamos				
	ghetto	ghettos				
	piano	pianos				
	portfolio	portfolios				
	radio	radios				
	studio	studios				

Nouns with No Singular Form

binoculars	pliers	shorts
clothes	police	slacks
glasses	premises	scissors
pajamas	scales	tongs
pants	shears	tweezers

Statement and Question Formation

the simple present and past tenses and *have* as a main verb*

	Question Word	Auxiliary Verb	Subject	Auxiliary Verb (and Negative)	Main Verb	Auxiliary Verb	Pronoun
Affirmative Statements			You		study.		
			(I, we, they)		study.		
			Ted		studies.		
			(he, she, it)		studies.		
			She		studied.		
			(we, they, etc.)		studied.		
Negative Statements			You	don't	(didn't) study.		
			Ted	doesn't	(didn't) study.		
Tag Questions			You		study,	don't	you?
			You	don't	study,	do	you?
			Ted		studies,	doesn't	he?
			Ted	doesn't	study,	does	he?
Yes/No Questions		Do(n't)	you		study?		
		Does(n't)	Ted		study?		
		Did(n't)	she		study?		
Short Responses			Yes, I do (did).	No, I don't (didn't).			
			Yes, he does (did).	No, he doesn't (didn't).			
Information Questions	Where	do	you		study?		
	When	does	Ted		study?		
	Who				studied?		

*Have as a main verb forms statements and questions in the same way as other simple present and past tense verbs.

	Question Word	Auxiliary Verb	Subject	Auxiliary Verb (and Negative)	Main Verb	Auxiliary Verb	Pronoun
Affirmative and Negative Statements			Ted	is (was) (not)	studying.		
			Ted	should (may, etc.) (not)	study		
			Ted	has (had) (not)	studied.		
Tag Questions			Ted	is	studying,	isn't	he?
			Ted	isn't	studying,	is	he?
			Ted	should	study,	shouldn't	he?
			Ted	shouldn't	study,	should	he?
			Ted	has	studied,	hasn't	he?
			Ted	hasn't	studied,	has	he?
Yes/No Questions		Is(n't)	Ted		studying?		
		Should(n't)	Ted		study?		
		Has(n't)	Ted		studied?		
Short Responses			Yes, he is.	No, he isn't.			
			Yes, he should.	No, he shouldn't.			
			Yes, he has.	No, he hasn't.			
Information Questions	Where	is	Ted		studying?		
	What	should	Ted		study?		
	How long	has	Ted		studied?		
	Who			is	studying?		

*Be as a main verb forms statements and questions in the same way as the auxiliary *be* does.

The with Proper Nouns

The has specific uses with proper nouns, especially with geographical locations. Because proper nouns identify specific places, *the* is often used. There are few exceptions to the rules. Study the following chart and use it for reference.

proper nouns with *the*		proper nouns without *the*	
Use *the* when the class of noun (continent, country, etc.) comes before the name: *the* + *of* + name.	the continent of Asia the Union of Soviet Socialist Republics (the USSR) the city of Paris	Do not use *the* with names of continents, countries, states, provinces, cities, and streets.	Africa Russia Ohio Quebec Austin State Street
Exceptions:	the Netherlands the Sudan the Hague the Champs-Elysées		
Use *the* with most names of regions.	the West the Midwest	*Exceptions:*	New England southern (northern, etc.) Ontario
Use *the* with plural islands, lakes, and mountains *Exceptions:*	the Hawaiian Islands the Great Lakes the Alps the Isle of Wight the Great Salt Lake the Matterhorn (and other mountains with German names that are used in English)	Do not use *the* with singular islands, lakes, and mountains.	Oahu Fiji Lake Superior Mt. Whitney Pike's Peak

proper nouns with *the*		proper nouns without *the*	
Use *the* with oceans, seas, rivers, canals, deserts, forests, and bridges.	the Pacific Ocean the Persian Gulf the Mississippi River the Suez Canal the English Channel the Sahara Desert the Black Forest the Golden Gate Bridge		
Note: The class name is often omitted with well-known oceans, deserts, and rivers:	the Atlantic the Nile		
Use *the* when the word *college, university,* or *school* comes before the name (*the* + . . . + *of* + name).	the University of California the Rhode Island School of Design	Do not use *the* when the name of a college or university comes before the word *college* or *university*.	Boston University Lawrence College
Use *the* with names of museums, libraries, and with most famous buildings.	the British Museum the Chicago Public Library the Louvre the Houses of Parliament the Palace of Fine Arts		

Modal Auxiliaries and Related Structures

Modal Auxiliaries

	meanings	examples
can	informal request present ability present impossibility	**Can** you help us? I **can** carry that for you. It **can't** be six o'clock.
could	request past ability present impossibility	**Could** you put the box on the table? Five years ago I **could** lift heavy things, but I can't now. That **couldn't** be John! He's in Hawaii!
may	request or permission present possibility	**May** I leave early today? Yes, you **may.** I **may** be late for dinner because we have a meeting.
might	present possibility	We **might** go to Chicago this weekend.
must	present need present prohibition present probability	You **must** let us know if you won't be able to come to the concert. You **must not** be late. She **must** be upset because she missed the beginning of the show.
ought to	present expectation present advice	They **ought to** arrive at any moment. You **ought to** call them to see if there is some problem.
should	present expectation present advice	The mailman **should** be here soon. You **should** write your parents more often.
would	request	**Would** you help me for a moment, please?
would like (to)	present desire or preference	**Would** you **like** to go to the movies?
would rather	present preference	I don't feel well. I would **rather** stay home.

Related Structures

meanings		examples
be able to	present ability past ability	I **am** not **able to** run very far now. When I was younger, I **was able to** run at least five miles.
had better	present advice	You **had better** do your home-work.
have to	present need present lack of need	I **have to** study. You **don't have to** read page 16 today.
	past need past lack of need	We **had to** read page 16 yesterday. He didn't **have to** take the test.

Verbs Followed by Gerunds or Infinitives

Verbs Often Followed by Infinitives

subject + verb + infinitive	
afford	We can't **afford** to go.
agree	They **agreed** to help.
appear	She **appeared** to be calm, but she was quite nervous.
be	We **were** to do the homework in Chapter 3.
be able	**Were** you **able** to finish the work?
be supposed	You **were supposed** to do it yesterday.
care	I don't **care** to go.
decide	He **decided** to stay.
deserve	She **deserves** to get a high grade.
fail	They **failed** to make the announcement.
forget	I **forgot** to buy eggs.
happen	Did he **happen** to stop by?
have	I **have** to leave.
hesitate	Don't **hesitate** to call!
hope	We **hope** to visit Rome next spring.
intend	I **intend** to stop there for several days.
know how	Do you **know how** to play squash?
learn	She **is learning** to play tennis.
manage	Somehow he **managed** to finish the race.
offer	They **offered** to help us.
plan	We **planned** to leave earlier.

prepare	They **prepared** to get on board the plane.
pretend	He **pretended** not to notice us.
refuse	I **refuse** to get up at 5:00 A.M.!
seem	He **seems** to be upset.
tend	She **tends** to forget things.
threaten	The employee **threatened** to quit.
volunteer	Several people **volunteered** to help us.
wait	She **waited** for the mailman to come.
wish	We **wished** to go, but we couldn't.

Verbs Often Followed by Infinitives

subject + verb +[optional (pro)noun] + infinitive

ask	We **asked** to come. We **asked** them to come.
beg	He **begged** to go. He **begged** us to go.
dare	I **dared** to go. I **dared** him to go.
expect	I **expect** to finish soon. I **expect** them to finish soon.
need	I **need** to go. I **need** you to go.
promise	She **promised** to help. She **promised** her mother to help.
want	They **want** to leave. They **want** us to leave.
would like	He **would like** to stay. He **would like** you to stay.
use	They **used** to live there. (habitual past) They **used** a hammer to fix the table. (method)

subject + verb + (pro)noun + infinitive

advise*	The doctor **advised** me to rest.
allow*	He won't **allow** you to swim.
cause*	The accident **caused** me to faint.
convince	She **convinced** us to try again.
encourage*	I **encourage** you to study languages.
force	The hijacker **forced** them to land the plane.
get	He **got** them to pay ransom.
hire	We **hired** you to do the job.
invite	They **invited** us to come.
order	I **am ordering** you to stop!
permit*	**Will** they **permit** us to camp here?
persuade	Perhaps we can **persuade** them to let us go.
remind	Did you **remind** her to buy milk?

subject + verb + (pro)noun + infinitive

teach*	He **taught** me to play tennis.
tell	I **told** him not to come.
urge	We **urge** you to change your mind.
warn	I **am warning** you to stop!

verb + infinitive or gerund (same meaning)

begin	She **began** to work (working) on the project.
can't bear	I **can't bear** to see (seeing) her work so much.
can't stand	She **can't stand** to stay (staying) alone at night.
continue	They'll **continue** to practice (practicing) several days more.
hate	He **hates** to play (playing) golf.
like	I **like** to play (playing) tennis.
love	Mary **loves** to read (reading) novels.
neglect	We **neglected** to tell (telling) her about that.
prefer	I **prefer** to go (going) alone.
start	We **started** to worry (worrying) about the situation.

verb + infinitive or gerund (different meanings)

mean	I **meant** to finish the project sooner.
	This **means** delaying the project.
quit (stop)	He **quit (stopped)** to take a long break.
	We **quit (stopped)** taking breaks in order to leave work earlier.
remember	**Did** you **remember** to tell her?
	I **remember** telling her about it, but she forgot.
try	We **tried** to call you, but the phone was out of order.
	I **tried** calling, and then I decided to write you a note.

---

*These verbs are followed by gerunds if no (pro)noun object is used after the main verb.

Appendix

Comparative and Superlative Forms of Adjectives and Adverbs

rules	positives	comparatives	superlatives
Add -er and -est to: one-syllable adjectives	nice	nicer	the nicest
	young	younger	the youngest
adjectives and adverbs that have the same form	early	earlier	the earliest
	fast	faster	the fastest
	hard	harder	the hardest
	late	later	the latest
Add -er and -est or use more, less, the most, the least with two-syllable adjectives	funny*	funnier	the funniest
		more funny	the most funny
	shallow	shallower	the shallowest
		more shallow	the most shallow
	slender	slenderer	the slenderest
		more slender	the most slender
Use more, less, the most, the least with longer adjectives and most -ly adverbs	difficult	more difficult	the most difficult
	interesting	more interesting	the most interesting
	quickly	more quickly	the most quickly
	slowly	more slowly	the most slowly

*With words ending in -y, the -er and -est forms are more common, although both forms are used.

Irregular Adjectives and Adverbs

adjectives	adverbs		
bad	badly	worse	the worst
good	—	better	the best
well	well	better	the best
far	far	farther	the farthest
—	—	further	the furthest
little	—	less	the least
many	—	more	the most
much	much	more	the most

Index

A

a(n), 60, 68, 89
a lot (of), 64, 70
(a) few, 70, 79, 80, 89
active voice, 283, 287, 288, 292, 302, 356
adjective clauses
  focus on testing, 327
  introduction to, 309
  restrictive and nonrestrictive, 316–317, 319, 320, 327
  with *that,* replacement of objects, 319
  with *that,* replacement of subjects, 309–310
  with *when* and *where,* 324–325
  with *who* and *which,* replacement of subjects, 314
  with *whom,* replacement of objects, 320, 327
  with *whose,* replacement of possessives, 315
adjectives
  with *as,* 251
  comparative forms of, 258
  with coordinating conjunctions, 190
  indefinite, 70
  participles used as, 249
  possessive, 315
  followed by prepositions, 178
  with *so . . . that,* 254
  superlative forms of, 267
adverb clauses
  of condition and time, 193–194, 203–204, 206–207
  of contrast, purpose, and reason, 193, 194
adverbs
  with *as,* 251
  comparative forms of, 262
  with coordinating conjunctions, 190
  of frequency, 8
  with present perfect tense, 125
  with *so . . . that,* 254
  superlative forms of, 267
after, 203, 207, 229
agent, 283–284, 286–288
agreement of nouns and verbs, 62, 89

already, 125, 126
and, 188, 190
anticipatory *it,* 339
(not) any, 64, 68, 70
(not) as . . . as, 251
articles, 78, 85, 89
(not) as . . . as, 251
auxiliary verbs
  and adverbs of frequency, 8
  and information questions, 43
  modal, 93–95 (*see also* modal auxiliaries)
  with tag questions, 41
  with *too, either, so,* and *neither,* 38, 39

B

be
  with adverbs of frequency, 8
  in information questions, 43
  with noncount nouns, 78
  with passive voice, 284, 297, 302
  with past participles, 176
  present tense forms of, 3
  in tag questions, 41
  with *there,* 62
  with *too, either, so,* and *neither,* 39
be able to, 100
be going to, 29, 30
before, 203, 207, 229
borrow versus *lend,* 96
but (yet), 188, 190
by + agent, 284, 286–287
by the time (that), 229

C

can
  expressing ability, 100
  requesting action, 94
  with clauses of purpose, 199
  as modal auxiliary, 93
  requesting and giving permission, 94, 109n
can't, 114
causative and structurally related verbs, 356
clauses: *see* adjective clauses; adverb clauses; dependent clauses; main (independent) clauses

commas
  with adjective clauses, 316–317
  with coordinating clauses, 187, 188, 190
  and clauses of purpose, 199
  and clauses of time and condition, 203–204, 207, 229
  after dependent clauses, 198
  with subordinate clauses, 241
  after transitions, 219, 220
comparisons , 251, 258, 260–261
complex sentences
  focus on testing, 213, 246
  introduction to, 192–193
  and simple and compound sentences, 241
  with *that,* 309–310
  with *when* and *where,* 324–325
  with *who* and *which,* 314,
  with *whom,* 320
  with *whose,* 315
compound sentences
  and coordinating conjunctions, 188
  focus on testing, 213, 246
  introduction to, 187
  and simple and complex sentences, 241
conditional sentences: *see* sentences, conditional
conjunctions
  coordinating, 187–188, 190, 199n, 241
  subordinating, 194, 198, 241
connecting words, 203, 213, 241
consonant sounds with indefinite article, 60
continuous tenses: *see* tenses
coordinating conjunctions: *see* conjunctions, coordinating
could
  expressing ability, 100
  requesting action, 94
  with clauses of purpose, 199
  as modal auxiliary, 93
  with *(not) have* + past participle, 373, 381, 382
  requesting and giving permission, 94
  expressing possibility, 112, 113

Index

could, (continued)
  expressing present and future
    wishes, 367
couldn't, 114
count/noncount nouns
  with *a, an, some,* 60
  with *any, some, a lot of,* 64
  with *as many, as few, as much, as*
    little, 251
  introduction to, 59
  noncount versus count, 68, 77
  with *how much, how many,* 70
  with *more/less, more/fewer,* 259
  with *most/fewest, most/least,* 267
  with *so much, so little, so many,*
    so few, 254
  with *there + be,* 62, 78, 79

D
definite articles: *see* articles
dependent clauses
  in complex sentences, 192,
    193–194
  in hopes and wishes, 367
  in past wishes, 381
  in simple past and past perfect
    (continuous) tenses, 229
  of time and condition, 203–204,
    206–207
direct object, 283

E
either, 38–39
(not) enough, 344–345
-er ending . . . *than,* 258, 262
-est ending, 267
ever, 8, 125

F
(a) few, 70, 79–80
fewer, 258–259
fewest, 267
focus on testing
  modals and related structures, 118
  nouns and articles, 89
  phrasal verbs and related struc-
    tures, 182
  present and past perfect tenses, 143
  review of problem areas from
    Chapters 5–8, 279
  review of problem areas from
    Chapters 9–12, 390
  use of adjective clauses, 327

use of compound and complex
  sentences, 213, 246
use of gerunds, infinitives, and
  other verb forms, 363
use of passive voice, 305
verb tenses, 55
for
  as coordinating conjunction, 188
  and period of time, 130,133, 236
future tense: *see tenses*

G
gerunds
  focus on testing, 363
  and infinitives, 331
  after prepositions, 332–333, 363
  uses of, 331–332
  after verbs, 335
  verbs followed by, 336, 351–352,
    363
get, 356
go with *the,* 85

H
had better, 107
had to, 109
have, 4, 356
(not) have to, 109, 199
help, 356
hope, 367
how, 44
how much versus *how many,* 70
however, 220n

I
if clauses
  of condition and time, 203, 204,
    206–207
  in conditional sentences, 373, 382
in order to, 347
indefinite articles: *see* articles
independent clauses: *see* main
  (independent) clauses
infinitives
  with causatives, 356
  focus on testing, 363
  and gerunds, 331
  of purpose, 346–347
  with *too* and *(not) enough,*
    344–345
  uses of, 339
  verbs followed by, 336, 342,
    351–352

-ing ending, 14, 175, 176, 331
inseparable phrasal verbs: *see*
  verbs, inseparable phrasal
it, 288, 339

J
just, 125–126, 251

L
(the) least, 267
lend, 96
less, 258–259, 262
let, 356
(a) little, 70, 79–80
lots of, 70

M
main (independent) clauses,
  expressing cause or reason, 254
  in complex sentences, 192, 193
  in conditional sentences, 373, 382
  of time and condition, 203,
    206–207
  in present perfect or present per-
    fect continuous tense, 236
  in simple past and past perfect
    (continuous) tenses, 229
main verbs, 8, 43
make, 356
many, much, 70, 79–80, 258–259
may
  as modal auxiliary, 93
  requesting and giving permission,
    94–95, 109n
  expressing possibility, 112, 113
measurement: *see* units of measurement
might
  with clauses of purpose, 199
  in conditional sentences, 373
  and *(not) have* + past participle,
    378, 382
  as modal auxiliary, 93
  expressing possibility, 112–113
modal auxiliaries
  with clauses of purpose, 199
  with clauses of time and condi-
    tion, 203–204, 207
  in conditional sentences, 373, 382
  focus on testing, 118
  introduction to, 93–95
  with passive voice, 283, 302
  perfect, 377–378, 381

with present and future hope, 367
simple forms of, 93–94
following *so that,* 213
(not) much/(not) many 70, 79–80
(much/many) more, 258–259, 262
(the) most, 267
must, 93, 109, 115, 118

N

neither, 38, 39
never, 125, 126
noncount nouns: *see* count/non-
count nouns
nor, 188
not, 93, 339
not any/not many, 70
not as . . . as, 251
not ever, 126
not have to, 199
not much versus *not many,* 70,
79–80
not quite as, 251
nouns
abstract, 77
and adjective clauses, 324–325
agreement with verbs, 62, 89
with *as,* 251
with coordinating conjunctions,
190
count/noncount: see count/non-
count nouns
focus on testing, 89
and gerunds and infinitives, 331,
339
and irregular noun plurals, 59
and phrasal verbs, 154
plurals, 60, 64, 79
possessive, 315
proper, 316
singular, 59, 60, 64, 68, 79
as subjects, 185
following *than,* 260–261
with verbs of perception, 358

O

objects
direct, 283
noun, 160
of prepositions, 331
pronoun, 160, 331
of, 70, 71
or, 188
ought to, 93, 102, 107

P

participles: *see* past participles;
present participles
particles, 153, 154, 155, 160–161,
182
passive voice
with *by* + agent, 286–287
with causatives and structurally
related verbs, 356
focus on testing, 305
introduction to, 283
with *it,* 288
modal auxiliaries, 302
with perfect tenses, 292
with present continuous tense,
297
with simple present and past
tenses, 284
past participles
as adjectives, 175, 176,
249–250
with causatives, 356, 363
with modal auxiliaries, 381, 382
placement of, 126
past tenses: *see* tenses
perfect tenses: *see* tenses
phrasal verbs: *see* verbs, phrasal
phrases, 185, 188, 190, 236
possessives, 261
prepositions
preceded by adjectives, 178
followed by gerunds, 332–333
with inseparable phrasal verbs,
153
preceded by participles, 175,
176
of place, direction/location, time,
48, 229n
with *the* and the verb *go,* 85
and verbs, 182, 284
present participles
as adjectives, 175, 249
with *am/is/are* + *being,* 297
with *had been,* 225
present tenses: *see* tenses
progressive (continuous) tenses:
see tenses
pronouns
indefinite, 70
and phrasal verbs, 154, 155
relative, 309, 320, 327
as subjects, 185
following *than,* 260, 261
with verbs of perception, 358

Q

question words, 43–44
questions
with *any,* 64
with count/noncount nouns, 70
information, 43–44, 94, 121, 131,
139, 225
tag, 41, 94, 121, 131, 139
yes/no: *see* yes/no questions

R

recently, 125, 126
relative clauses: *see* clauses, relative
restrictive/nonrestrictive clauses:
see adjective clauses, restric-
tive/nonrestrictive

S

semicolons, 187, 219, 220n, 241
sentences
basic structure of, 185
complete, 39, 185, 192, 241
complex: *see* complex sentences
compound: *see* compound sentences
conditional, 302, 373
focus on testing, 213, 246
incomplete, 193
simple: *see* simple sentences
with transitions, 219–220
separable phrasal verbs: *see* verbs,
separable phrasal
shall, 93
should, 93, 102, 107
simple sentences
and complex sentences, 192, 310,
314, 315, 320, 324, 325
and compound and complex, 241
introduction to, 187
since, 130, 133, 236
so, 38–39, 188, 213
so . . . that, 199, 213, 254
some, 60, 64, 68, 70
still, 125, 126
subjects
and active/passive voice, 283,
287
with auxiliary verbs, 38
and clauses, 192
in combination with verbs, 241
and complete sentences, 185

Index

409

subjects (*continued*)
  gerunds and infinitives as, 331, 339
  placement of, 43, 93, 225
  replacement of, in adjective clauses, 309, 314, 315
  following *than,* 260
subjunctive forms, 367, 373, 381
subordinating conjunctions: *see* conjunctions, subordinating

T

tag questions: *see* questions, tag
tenses
  with continuous and nonaction verbs, 13
  focus on testing, 55
  future, 207
  future continuous, 32, 41
  past continous, 18, 41, 233
  past perfect, 139, 143, 225, 229, 381, 382
  past perfect continuous, 225, 229
  present continuous, 11
  present perfect, 121, 125, 133, 143, 207, 236, 292
  present perfect continuous, 13, 14, 130–131, 133, 236
  simple future, 30, 41
  simple past, 21, 121, 229, 233, 236, 283, 284
  simple present, 3, 8, 41, 204, 207, 283, 284
than, 260–261
that
  adjective clauses with, 309, 316, 319–320
  optional in past wishes, 381
the, 84, 85
there + be, 62
time expressions
  with future continuous tense, 32
  guidelines for placement of, 8
  with past continuous tense, 18
  with past perfect continuous tense, 225
  with past perfect tense, 139
  with present continuous tense, 11
  with present perfect tense, 121
  with simple future tense, 30
  with simple past tense, 21

with simple present tense, 3
with *used to,* 25
to (the), 85
too, 38–39, 344–345
transitions, 219–220

U

units of measurement, 70–71
unless, 203, 207, 229
used to, 25

V

verbs: *see* also *be, be going to, go, have, used to*
  action, 133
  with adverbs of frequency, 8
  agreement with nouns, 62, 89
  auxiliary, 43
  causative and other structurally related, 356
  and clauses, 192
  with coordinating conjunctions, 190
  of feelings, opinions, or thoughts, 13
  formal/informal, 94
  and gerunds and infinitives, 331, 335, 336
  in information questions, 44
  -ing form of, 14
  inseparable phrasal, 153–154, 155–156, 160, 169n, 170, 182
  main, 43
  with modal auxiliaries, 93–94
  nonaction, 13, 133
  as past participles, 249
  of perception, 14, 358
  phrasal, 163, 165–166, 182 (*see* also verbs, separable phrasal; verbs, inseparable phrasal)
  of possessions, 14
  separable phrasal, 160–161, 169, 182
  with *too, either, so,* and *neither,* 38, 39
verb tenses: *see* tenses
voice: *see* active voice; passive voice

W

were in conditional sentences 373
when versus *while,* 233

what, 43, 44
when
  as common question word, 44
  in clauses of time, 203–204, 207, 229, 233
  as relative pronoun, 309
  in adjective clauses, 324
whenever, 203, 204
where, 44, 309, 324–325
which, 45, 309, 314, 316, 320
who(m)
  as common question word, 44, 45
  as replacement of subjects, 309, 314, 316,
  as replacement of objects, 319, 320, 327
whose
  as common question word, 45
  as relative pronoun, 309
  as replacement of possessives, 315, 316
  as replacement of objects, 319
will, 30–31, 43
while, 233
why, 45
wish, 367
would
  requesting action, 94
  with clauses of purpose, 199
  in conditional sentences, 373
  and (*not*) *have* + past participle, 377, 381, 382
  as modal auxiliary, 93
  requesting and giving permission, 94
  expressing present and future wishes, 367
would like, 103
would rather, 103

Y

yes/no questions
  with auxiliary verbs, 41
  with *be going to,* 29
  with future continuous tense, 33
  with *have* and other verbs, 4
  with modal auxiliarieis, 93
  with past continuous tense, 19
  with past perfect continuous tense, 225

with past perfect tense, 139
with present continuous tense, 11
with present perfect continous
   tense, 131

with present perfect tense, 121
with simple future tense, 31
with simple past tense, 21
with simple present tense, 3

with *there + be,* 62
with *used to,* 25
yet, 125, 126, 190